ROUTLEDGE LIBRARY EDITIONS:
AGRIBUSINESS AND LAND USE

Volume 25

# AGRIBUSINESS AND RURAL ENTERPRISE

T0271117

# AGRIBUSINESS AND RURAL ENTERPRISE

## B. H. KINSEY

Routledge
Taylor & Francis Group

LONDON AND NEW YORK

First published in 1987 by Croom Helm Ltd.

This edition first published in 2024
by Routledge
4 Park Square, Milton Park, Abingdon, Oxon OX14 4RN

and by Routledge
605 Third Avenue, New York, NY 10158

*Routledge is an imprint of the Taylor & Francis Group, an informa business*

© 1987 B. H. Kinsey © 2022 New Preface B. H. Kinsey

All rights reserved. No part of this book may be reprinted or reproduced or utilised in any form or by any electronic, mechanical, or other means, now known or hereafter invented, including photocopying and recording, or in any information storage or retrieval system, without permission in writing from the publishers.

*Trademark notice:* Product or corporate names may be trademarks or registered trademarks, and are used only for identification and explanation without intent to infringe.

*British Library Cataloguing in Publication Data*
A catalogue record for this book is available from the British Library

ISBN: 978-1-032-48321-4 (Set)
ISBN: 978-1-032-47279-9 (Volume 25) (hbk)
ISBN: 978-1-032-47292-8 (Volume 25) (pbk)
ISBN: 978-1-003-38543-1 (Volume 25) (ebk)

DOI: 10.4324/9781003385431

**Publisher's Note**
The publisher has gone to great lengths to ensure the quality of this reprint but points out that some imperfections in the original copies may be apparent.

**Disclaimer**
The publisher has made every effort to trace copyright holders and would welcome correspondence from those they have been unable to trace.

# Agribusiness and Rural Enterprise

## B. H. Kinsey

CROOM HELM
London • New York • Sydney

© 1987 B.H. Kinsey
Croom Helm Ltd, Provident House, Burrell Row,
Beckenham, Kent, BR3 1AT
Croom Helm Australia, 44-50 Waterloo Road,
North Ryde, 2113, New South Wales

British Library Cataloguing in Publication Data

Kinsey, B.H.
   Agribusiness and rural enterprise
   1. Rural development projects — Developing countries —
   Management
   I. Title
   330.9172'4      HC59.7

   ISBN 0-7099-1558-6


Published in the USA by
Croom Helm
in association with Methuen, Inc.
29 West 35th Street
New York, NY 10001

**Library of Congress Cataloging-in-Publication Data**

Kinsey, B.H.
   Agribusiness and rural enterprise.

   Authorized revision of a reference manual prepared under
contract for the Agribusiness Division in the Office of Agriculture of
the United States Agency for International Development.
   Bibliography: p.
   Includes index.
   1. Agricultural industries — Developing countries.
2. Small business — Developing countries. 3. Rural
development projects — Developing countries. I. United
States. Agency for International Development.
Agribusiness Division. II. Title.
HD9018.D44K55   1987     338.1'09172'4     87-471
ISBN 0-7099-1558-6


Printed and bound in Great Britain by
Biddles Ltd, Guildford and King's Lynn

# CONTENTS

Contents

# Contents

LIST OF TABLES

Tables

List of Tables

List of Tables

# Preface to the Reissue of 2023
## *Agribusiness and Rural Enterprise*

In the time since this volume was originally published, there have been major shifts in emphasis in development economics. One of these, spurred by the demands of policy-makers and practitioners alike, has been a growing insistence for more and better evidence illuminating the impact of development-targeted interventions. This demand has led to the rapid expansion in systematic reviews and meta-analyses examining interventions and their outcomes, a trend that has been mirrored in multiple arenas where public expenditure is involved.

A second major change in emphasis has been the alignment of diverse interventions under the rubric of sustainable development goals. Both these changes have been amplified by growing frustration with the failure of single-dimensional interventions to alleviate rural poverty.

Despite these significant shifts, however, there is still relatively little new evidence available on the potential role of agribusinesses and rural enterprises. Much of what is available consists largely of abstract general reviews or isolated case studies. The recently published *Handbook of Critical Agrarian Studies*, for example, devotes only a single page to addressing the promotion of agribusinesses (Akram-Lodhi *et al* 2021).

In considerable measure this dearth of evidence arises from the fact that national census and statistical services often continue to exclude enterprises below certain threshold sizes or outside certain functional categories, so there is little relevant comprehensive data for analysts to utilise. Since nonfarm entrepreneurship includes any kind of business activity in the nonfarm economy undertaken by rural residents, it is a challenging sector to study. Such enterprises typically include numerous heterogeneous activities, such as food-processing, trade and sales, services, as well as construction and transportation activities (Wiggins and Hazell 2011). Although commonly referred to as *nonfarm*, many of these activities are closely linked to agriculture and may in fact be located on a farm (Rijkers and Costa 2012). Some analysts (Dorosh and Thurlow 2018) note that, when the heterogeneity of nonfarm enterprises is decomposed by subsector, agro-processing in particular might be just as effective as agriculture in benefiting the poor.

The default approach, then, is either to use more macro-scale but less-focused data or to undertake primary data collection. An example of the former is the review of structural transformation in sub-Saharan Africa by Deudibe *et al* (2020), who note that the movement of labour from agriculture to the non-agricultural sector is occurring more slowly and with less variation from country to country than expected and is only modestly correlated with poverty reduction. Examples from primary case studies are cited below.

The standard arguments in favour of small-scale rural enterprises have been summarised by Ellis (2000, 2007). The rural nonfarm economy is conceptualised as playing an intermediary role in a pro-poor growth process. The argument goes that this economy is dynamic and vibrant, characterised by small-scale, domestic, and labour-intensive enterprises offering a potentially important contribution to a pro-poor growth trajectory. This contribution builds upon improved agricultural productivity first to widen options for employment and income generation in rural areas, and then acts as a wider pathway to an eventual transition to the urban sector. This viewpoint lay at the heart of the World Bank's 2008 *World Development Report* on agriculture (World Bank 2008).

Other researchers (de Janvry and Sadoulet 2010) expand on the critical role of the links between agriculture and poverty reduction. They point out that poverty reduction has been associated with growth in farm production and in agricultural labour productivity, but that this relationship varies across different contexts. The centrality of agriculture comes not only from its direct poverty reduction effect but also from its potentially strong growth linkage effects on the rest of the economy. Overall, synergy between agricultural production and rural- and urban-based enterprises can stimulate the development of more dynamic local economies and to less unequal and more pro-poor economic growth. This mutually beneficial economic interdependence leads to transformations in the livelihoods of different groups and has opened pathways out of poverty for farming households.

A central feature of this interpretation of non-farm activities in rural areas is that they constitute an entrepreneurial training ground for individuals and families that can later be built upon when migration to towns or cities occurs. Through setting up and running small-scale rural enterprises, individuals learn new trades and develop business management skills. New pathways are thus opened up that allow individuals to diversify income sources away from excessive reliance on unreliable agriculture and lay the foundation for a complete departure from agriculture for those who wish to do so.

Ellis, however, goes on to critique the stereotypical rosy perspective of African agriculture's potential as a driving force. He argues that this standpoint "fails in almost all respects to describe real events, trends, and outcomes for agriculture and rural poverty in [sub-Saharan Africa] in the past 40 years" (2007 p1) and that the Asian Green Revolution provides no blueprint for Africa. Agriculture in sub-Saharan Africa (SSA) provides such a weak and unreliable livelihood platform, Ellis argues, that most rural families have to cope by diversifying into nonfarm activities or by relying on remittance income.

Structural transformation in the form of rural-urban transitions represents a formidable challenge within pro-poor development policy. Some researchers maintain that enabling a rapid transition out of rural areas is one of the most urgent tasks facing development policy in Africa, a challenge made even more urgent by the probable adverse impacts of climate change on the security of agriculture-based livelihoods (Collier and Dercon 2009).

Ellis maintains that rural-urban transitions have been largely neglected by donors and policy-makers. The failure to improve urban infrastructure to make these areas the basis of dynamic economic and social change underscores that it is human mobility rather than production increases in agriculture that is the single most decisive factor explaining rapid and progressive economic and social change. Rural poverty in SSA will only sustainably decline when, according to Ellis, people exit agriculture to participate in the growth of other sectors, thereby creating rising urban demand for food to ensure higher, more stable incomes for those farmers who remain behind.

The livelihood support requirements of the rural-urban transition differ significantly from the search for yield-improving innovations for small farms. Even when agriculture plays a primary initial role in the transition process, rising incomes and wealth are associated with the passage from mainly rural to mainly urban lifestyles. As Ellis (1998) notes, the livelihoods that individuals and families are able to shape for themselves in towns and cities tend to be portrayed by labels such as *the informal sector*. This characterisation is most visible in the expanding shantytowns and slums that mark the transition for so many rural-urban migrants into the urban economy.

Welcome contributions to bridging existing lacunae in empirical evidence are the comparative study of rural nonfarm enterprises reported by Liedholm and the analysis of income diversification through rural households investing in nonfarm activities by Reardon *et al*, chapters in the thematic volume edited by Haggblade *et al* (2007).

Liedholm's focus is the start-up of rural enterprises, their expansion, and their closure based on firm-level data from household surveys in six different countries (five African and one Latin American). He addresses causes and magnitudes of rural enterprise dynamics as well as how these vary across locations. In contrast to the aggregated studies of functionally related enterprises, Liedholm examines the micro determinants of the patterns of growth of small rural nonfarm enterprises in contrast with those of their urban counterparts. The birth rates of new firms present a mixed picture, with small enterprise start-up rates substantially higher in rural than in urban areas in some countries, whereas the opposite pattern is found in other countries.

Rural enterprises close for multiple reasons. Roughly half of closures result from a lack of economic or financial viability while about a quarter arise from personal reasons, such as poor health or age. For some, better options become available or they are forced to shut down by administrators. Most closures due to business failure occur fairly early in the life of the enterprise.

McPherson (1995) provides a profile of the characteristics of enterprises that are most likely to close. Holding other things constant, a rural firm is more likely to close during a given year if it starts large rather than small; does not grow; operates in a retail trading sector; operates from a domestic setting; and is owned and operated by a female entrepreneur.

The growth rate of small enterprises has similarly been found to be mixed. Although new enterprises are being created at a high rate, the majority of them in many cases disappear within the first three years. The annual growth rate of surviving rural nonfarm enterprises is high, but only a tiny minority of enterprises benefit from this expansion.

A further contribution to filling some of the existing gaps comes from the work on nonfarm entrepreneurship in rural sub-Saharan Africa by Nagler and Naudé (2017), who use comparative data from the World Bank's Living Standards Measurement Study-Integrated Surveys on Agriculture. They examine the prevalence and patterns of nonfarm enterprises in six SSA countries in terms of their performance as measured by labour productivity, survival, and exit. Rural households, they report, operate enterprises due to both push and pull factors and tend to do so mainly in activities with easy entry, such as sales and trade, rather than in activities that demand higher cost thresholds, such as transport or specialised services. Labour productivity presents a mixed picture: rural and female-headed enterprises, those located further away from population centres, and businesses that operate irregularly have lower levels of labour productivity compared to urban and male-owned enterprises, or enterprises that operate throughout the year.

In a Ghanian case study, Kuwornu *et al* (2014)find that households diversify their livelihood activities to both agro-processing and activities unrelated to agro-processing. Most likely to diversify are females who are high income earners with small farm sizes. Further, educated and asset-rich farmers who produce for subsistence only are more likely to diversify into agro-processing, while access to credit influences diversification but not necessarily into agro-processing. And, as reported also by Liedholm, rural enterprises leave the market primarily due to a lack of profitability or finance, and due to idiosyncratic shocks.

Other studies deviate from starting with smallholders as the point of departure and instead analyse the relationships between existing large-scale commercial enterprises and small-scale farmers. For example, Gaffney *et al* (2019) review multinational agribusinesses as potential spearheads to stimulate local agribusiness innovation and to support smallholder farmers. In a case study from Mozambique, Glover and Jones (2019) explore the impact of commercial farms on smallholders. Drawing on survey data covering all large commercial farms in Mozambique and linked to a nationally-representative survey of 6000 smallholders, they find that commercial farms are selective in their preferred locations, choosing areas close to existing infrastructure and markets. The presence of a commercial farm is associated with somewhat higher incomes among neighbouring smallholders but a lower incidence of wage employment, however the effects vary by the type of commercial farming. Commercial models such as those associated with outgrower schemes appear to generate larger benefits, but Glover and Jones caution against broad generalisations about commercial farming investments because of the need for more nuanced examination of alternative investment models

The rural-urban transition will be affected by resource flows in both directions, as off-farm work may affect farm production decisions through reinvestment in farm inputs and intensification. Mathenge and Tschirley (2007), however, find that the possible use of nonfarm earnings for input purchases is tempered by the higher cost of improved technology and fertilizer-seed packages. These costs may represent a substantially greater investment of money and commitment than households with supplemental nonfarm earnings are willing to invest, especially for those without access to credit. Engagement in nonfarm work may therefore allow some partial agricultural intensification but such work may also compete with taking the farming enterprise to higher levels. Mathenge and Tschirley find that access to a regular source of earnings in the form of a salary, wage or pension seems to be the driving force behind any reinvestment behaviour.

Although diversification away from small farm livelihoods may represent a growth trajectory, it may also be a reflection of extreme stress. As Cunguaraa et al (2011) observe, agricultural households are more likely to engage in at least one nonfarm income-generating activity during a drought year. Poorer households are more likely to engage in nonfarm activities, but they are less likely to participate in high-return nonfarm activities. Similarly, on the basis of three waves of the Tanzanian National Panel Surveys, Khan and Morrissey (2020) find that increased diversification is associated with higher welfare, but that there are significant differences by gender and activity type.

Asfaw et al (2019) explore empirical linkages between crop and livelihood diversification strategies, extreme weather events, and household welfare across three African countries. As others find, exposure to extreme climate events is positively associated with either crop or livelihood diversification in all the countries analysed, suggesting that climate-related shocks are key push factors for diversification. Moreover, the effects of diversification on household income are varied across countries and diversification strategies. Importantly, the impact of both crop and income diversification on household welfare is generally higher for the poorest, while it decreases, and in some cases turns negative, moving toward the upper end of the income distribution. Their findings, therefore, highlight the pro-poor impact of diversification strategies in multiple rural African contexts, but they also illustrate the need to tailor diversification interventions toward specific socio-economic segments of the rural population.

This last point is stressed by Ørtenblad et al (2019), who find that even in dynamic regions with apparently positive levels of development and emerging opportunities, local spatial variations and differences in household characteristics and strategies influence the degree to which people can benefit from diversification. The positive aspects of changed and increased links between rural and urban areas are not uniformly shared. The transformations of rural areas that generate benefits for many also have the potential to increase inequalities and encourage processes that exclude some.

A large literature has focused on whether income diversification is a means of survival or a means of accumulation, but the available evidence remains inconclusive regarding motivations and outcomes. Ellis (2000) explores the reasons households adopt multiple livelihood strategies and distinguishes between diversification of necessity and diversification of choice. He considers six determinants shaping diversification: seasonality, risk, labour and product markets, credit markets, asset strategies, and coping strategies. The conclusion is that, given the precarious conditions that characterise rural livelihoods in many low-income countries, diversification does lead to rural livelihoods that are less vulnerable than undiversified ones.

Dimova et al's (2021) study of long-run diversification in Tanzania supports the accumulation hypothesis: wealthier households engage in more income diversification than poorer households, and the greater diversification of better-off households persists over time. At the same time, households that were originally poorer are found to achieve higher incomes by diversifying into nonfarm self-employment activities. Available infrastructure, including access to a daily market and public transport, helps explain these improvements.

Using household panel data, Dzanku (2015) finds that livelihood diversification is the norm in Ghana although, aside from farming, many rural economic livelihood options are transient. Evidence suggests that more than half of households exhibit considerable instability in livelihood diversity behaviour. Rural household welfare is shaped strongly by multiple factors: spatial location of the household, demographic factors, education, and market forces such as consumer-producer price differentials.

As the small selection of materials cited here shows, livelihood diversification is a widespread phenomenon characterising the survival and income strategies of individuals and families in rural areas of low-income countries. As Ellis (2007) notes, diversification is an infinitely heterogeneous social and economic process that responds to innumerable forces in the rural economy. While it may be tempting to seek generalisations relating to the causes and effects of diversification, livelihood diversification is highly differentiated in its causes and effects by multiple factors. The absence of many universal patterns emphasises the importance of local contexts and thus the necessity to tailor local policies to local circumstances. And local policies include those at national level. Macroeconomic policies are frequently adopted with little awareness as to the changes in rural livelihoods that they provoke. In order to inform researchers, donors and national policy-makers of the consequences for rural livelihoods of the policies being pursued, the missing element of household monitoring systems needs to be introduced.

The purpose of this second preface has been to update the empirical evidence bearing on the design and performance of agribusinesses and rural enterprises as instruments to improve welfare and reduce poverty. While there is still considerable controversy among analysts over emphases and priorities, the issues of overt poverty and unemployment have only become more pressing over recent decades. Similarly, a growing appreciation of the enormous heterogeneity across rural settings rules out a one-size-fits-all approach. The basic toolkit provided in this volume still provides a systematic framework for conceptualising and constructing projects to address poverty through interventions in agribusiness and rural enterprise. What the analysis of experience over recent years tells us, however, is that such interventions need to be multidimensional in character and designed in collaboration with specific stakeholder communities and drawing upon local knowledge and experience. And these interventions need to be implemented in sympathetic policy environments.

B. H. Kinsey

January 2023

## References

Akram-Lodhi, A. H., K. Dietz, B. Engels and B. M. McKay (eds.). 2021. The *Handbook of Critical Agrarian Studies*. Cheltenham: Edward Elgar Publishing Ltd.

Asfaw, S., A. Scognamillo, G. Di Caprera, N. Sitko and A. Ignaciuk. 2019. Heterogeneous impact of livelihood diversification on household welfare: Cross-country evidence from Sub-Saharan Africa. *World Development* 117: 278–295.

Brockington, B. 2021. Persistent peasant poverty and assets. Exploring dynamics of new forms of wealth and poverty in Tanzania 1999–2018, *The Journal of Peasant Studies* 48, 1: 201-220.

Collier, P. and S. Dercon. 2009. African agriculture in 50 years: Smallholders in a rapidly changing world? Paper prepared for the Expert Meeting on How to Feed the World in 2050, 24-26 June 2009. Economic and Social Development Department. Rome: Food and Agriculture Organization.

Cunguaraa, B., A. Langyintuoc and I. Darnhofera. 2011. The role of non-farm income in coping with the effects of drought in southern Mozambique. *Agricultural Economics* 42: 701–713.

de Janvry, A. and E. Sadoulet. 2010. Agricultural growth and poverty reduction: Additional evidence. *The World Bank Research Observer* 25, 1: 1-20.

Deudibe, G., J. Merfeld, J. Ndoutamou and D. Newhouse. 2020. Structural Transformation in Sub-Saharan Africa. *Poverty & Equity Notes* February, Number 19. Washington, DC: The World Bank.

Dimova, R., S.K. Halvorsen, M. Nyyssölä and K. Sen. 2021. Long-run rural livelihood diversification in Kagera, Tanzania. WIDER Working Paper 2021/9. Helsinki: The World Institute for Development Economics Research.

Dorosh, P. and J. Thurlow. 2018. Beyond agriculture versus non-agriculture: Decomposing sectoral growth poverty linkages in five African countries. *World Development* 109: 440–451.

Dzanku, F. M. 2015. Transient rural livelihoods and poverty in Ghana. *Journal of Rural Studies* 40: 102e110.

Ellis, F. 2000. The Determinants of Rural Livelihood Diversification in Developing Countries. *Journal of Agricultural Economics* 51, 2: 289-302.

Ellis, F. 2007. Strategic dimensions of rural poverty reduction in sub-Saharan Africa. Paper presented at the workshop: Rural Development Retrospect and Prospect: A Workshop for Judith Heyer. Oxford, 14-15 September.

Ellis, F. 1998. Household strategies and rural livelihood Diversification. *The Journal of Development Studies* 35, 1: 1-38.

Gaffney, J., M. Challender, K. Califf and K. Harden. 2019. Building bridges between agribusiness innovation and smallholder farmers: A review. *Global Food Security* 20: 60-65.

Glover, S. and S. Jones. 2019. Can commercial farming promote rural dynamism in sub-Saharan Africa? Evidence from Mozambique. *World Development* 114: 110–121.

Haggblade, S., P.B.R. Hazell and T. Reardon (eds.). 2007. *Transforming the Rural Nonfarm Economy: Opportunities and Threats in the Developing World*. The International Food Policy Research Institute. Baltimore: The Johns Hopkins University Press.

Khan, R. and O. Morrissey. 2020. Income diversification and household welfare in Tanzania 2008–13. WIDER Working Paper 2020/110. Helsinki: United Nations University World Institute for Development Economics Research.

Kuwornu, J.K.M., M. Bashiru and M. Dumayiri. 2014. Farm households' livelihood diversification into agro-processing and non-agro-processing activities: Empirical evidence from Ghana. *Information Management and Business Review* 6, 4: 191-199.

Liedholm, C. 2007. Enterprise dynamics in the rural nonfarm economy. In Haggblade *et al* (eds.). *Transforming the Rural Nonfarm Economy: Opportunities and Threats in the Developing World*. The International Food Policy Research Institute. Baltimore: The Johns Hopkins University Press.

Mathenge, M. K. and D. Tschirley. 2009. Off-farm work and farm production decisions: Evidence from maize-producing households in rural Kenya. WPS 33/2008. Nairobi Tegemeo Institute of Agricultural Policy and Development.

McPherson, M. A. The hazards of small firms in southern Africa. *The Journal of Development Studies* 32, 1: 31-54.

Nagler, P. and W. Naudé. 2016. Non-farm entrepreneurship in rural sub-Saharan Africa: New empirical evidence. *Food Policy* 67: 175-91.

Ørtenblad, S. B., T. Birch-Thomsen and L. R. Msese. 2019. Rural transformation and changing rural–urban connections in a -dynamic region in Tanzania: Perspectives on processes of inclusive development. *European Journal of Development Research* 31, 1: 118-38.

Reardon, T., J. Berdegué, C. B. Barrett and K. Stamoulis. 2007. Household income diversification into rural nonfarm activities. In Haggblade *et al* (eds.) *Transforming the Rural Nonfarm Economy: Opportunities and Threats in the Developing World*. The International Food Policy Research Institute. Baltimore: The Johns Hopkins University Press.

Rijkers, B. and R. Costa. 2012. Gender and rural nonfarm entrepreneurship. Policy Research Working Paper 6066. Washington DC: The World Bank.

Wiggins, S. and P. Hazell. 2011. Access to rural non-farm employment and enterprise development. *Background Paper for the IFAD Rural Poverty Report*. Rome: International Fund for Agricultural Development.

The World Bank. 2008. *World Development Report 2008: Agriculture for Development*. Washington, DC: The World Bank.

For my parents

PREFACE

The last two decades have seen many changes in
the focus of development programmes and policies.
International donors and developing countries have
become increasingly concerned about the distribution
of the benefits of economic growth. This concern
has brought with it a sharper focus on rural employment which has led in turn to expanded interest in
agribusiness and small-scale rural enterprises.
Agribusinesses and rural enterprises of all types
have attracted substantial attention as potential
sources of increased rural employment and income,
both directly in themselves and indirectly through
their impact on the small-farm sector.
    Analysts of development have directed a great
deal of emphasis to the apparent conflict between
economic growth on the one hand and social equity on
the other. One of the most important potentials of
agribusiness and rural enterprise projects lies in
their apparent ability to generate possibilities for
growth with minimal or no conflict with equity
objectives. Labour-intensive, small-scale and relatively efficient enterprise systems exist in most
countries, and their expansion has favourable
impacts on employment and incomes of the rural
landless and poor as well as beneficial linkages to
the small-farm sector.
    While all these potentials exist, they are not
simple to harness: care must be taken in project
identification, design and implementation in order
to achieve meaningful contributions to both growth
and equity objectives. Much is yet to be learned
about agribusiness and rural enterprise systems in
developing countries and how to promote their
development successfully. The purpose of this
manual, therefore, is to provide an overview of what
is known about the role of projects to assist agribusiness and rural enterprises, to summarise a

growing body of experience and to outline methods of project analysis for the identification, design, and monitoring and evaluation of such projects. In subject matter and approach, the manual attempts to strike a balance between the level of technical detail desired by the practitioner and the kind of comprehensive overview wanted by the reader with more general interests. This manual is designed primarily for planners, public administrators and project personnel in countries or international agencies implementing or considering a development strategy in which agri-business and rural enterprise projects are viewed as desirable as a policy instrument for generating employment and income. Its objective is to make available to project and other personnel the back-ground and methodology of project analysis necessary so that agribusiness and rural enterprise projects can be designed, implemented and reviewed effec-tively in a wide variety of circumstances. The manual is intended to be a management-oriented guide; it is not aimed at the narrow interests of the subject-matter specialist and does not attempt to provide a comprehensive review of existing liter-ature and experience, but rather selects from these useful examples which will either provide an overview of the field or illustrate viable methods of project analysis. The manual outlines how to establish objectively the potentials and limitations of agribusiness and rural enterprise projects, provides guidelines for deciding whether a project can be effective in a given area, considers the policy issues relating to such projects, and suggests techniques for judging project performance. Because the problems of overt poverty and unem-ployment are so widespread, and likely to become even more pressing, the issues addressed by the manual are of focal policy and practical importance in virtually all countries and development agencies. Addressing these problems effectively will require the involvement of many types of expertise and ability. It is hoped, therefore, that the manual will fill a need for a wide range of personnel: operational project staff, development planners and policy-makers at national and local levels, staff of international funding agencies and other policy-making bodies, development researchers and teachers, and specialised training institutions.

B. H. Kinsey

## ACKNOWLEDGEMENTS

This work is based substantially upon the preliminary version of a reference manual prepared under contract for the Agribusiness Division in the Office of Agriculture of the United States Agency for International Development (USAID). This earlier version was prepared by S. R. Daines, Bryant Smith, William Rodgers and Fred Mann. The audience for the original version of the manual was taken to be primarily USAID project personnel. Through the revisions and modifications made for this publication, the intention is to reach a wider group of policy makers and programme and project administrators, both in bilateral and multilateral development agencies and in developing countries.

USAID supports the revision of this work in the conviction that it will promote development, and it is on this basis that the present version is authorised--and justified. Any errors or misjudgments in the revision remain, of course, the sole responsibility of the author.

The author would like to express his appreciation to the Office of Development Information and Utilization in the Bureau for Science and Technology, USAID for permission to publish the manual.

# CHAPTER 1

## INTRODUCTION

The past 20 years have seen numerous changes in the focus of development programmes and policies. Many international donors have become increasingly concerned, along with most developing countries, about the distribution of the benefits of economic growth. This new focus has brought with it increased concern for rural employment which has in turn led to expanded interest in agribusiness and small-scale rural enterprises. Agribusinesses (which include the processing of food and fibre products, agricultural marketing services and agricultural inputs) and rural enterprises of all types have recently received substantial attention as sources of increased rural employment and income. Not only can these activities provide income and employment directly, but perhaps just as important is the indirect impact they have on small farms from which they purchase produce and to whom they provide inputs and services. Agribusinesses and rural enterprises occupy an important intermediate position between farms and consumers of farm products, and their expansion can be a catalytic factor in stimulating rural development at all levels.

Much of the recent emphasis in thinking on development assistance has been related to what some perceive as a conflict between growth and equity. One of the most important potentials of the agribusiness and rural enterprise sector is in providing growth possibilities without sacrificing the equity dimension. Labour-intensive, small-scale and relatively efficient enterprise systems exist in most countries and their expansion can have favourable impacts on the incomes and employment of the rural landless and the nonfarm poor as well as favourable linkages to the agricultural subsector characterised

1

Introduction

by small farms.

While all of these potentials exist, they are not simple to unlock; care must be taken in project identification, design and implementation in order to achieve important contributions to both growth and equity. Much is yet to be learned about the agribusiness and rural enterprise systems in developing countries and about how to provide development assistance in the most effective and successful ways. Twin objectives in this volume are to provide an overview of what is known about the role of activities which could be developed as possible components in projects formulated by governments and aid agencies and then to outline methods of project analysis for the identification, design, monitoring and evaluation of development assistance projects in this area.

## PURPOSE AND SCOPE OF THE VOLUME

The purpose of this volume is to serve as a practical manual in order to give the background to and a set of methods for the analysis of agri-business and rural enterprise projects. The volume is written basically for three different groups. The first is those who are concerned with the design, implementation and/or the evaluation of agricultural and rural enterprise projects. This group, whether officials from government or from a donor agency, is closest to the day-to-day and month-to-month operational level as well as being intimately concerned with the design and funding processes. The second group of potential users is those who are involved only part time with agricultural and rural enterprise projects. This would include central and regional staff, as well as aid officials involved in project review. The third group includes development agency and national government personnel who have only a peripheral interest in agricultural and rural enterprise projects as one among many possible development interventions. For all these groups, the volume should be useful as a guide and a signpost to the major issues likely to be encountered in agricultural and rural enterprise projects.

It is difficult to design a manual which can satisfy the reader with a general interest as well as meet the needs of the practitioner with a day-to-day concern with effective project management. When one is directly involved in conducting a cost-

benefit analysis of a project, for example, the
level of interest in exploring the technical detail
related to the task at hand will be greater than it
will be for the reader seeking a broad overview.
The volume attempts to strike a balance between
these varying levels of interest. While it does not
provide a project analyst with the detail of the
"cookbook" approach to designing and appraising a
project, it does intend, for example, to provide a
project manager with the necessary understanding to
define terms of reference for a project analysis and
the background necessary to monitor adequately the
work of a contractor engaged in project analysis.
The volume, therefore, is intended to equip project
personnel with sufficient skills and background so
that they can systematically manage the specialists
involved in project identification, design, implementation and evaluation. This is simply another
way of saying that the volume is oriented more to
the requirements of the project manager (with
"management" defined broadly) than to those of the
subject-matter specialist.

The volume is thus intended to be a management-
oriented guide; it does not  attempt to provide a
comprehensive review of existing literature and
research but rather selects from the literature
useful examples to provide an overview or to illustrate viable methods of project analysis. Technical
and theoretical material has been deliberately mini-
mised in order to place emphasis on the more basic
and practical aspects of project-related work in
this area. The reader is cautioned however that
simplicity in presentation (which it is hoped has
been achieved) is not meant to imply that the
process of designing and implementing projects to
assist agribusinesses and rural enterprises is
either simple or easy.


ORGANISATION OF THE VOLUME

Chapters 2 and 3 elaborate in greater detail
what is provided only as an overview in the following section: the major issues which suggest that
agribusiness and rural enterprise projects have
considerable potential as instruments to promote
meaningful development. Chapters 4 through 7 deal
with the approaches and techniques useful in the
process of project design--from the identification
of participating groups to the cost-benefit analysis
of project components and overall project design.

Introduction

Chapter 8 presents a typology of the kinds of data
used in the analysis of agribusiness and rural
enterprise projects and sets out optional approaches
for collecting the various types. Finally, Chapter
9 deals with the critical issues of implementing,
monitoring and evaluating agribusiness and rural
enterprise projects. Chapter 10 concludes with a
brief summary of the major themes of the volume.
The bibliography lists useful supplemental
references as well as the works cited in the
footnotes.

## THE SETTING OF RURAL ENTERPRISES

Agribusinesses and rural enterprises are small-
to-medium scale enterprises located predominantly in
nonmetropolitan areas. While they typically process
agricultural raw materials--including food, fibre
and forest and livestock products, many do not
produce any product but instead provide marketing,
transport or other services. To the extent that
larger-scale enterprises in urban or peri-urban
areas have particularly strong backward links to
small-scale, labour-intensive rural producers of raw
materials, they are also included in the scope of
this volume. The central focus of most of the
volume then is on the provision of development
assistance to indigenous small-scale enterprises in
rural areas, or in urban areas but involved in
processing or distributing agricultural products.
Agribusiness and rural enterprise projects hold
significant potential for promoting growth with
equity. Many of the activities suitable for assistance in such projects are labour intensive, owned
and operated by families in priority target groups,
provide employment and income for landless rural
populations, and at the same time are relatively
efficient. The efficiency of resource use of many
of these enterprises implies that scarce capital
resources can be appropriately expended in these
projects from the point of view of promoting both
"growth" and "equity".
The rural economy in developing countries is a
complex and interknit system. Farms, small-scale
enterprises, commerce and services operate in an
interrelated fashion whether or not a money economy
predominates. Growth and development in this system
also take place in a linked manner, although this
fact does not necessarily imply that each subsector
will grow at an even pace. Growth may stem from an

initiative in a single part of the system and spread unevenly to other components of the rural economy.

Almost all agribusinesses and rural enterprises in developing countries are in the private sector, and projects seeking to assist such enterprises must interact with the private sector system. Public sector banking channels, technical assistance organisations and research capability may be critical to project success, yet the projects are basically oriented toward the private sector. Unlike agricultural technology, which has been substantially developed and disseminated through public channels, the technologies which can be drawn upon to assist the development of agribusiness and small-scale rural enterprise have largely originated in or been developed by the private sector. For some development agencies, attempting to operate with the private sector will be a new experience, and there will be a need to be innovative and to draw on the experience of others.

Agribusinesses (whether rural or urban, or large or small scale) utilise farm and other rural products as their major raw material inputs. Attempts to promote the development of agroindustry and rural enterprises need to be targeted so as to stimulate the volume and value of transactions flowing along the linkages backward to agriculture and forward to final consumers. Well-designed interventions are ideally situated to draw the system more closely together and to distribute the benefits of growth in one subsector to other segments of the economy by connecting potential producers with final markets.

Because the focal group of enterprises operates in the private sector and at the fulcrum between agriculture and consumers, it is in a position to be influenced positively by a very wide range of public policies and--equally but negatively--by the absence of appropriate policies or by contradictory policies. The policy setting is therefore critical and constitutes an essential part of the base of knowledge required in order to design projects with a reasonable prospect of success in improving the lot of the rural poor. Much greater attention will be directed to this point in the chapters which follow.

Further discussion at this level of generality serves little purpose here, and it is the task of the two chapters which follow to extend and elaborate the issues raised here.

CHAPTER 2

PUBLIC POLICY OVERVIEW OF AGRIBUSINESS AND RURAL
ENTERPRISE PROJECTS

The last two decades have seen many changes in the
focus of development programmes and policies.
International donors have become increasingly
concerned, along with most developing countries,
about the distribution of the benefits arising from
economic growth. This new focus brought with it
increased concern for rural employment which in turn
led to increased interest in agribusiness and small-
scale rural enterprises. Agribusinesses and rural
enterprises of all types have received growing
attention as potential sources of increased rural
employment and income. Not only can such enterprises provide income and employment in a direct
fashion, but perhaps as important also is the
indirect impact they can have on the small farms
from which they purchase produce and to whom they
provide inputs. Agribusinesses and rural enterprises occupy a pivotal intermediate position
between farms and consumers and can have powerful
and far-reaching catalytic effects in accelerating
rural development.

Much of the recent emphasis in development
assistance thinking has been related to the apparent
conflict between "growth" and "equity". One of the
most important potentials of the agribusiness and
rural enterprise sectors is in providing growth
possibilities without an equity conflict. Labour-
intensive, small-scale and relatively efficient
enterprise systems exist in most countries and their
expansion has favourable impacts on the income and
employment of the rural landless and nonfarm poor as
well as favourable linkage to the small-scale farm
sector. While all these potentials exist, they are
not simple to unlock; care must be taken in project
identification, design and implementation in order
to achieve important contributions to both growth

and equity. Much is yet to be learned about agribusiness and rural enterprise systems in developing
countries and about how to provide development
assistance in ways that will ultimately prove successful. The purpose of this volume is to provide
an overview of what is known about the role of such
enterprises and then to outline methods of analysis
for the identification, design, monitoring and
evaluation of projects intended to assist in the
development of agribusinesses and rural enterprises.

## FUNDAMENTAL CONCEPTS

The terms "agribusiness" and "rural enterprise"
are used in this volume to refer to small- and
medium-scale rural enterprises (SMREs) located in a
non-metropolitan area. Defining "small" and
"medium" is difficult, as the terms have different
implications in almost every country. In Ecuador,
for example, "small" has been defined as those
enterprises with less than $11,000 in fixed assets,
while in Korea the term is used to refer to firms
with less than $200,000 in fixed assets. [1]
Working definitions should ideally include
three dimensions: number of workers, fixed assets,
and labour intensity. Small-scale enterprises by
definition would, for example, be those with a
maximum of 20 workers, $50,000 in total assets, and
maximum capital costs per workplace provided of
$5,000. A workplace should be defined as 12 person-
months of work, not by the number of employees or
workers. Medium-scale enterprises would be those
with a maximum of 150 workers, $500,000 in total
assets and capital costs for providing one workplace
of $15,000. (It should be noted that medium-scale
enterprises in particular may provide substantial
indirect employment which should be considered when
evaluating labour intensity.) These definitions
underlie the remainder of this volume.
While these definitions are admittedly arbi-
trary, they attempt to capture those types of agribusinesses and rural enterprises with the largest
potential for the achievement of broad-based
development objectives. There is a need for
restrictive definitions because of the very real
tendency in all countries for the larger enterprise
to be more agile in obtaining scarce resources,
money, and other assistance. If there are no
restrictions on the types of enterprises to be
included, or if the limits are set so that few types

of enterprise are excluded, the bulk of the assistance may be concentrated among the larger firms
with access to conventional forms of assistance. In
this section, the use of either "small" or "medium"
on its own should be understood to include both
small and medium together.

The measure of labour intensity, that is, the
capital costs per workplace created, is important
since size and locational characteristics do not
determine the cost per job for a given enterprise.
Labour intensity, for example, varies much more
widely by type of product than by scale of operation or location. The potential of rural enterprises to generate income for the poor is significantly different depending on the type of industry.
This is not to say that scale and location are not
important characteristics which should be used to
define an area of interest, but only to caution
against the exclusive use of these characteristics
in determining the boundaries of that interest.
Smaller scale does tend to increase labour intensity, [2] rural industries are on the average
more labour intensive, yet these averages conceal
large differences between the labour intensity and
income potential of different types of enterprises
as defined by product and service. For example, the
amount of capital required to provide one workplace
varies widely within the SMRE subsector. A study in
El Salvador indicated that approximately one-third
of the small enterprises require less than $1,000
per worker, approximately half from two to eight
times as much, and a small but not unimportant
number from $8,000-15,000. [3] It is therefore
important to segment this group into subgroups, not
only by fixed assets and employment levels, but also
according to their labour intensity in order to
determine which set of firms best meets specific
development objectives.

As the size, location and labour intensity of
specific industries varies by country, no attempt
will be made to define or limit the types of industries to be emphasised. Small firms considered for
project support should initially include all enterprises found in nonmetropolitan areas. Many of this
group will not produce a product, but rather provide
marketing, transport, or other services. At least
one-third of the priority firms in most developing
countries will come from the service category.
Food, fibre, and wood processing make up almost all
of the remaining small-scale enterprises, and only a
very small percentage consists of makers of handi-

craft products. Firms may range from very small, craftsman-type operations to fairly sophisticated businesses with complex internal organisation and production processes. [4] (See Table 2.1.)

## THE ROLE OF SMALL- AND MEDIUM-SIZED RURAL ENTERPRISES IN A DEVELOPING ECONOMY

Small firms can play an important role in developing economies, although their ability to do so depends on the existence of an adequate environment to support their growth. As the largest percentage of such firms will generally be dependent on the demand of the domestic population for their goods, their development requires the existence, or at least the simultaneous development of, an expanding agricultural sector. Stagnation or slow growth in agriculture will generally restrict the opportunity for substantial development of new or existing enterprises.

In general, the potential contributions which small- and medium-sized rural enterprises can make to a country's economy include the following: first, as they usually tend to be more labour intensive than larger enterprises, the opportunities for increasing rural employment can be enhanced by encouraging the development of small firms. As most developing countries underutilise their rural populations, the reduction of this waste of human resources and the stream of attendant economic and social ills which it carries in its wake must be a first priority. Much of the problem can and should be attacked through agriculture directly; many poor rural families rely on small-scale farming and will benefit directly from programmes aimed at expanding and diversifying their production. Yet agriculture cannot hope to absorb all the existing, and expanding, labour force. Recent research [5] indicates that in Asia the landless and near landless constitute a majority of the labour force, and the figures approach 90 per cent in Bangladesh and Pakistan. In Latin America the landless and near landless are also a majority, and exceed 80 per cent in Bolivia, El Salvador, Guatemala and the Dominican Republic. At prevailing rates of population growth and allowing for net outmigration from rural areas of one-third of the projected population increase, the rural labour force will grow by at least 50 per cent in most of these countries by the end of the century. Rural enterprise projects of all

9

Table 2.1.--Composition of Rural Nonfarm Employment, Selected Countries [a]

| Sector | Zambia (1975) [b] | Nigeria (1966) [c] | India (1966-67) | West Malaysia (1970) | Indonesia (1971) | Philippines (1970) | Republic of Korea (1970) | Taiwan [d] (1966) | Chile (1970) | Colombia (1970) | Brazil (1970) |
|---|---|---|---|---|---|---|---|---|---|---|---|
| | | | | | (Percentages) | | | | | | |
| Manufacturing | 10.4 | )49.0 | 38.7 | 15.3e | 24.7 | 34.1 | 30.3 | 23.0 | 19.4 | 33.0 | 24.1 |
| Construction | 12.1 | ) | 13.6 | 3.7 | 4.7 | 10.7 | 10.3 | 3.2 | 10.4 | 8.4 | 14.7 |
| Utilities | 2.8 | n.a. | 0.5 | 1.3 | 4.4f | 0.4 | 0.6 | 0.9 | 1.1 | 0.4 | 0.9 |
| Commerce | 34.9 | 25.3 | 13.6 | 15.3 | 29.1 | 15.2 | 23.4 | 11.5 | 10.1 | 18.9 | 12.9 |
| Transport | 5.1 | 6.6 | 4.7 | 5.6 | — f | 9.6 | 5.7 | 4.7 | 6.7 | 6.2 | 7.8 |
| Services | ) | ) | ) | 12.3 | ) | ) | 8.6 | 25.5 | ) | ) | 1.7 |
| Government | )31.3 | )19.1 | )24.1 | | )22.5 | )30.0 | | | )26.9 | )33.0 | |
| Other | ) | ) | ) | 16.3 | ) | ) | 20.6 | 17.9 | ) | ) | 31.9 |
| Miscellaneous | 3.5 | - | 4.7 | 30.2 | 14.5 | - | 0.6 | 13.4 | 25.4 | - | 6.0 |
| Total | 100.0 | 100.0 | 100.0 | 100.0 | 100.0 | 100.0 | 100.0 | 100.0 | 100.0 | 100.0 | 100.0 |

Source: D. Anderson and M. W. Leiserson, Rural Enterprise and Nonfarm Employment (The World Bank, Washington, 1978), p.24.

a Details may not add to totals due to rounding.
b Data are for the rural province of Puapula.
c Rural districts of Ifo, Otta, and Ilaro in Western State. Data include rural towns.
d Excludes rural towns.
e Excludes rubber processing.
f Data on transport, communications, and utilities are combined.

types offer a viable and indeed critical possibility for providing productive workplaces for rural labourers. In some areas, they may also have the advantage of opening employment opportunities for women, who may be culturally or economically excluded from agricultural pursuits.

Second, small rural firms may contribute to the income and employment of families on small farms. It has been demonstrated in many countries that the most profitable options for small-scale farmers are intensive crops which carry attendant high risks, involve increased credit, require post-harvest processing and/or efficient marketing links to prevent losses through spoilage. Enterprises involved in processing and marketing can be catalytic in allowing small farmers to pursue this high-income option. In fact, in many cases it is the development of these firms which <u>precedes</u> the entrance of small-scale farmers into intensive crop production. These enterprises can open markets, provide credit and technical links to small-scale farmers which will directly expand the employment of both farm and landless families in agricultural production. In addition, on-farm enterprises owned and managed by the small-scale farm family can absorb labour during the slack season, and provide additional sources of income from added value to farm production. Capturing as much income as possible from adding value to farm production before it leaves the farm gate may be an important alternative in some commodities. Livestock, fibre and wood products are the best commodities for on-farm processing enterprises.

Third, these enterprises have the potential to improve income distribution by increasing the number of workers participating in the labour force, improving income-earning possibilities for small-scale farmers, and, in the case of very small establishments, providing landless families with opportunities to become entrepreneurs rather than labourers. New opportunities for the landless are particularly important in developing countries where expanding rural populations and sluggish economic growth have resulted in a large and growing pool of unemployed. While product markets have remained reasonably responsive and prices for products have risen fairly consistently, wages have not. This situation, characteristic of much of the developing world, has meant that people whose income comes from the sale of products have a brighter <u>potential</u> future than those who must enter the depressed labour markets.

11

In some countries the small-scale farmer makes twice as much income from each day productively worked on his farm as he makes from each day worked as a labourer, due largely to the disparity between the markets for labour and for products. Hence, farm employment should be looked to as a relatively more attractive income-generating activity. For the landless, more income will come to labourer-entrepreneurs in most depressed labour market situations than to labourers alone. Attention has focused in many international development institutions on the plight of the landless families who constitute a large proportion of the rural poor, and probably the poorest of the rural poor. More than one-half of all rural poor lack any income-producing assets other than their own labour and are thus locked into obtaining what income they can from the depressed labour markets. One of the largest potential contributions of the very small enterprises is to convert these landless labourer families into small-scale entrepreneurs and allow them to enter product, not labour, markets for their incomes.

In attempting to evaluate the potential of small- and medium-scale rural enterprises, some analysts have measured labour productivity, and finding it significantly lower in small-scale establishments, have reached the incorrect conclusion that they had little income-generating potential. In some countries, labour productivity is four or five times higher in large-scale enterprises than in small-scale ones, and one might think therefore that it would be better to expand large-scale enterprises and provide increased benefits to the rural poor by employing them rather than to spread inefficiency by emphasising expansion of small-scale enterprises. This argument ignores two important facts usually characteristic of the rural sector in developing countries. First, much of the added labour productivity is due to substitution of capital for labour, not increased labour efficiency, and may result in larger payments to owners of capital, while labourers stay on minimum wages. Second, even at lower labour efficiencies, labourers will capture a larger share of income in very small-scale, labourer-owned-and-operated enterprises. Empirical studies [6] have indicated that in food, clothing and wood products, even though labour productivity is one-fourth that of large-scale establishments, net income per worker is 15-55 per cent higher in firms with fewer than five workers.

Fourth, by focusing on areas outside of the major metropolitan areas, governments can encourage decentralisation of industrial development. Decentralisation is a factor in improved income distribution and can contribute to stemming migration to metropolitan areas. The potential of small- and medium-scale rural industry to decentralise the process and benefits of growth has been found to be particularly important in studies of Brazil and Columbia. [7]

Finally, these firms in appropriate lines of activity can contribute to growth of the overall economy by being efficient users of capital. Though the evidence is not conclusive, studies [8] do indicate that in many industries, the output per unit of capital is higher for small-scale than large-scale enterprises. Hence, in industries where this holds true, support of labour-intensive SMREs will not be at the cost of increased output, but will rather be the best means to achieve improved social and economic welfare.

## SELECTIVE SUPPORT FOR THE DEVELOPMENT OF SMREs

If an underlying dynamism exists in the agricultural sector, small and medium-sized rural enterprises will undoubtedly grow without government efforts. Reasonable support, however, has the potential to accelerate their development in appropriate industries by improving the efficiency and effectiveness of their operations. Generally, specific efforts to support the development of these enterprises will realise the best results in areas where they enjoy comparative advantages. Trying to stimulate firms which have significant employment potential but which have no advantage vis-a-vis larger, metropolitan enterprises often proves difficult, if not impossible, and fosters inefficiency.

Three primary influences have been identified which significantly bear on the relative advantages of small and large enterprises: location, processes, and markets. [9] Specifically, it has been argued that smaller enterprises are most suited where factors encourage dispersed locations, where scale economies are not pronounced or process advantages exist in small-scale operations, and where markets are small or highly differentiated.

Locational influences favouring small and dispersed enterprises might include industries

13

where: a) local markets and high transfer costs make localised production more economical (for example, prepared animal feed, concrete blocks and bricks, ice cream, and soft drinks), b) raw material is dispersed (for example, butter, cheese, grease, tallow, or wood products), and c) localised services are required to ensure timely and flexible customer contact (for example, printing, typesetting, grain storage and milling).

Favourable influences relating to process include those where: a) operations are based on localised skills, which may include craft or precision handwork (for example, furniture, leather goods, and blacksmithing), b) manufacturing operations are separable (for example, machine shop products, castings, and dies and tools), and c) operations require simple assembly, mixing and finishing (for example, food flavourings, footwear, fertiliser mixing, and wood products).

Industries with market influences favouring small enterprises would include those with: a) differentiated products which have low scale economies (for example, women's dresses), and b) small markets which are best served by a locally based enterprise (for example, fresh/frozen fish, cottonseed oil mills, carts and wheelbarrows). [10]

In general, enterprises engaged in activities in these classifications should enjoy a natural advantage. By direct support selectively to these SMREs, government or other donor efforts have the potential to stimulate those enterprises which can theoretically make the most positive contribution to the economy as a whole.

## PROBLEMS COMMON TO SMREs

The form of government support will vary with the problems specific to a particular country's small-scale enterprise subsector. Following is a general discussion of problems which are common in many industries in many countries, although they may not be universal. Some of these problems are shared by large-scale operations. In general, however, the problems are more pronounced for smaller enterprises which, by virtue of their size, are unable to resolve many of them without external support, be it private or public. Common difficulties include:

1. Government disincentives. One of the most serious problems faced by these enterprises is disincentives created through government actions.

These can include:

     a.   Distortions in factor prices which result in investment in large, overly capital-intensive operations. Artificially low interest rates and overvalued foreign exchange make purchase of capital equipment more attractive when abundant, cheap labour and scarce capital should favour the development of labour-intensive operations.

     b.   Burdensome rules and regulations, such as those requiring overly detailed reports, records and licensing, which can consume valuable time and may discourage growth, as many of these requirements often become more involved as firms grow larger.

     c.   Taxes and tariffs which favour large firms, giving them artificial advantages in comparison to SMREs, and a tax structure which discourages growth of small enterprises by rapidly increasing taxes once enterprises reach a certain size.

    2.   Management. In many small firms, one individual is responsible for the production, management, marketing and financial operations. The entrepreneur, who, for example, may be a skilled craftsman, often lacks expertise in all of these areas. Although the firm's operations may appear to be fairly straightforward, for example dressmaking, the entrepreneur still has to make decisions relating to each of the above functions, for example, how many machines to purchase or workers to hire, how much money to borrow, and how better to sell his or her services.

The ill-informed businessperson can easily make decisions resulting in an inefficient use of resources and thereby seriously affect the enterprise's ability to compete effectively. These entrepreneurs are often reluctant to accept outside assistance and are unable to identify their specific problems. Many of the other difficulties outlined below stem largely from this lack of specialised management.

    3.   Technical information. The entrepreneur's limitations are further aggravated by the lack of access to current technical information. Consequently, decisions regarding technology, production processes and planning, inventory levels, and related matters are often based on outdated and inefficient practices.

    4.   Marketing. Whereas large firms usually have the staff and contacts to keep abreast of

market developments, smaller rural firms do not.
Consequently, their knowledge of new or changing
opportunities is limited to their environs.  In
addition, large firms can afford transport and
storage facilities, advertising and product development efforts which an individual SMRE cannot.
    5.    Credit.  Most small-scale enterprises and,
to a slightly lesser degree, medium-scale enterprises are forced to rely on personal savings, money
from friends or relatives, and moneylenders.  They
therefore find it difficult to obtain working
capital or long-term credit needed for capital
investment on an adequate or timely basis and on
reasonable terms.
    Formal credit channels are often closed for
several reasons.  The general problems faced by
rural industries, compounded by the lack of
accounting records, make them more risky for credit
institutions which can lend to more stable
customers.  Also, lending to smaller rural enterprises rather than larger, metropolitan-based
industry usually means higher administrative costs
due to the smaller size of the loan and the additional time bank personnel may need to spend in
reviewing, monitoring, and assisting the rural
customer.  Banking practices further complicate the
situation.  They often require substantial collateral to guarantee the loan, and commercial banks in
particular are often unable to lend on a long-term
basis because most of their funds are loaned for
short or medium terms.
    Government policies tend to aggravate the
situation further when approaches such as those
discussed above foster "over-development" of larger,
more capital-intensive operations and thereby make
them favoured customers.
    6.    Raw materials/equipment.  Large-scale
enterprises usually enjoy several advantages in
purchasing raw materials and equipment; they can
make bulk purchases, have specialised procurement
staffs, and have more political, social, and financial influence with government and suppliers.  This
affords a significant price advantage and invaluable
control in developing countries where the supplier
and sales networks are often inadequately developed
and raw materials and equipment are usually in
chronic short supply. [11]
    7.    Socio-cultural factors.  Socio-cultural
factors may be a serious handicap to the development
of SMREs.  The rural entrepreneur may be expected to
share his/her wealth among relatives, which limits

funds available for reinvestment; profits may be discouraged by the community, thereby discouraging ambition and growth; leisure time may be highly regarded and consequently efforts are discouraged to utilise equipment at full capacity, etc.  In addition, the social structure in some countries may be such that an elite can control access to government, sources of credit and supplies, markets, etc., so effectively that it denies small enterprises support needed for development.  These considerations may seriously affect any programme intended to develop SMREs and should be carefully assessed.

8.  Infrastructure.  Many of the less-traditional and larger SMREs require access to basic infrastructure such as roads, electricity and water. Inadequate or unreliable access to such services can seriously hamper or even prevent new growth of SMREs.  Hence, external efforts to stimulate rural enterprises may often follow development of infrastructure.

THE POLICY FRAMEWORK

A public policy structure frames the environment within which small-scale enterprises function in any country, and this framework must be a part of the base of knowledge which the planner addresses prior to identifying optional project interventions.

The characteristics of some of the more important policy areas are discussed in this section.  The purpose here is to make project planners aware of what to look for in reviewing public policy and of the opportunities that may be available for project interventions at the policy-making level.

Credit Policy

Credit is a tool by which adjustments in all factors of production can be achieved.  Thus, public policies affecting the availability and conditions of credit and capital supply to rural enterprises and agroindustry are particularly important.

In looking at credit policies, it is important to examine not only those policies that seek to make credit accessible to SMREs on acceptable terms, but also those policies which provide access by large-scale enterprises to capital (often at subsidised interest rates) that generally cannot be tapped by

17

smaller rural enterprises. Capital markets in developing countries often are not well developed, being generally limited to the capital city in smaller countries, and generally not reaching beyond major regional centres in larger countries. Although bank branches may exist in more remote areas, they exist primarily as deposit-takers and to facilitate noncredit transactions between the hinterland and the capital city.

In many cases, large-scale enterprises have access not only to national capital markets but to international capital markets as well. In addition, special government industrial promotion programmes often provide special lines of credit at subsidised interest rates. Such programmes usually are administered from one office in the capital city or a limited number of offices in other major commercial centres. Paperwork generally is substantial and insurmountable for many small enterprises. Because of geographic isolation and the sophistication required to access these special lines of credit, these firms do not benefit from such programmes, although they are not formally excluded. Their situation can be characterised as one of "benign neglect". Nevertheless, the net result of such programmes can often be negative for SMREs, since they enhance the relative competitive position of larger-scale enterprises. [12]

As credit policies are examined, both in terms of existing policies and apparent gaps for targeting credit, it is important to be aware of the potential pitfalls of what has been termed the "need-creed" syndrome. [13] It is common to assume that all small-scale enterprises need loan funds to purchase raw materials and equipment, to finance inventories and marketing costs, etc. The view is that, because of meagre internal resources, the small entrepreneur automatically needs outside resources in order to modernise and expand.

Some assumptions upon which this need-creed is based may not be valid in specific rural enterprises. Credit proposals often assume that prior to the project, there were no stocks and flows in the enterprises to be assisted, or that they are so small as to foreclose any realistic alternatives, and that financial input requirements are relatively large and indivisible. However, it often may be the case that improvements in the output and profitability of the enterprise do not require credit, or that improvements can occur gradually by a succession of small increments. Incremental change might

18

well be financed largely through re-investment of savings of the enterprises themselves.

The point is that credit should not be looked on as one of the essentials of developing small enterprises or in the same category as availability of raw materials, markets for output, managerial capability, etc. If these essentials do exist, then credit may accelerate the growth of enterprises, if the potential exists. Rural entrepreneurs may not lack capital or credit so much as the motivation to use resources to develop their enterprises. There is ample evidence that credit programmes for small businesses often can be wasteful of funds, or even counterproductive. [14]

Despite the pitfalls, credit may be an important component of a project intervention aimed at ensuring that the essentials to the growth and development of smaller rural firms are in place. Credit policies then become important variables to be taken into account by the project planner.

Credit policies generally fall into one of the three following categories:

1. Credit Terms. The terms under which credit is offered often determine whether or not it can be useful to specific firms. Interest rates, security requirements, repayment terms (length of loan and repayment flexibility), and purposes to which loans may be put are the major policy components of credit terms.

In the past, many developing countries, often at the urging of donor agencies, have instituted credit programmes for small-scale farmers and other small enterprises at subsidised interest rates, that is, interest rates that do not cover the opportunity cost of capital, the cost of administering the credit, and the cost of risk and default. The rationale is that small-scale enterprises are operated by poor people who ought not to be charged interest rates high enough to cover the lender's costs because they cannot afford it, or because they need to be introduced to the borrowing process gradually.

The concept that poor producers need low interest rates to be able to use credit became a truism for many credit programmes. More recently, many specialists have marshalled impressive evidence that this may not be the case, and that subsidised interest rates may be self-defeating in terms of making credit effectively available to these target groups. It should be kept in mind that if the profitability of the credit investment depends upon

19

a few percentage points of interest, the investment
probably is not sufficiently profitable to justify
the use of credit in the first place.

The most telling argument in favour of charging
true interest rates is that economic viability of
the lending institution cannot otherwise be
sustained. Even in the case of a state lending
institution, the government is not likely to conti-
nually replace the capital of a subsidised credit
fund, and it will eventually become depleted. Additionally, a subsidised credit fund administered by a
state institution may draw customers from cooperative and other private institutions, thereby putting
these sources of credit out of business, or
seriously limiting their ability to capitalise and
expand. Once the state fund is depleted, the client
group has access to neither the state subsidised
credit nor a private institution. Furthermore, even
if a subsidised credit fund can be maintained at a
given level, there is no opportunity to capitalise
earnings and thereby expand the funds available for
lending to more clients.

The project planner should carefully weigh the
potentially negative aspects of a subsidised
interest rate before deciding whether or not to
incorporate it into a credit programme.

There is one instance where subsidised interest
rates may be used to improve the economic viability
of lending institutions. Some projects have successfully accelerated capitalisation and lending
capacities of cooperative lending institutions by
providing funds on concessional terms to the
national level of the organisation for on-lending to
local cooperatives (and in turn to members) at
market rates of interest. In this manner, the
national level organisation is permitted to capitalise and expand services more rapidly than otherwise
would have been possible. At the local level, more
membership can be served, while at the same time
improving economic viability of the various levels
of lending institutions.

Subsidised interest rates also may distort the
purposes for which loan funds are sought and used.
This may mean that scarce capital supplies are not
used in their most productive way. The usual role
of interest rates--a rationing mechanism for distributing scarce credit to its most productive uses--is
subverted, and other, less-effective rationing
mechanisms must be sought. These often become political criteria and/or expediency of administration,
for example, larger loans going to borrowers who can

offer better security.

Often, banking and internal regulations of state lending institutions require that borrowers pledge some collateral as loan security. Documentation and paperwork involved in meeting these collateral requirements, or the lack of adequate collateral, will discourage or disqualify some firms. A more forward-looking lending policy is to emphasise repayment capacity of the borrower based on the income-producing potential of his or her enterprise. However, for many small-scale enterprises, documentation of income-producing capacity also may be difficult. Alternatives include lending on the basis of reputation in the community and joint liability loans to small groups. For example, credit unions often require a borrower to have one or more guarantors who are credit union members in good standing.

The degree of flexibility in amortisation arrangements may have considerable bearing on the ability of enterprises to make effective use of credit. Although lending institutions must be aggressive in encouraging repayment, it is also necessary to be sufficiently flexible to allow for rescheduling loan repayment when unforeseen circumstances warrant. Often, state lending institutions have unrealistic and inflexible repayment requirements which do not adjust to the needs of smaller rural firms. This results in defaults that otherwise could be avoided. It also leads to a large delinquent portfolio. These delinquent loans remain uncollected in many cases because of political pressures and public image, or because of lack of collection staff and capability, and the corollary high cost of enforcing collection of large numbers of small loans.

Such a situation creates problems for the lender and acts as a bar to further credit by the borrower. A clear-cut and strictly enforced policy for treating delinquencies in terms of renewal, collection, forgiveness and bad debt treatment are preferable both from the viewpoint of the borrower and the lender.

Many credit programmes define a relatively narrow purpose for which loan funds may be used. There is considerable diversity in rural enterprises and in their credit needs. Also, most cottage-type enterprises do not distinguish between funds used in the business and funds used for family consumption. Too narrow a definition in a credit programme can result in lack of loan placement, or placement

ostensibly for one purpose while, in fact, the funds
are used for other purposes. In this respect,
credit policies affecting producers of raw materials
may have a negative impact on SMREs. For example, a
credit programme for small-scale farmers which is
limited to loans for production of staple grains may
have a negative effect on the supply of vegetables
to an enterprise using them as raw materials.

    2. Credit channels. Policies related to
promoting different credit channels may be of more
importance in providing access to adequate credit
supplies than are credit terms. In fact, devising
workable terms for credit depends to a certain
extent upon the channels through which credit is to
flow.

Non-commercial (or informal) channels supply
nearly all credit to small rural enterprises in most
traditional economies. Professional moneylenders,
traders, raw materials suppliers, family members and
friends channel most non-commercial credit to SMREs.
Another informal system that has received attention
is indigenous savings and credit, or rotating
credit, associations or societies. Although there
are many variations, these can be defined as a
group of participants who make regular contributions
to a fund which is given, in whole or in part, to
each member in turn. [15] These informal associations appear to provide capital in many countries
for members to start small rural businesses and
shops.

    Informal credit systems, especially money-
lenders, are often criticised because they are considered to be exploitative through charging
unusually high interest rates. However, some
observers suggest that these rates may be necessary
for the lender to cover the costs and risks of
lending money. In any event, experience has shown
that it is extremely difficult for formal institutional channels to reach the poor, isolated target
groups served by these informal channels. Public
policy related to informal credit often attempts to
limit maximum interest rates that can be charged.
This usually is not effective since informal systems
are difficult to monitor.

    Part of the motivation for establishing formal
government channels for credit is to provide poor
borrowers with an alternative to being in the "grip
of unscrupulous moneylenders." Yet, informal
channels of credit continue to function.

    An alternative policy choice is to attempt to
upgrade informal channels and link them into

supplies of funds that can permit expanded credit availability and result in lower interest rates because of less rationing. There is a case to be made for integrating the indigenous savings and credit societies into the modern financial sector. [16] In India, banks organise so-called "chitties" that are similar in principle to these societies. [17]

Formal credit channels include: 1) state-administered systems such as development banks and special credit programmes, 2) private channels such as commercial banks and finance companies, 3) cooperatives, whether service cooperatives (providing not only input, marketing or other services, but also credit for financing these services) or savings and credit cooperatives (receiving savings deposits from and lending to members), and 4) mixed public and private systems. In the latter systems, public institutions wholesale credit, while regional and local private institutions perform the intermediate distribution and local level retailing functions.

Public policies conducive to providing small rural enterprises with effective access to credit when needed and profitable are those which encourage: 1) local control and responsibility over resource allocation, 2) distribution of credit resources through small groups or with group guarantees of repayment, 3) linkage of local institutions to capital supplies within the larger credit system, and 4) rates charged for credit that permit the various levels of institutions involved to capitalise earnings and strengthen their ability to expand credit supplies.

3. Other credit policies. Equity participation may be an important alternative to credit for some agroindustrial enterprises and other enterprises embarking on non-traditional undertakings such as manufacturing a new product where market demand depends on recent changes in the local or national economy. Instead of establishing a debtor-creditor relationship between the outside capital-supplying institution and the local entrepreneur, the capital supplier takes shares in the business, or builds the plant and supplies the equipment on a profit-sharing basis, while sharing the business risks involved. In most cases, it is likely that the equity participation is practical only for medium-size, agribusiness enterprises.

Credit may be tied to some form of supervision or mandatory management advice. In fact, it may be a wise policy to include training and technical assistance for both the borrower and the lender in credit projects. [18]

In addition, the inclusion of other, noncredit services to small-scale borrowers may be more useful in terms of viability and growth than the provision of credit. Such services as bookkeeping assistance or skills-focused training are examples of important non-credit services that can and in many cases should be coordinated with credit.

## Agrarian Reform and Agricultural Policy

Present conditions and expected future trends for raw materials and markets are of critical importance to enterprises that are linked either backwards or forwards (or both) into the local economy or into the rural sector as a whole. Agrarian reform policies may have either negative or positive effects on the size and dynamism of the supply and product markets for these firms.

In cases where land previously held in absentee ownership or concentrated in large units is distributed to the former landless labourers or share-croppers, disposable incomes in the local area may increase even if output does not increase (or even declines somewhat). This is because more of the total agricultural income is retained by local people and spent in the area rather than being spent in the capital city or outside the country. Thus, an agrarian reform that results in nothing more than income transfer can be expected to increase local demand for goods and services. If productivity increases also are achieved as the result of programmes supporting agrarian reform, the increase will be even more substantial. This results in an economic climate that should have a positive impact on those small enterprises that provide goods and services for local consumption.

The positive impact on income of effective agrarian reform is demonstrated by the case of Taiwan. There the index of farm family incomes increased in real terms from 100 to 160 in the 15-year period following the Agrarian Reform. [19] Further, non-agricultural incomes of farm families increased at an even greater rate than did agricultural incomes. This suggests that the stimulus of increased incomes from agriculture may have a high multiplier effect on rural non-farm incomes.

Of course, it may be possible that income transfers from agrarian reform will be absorbed entirely in increased on-farm consumption. In that case, the impact on SMREs may not be positive and could possibly be negative. It also is possible that an agrarian reform that creates large-scale communal or collective farm enterprises could depress local demand served by small enterprises, if such tenurial forms are associated with centralised purchasing and marketing and internal distribution systems for items consumed by farm workers.

Other agricultural policies can affect the raw materials supply and/or product market structure of small enterprises. This is true for those depending on local markets as well as those serving broader markets.

Pricing policies that establish support prices for agricultural products used as raw materials may raise their costs to a point that destroys market competitiveness for agroindustries. Or high support prices for one product may cause farmers to shift out of the production of another product which served or could serve as raw material for agro-industry.

Policies of providing agricultural inputs, or market outlets for farm production, through state-owned channels at subsidised prices or costs may preclude the establishment and expansion of private and cooperative farm input supply and output marketing firms. For example, the practice of marketing fertiliser at subsidised prices through the state-owned agricultural development board in Guatemala resulted in considerable difficulties for agricultural input supply cooperatives in expanding fertiliser sales to small farmers until the government adopted a programme of passing on to the co-operatives the subsidy margin being applied by the state-owned distribution system. [20]

## Labour Laws and Employment Policy

Labour laws that impose minimum wages and relatively high levels of fringe benefits are common in developing countries. Where these affect small- and medium-scale rural enterprises, they can seriously limit ability to maintain viability and to expand. In many cases such labour laws exempt enterprises under a certain size, for example, those with fewer than five employees. Exemptions set at low levels may be an important disincentive to expansion by SMREs, even where other factors are favourable.

Other legislation affecting things such as

unionisation and contracts, severance, vacation and
disability allowances, maternity leave, pensions,
funeral expenses, food allowances, clothing, holiday
pay, etc., all act together to exert an upward
distortion in the price of labour which may effectively bar a significant percentage of the labour
force from participation in employment. Although
much of this legislation does not apply to many
smaller firms, it may well serve as a disincentive
to expansion because of concern about coming under
its provisions at some later time.

Job protection provisions of labour laws, such
as severance pay and disability allowances, often do
apply to all non-agricultural employment. This may
encourage enterprises to operate on the basis of
family labour, or limit outside employees to
temporary work, in order to avoid having employees
qualify for such benefits.

Government policies designed to provide employment to landless rural families may disrupt local
labour markets and serve as disincentives to establishment or expansion, or actually cause existing
enterprises to go out of business. This can occur
when extensive public works projects are sited in
areas where an equilibrium already exists in terms
of employment levels. [21] For example, small rural
enterprises were thought to have been negatively
affected by the increased and sustained demand for
employment generated in areas of Guatemala by
extensive earthquake rehabilitation construction
after 1976.

## Internal Fiscal and Tax Policies

Nationally administered property and income
taxes probably do not have a negative impact on
smaller rural enterprises in most developing
countries. Small enterprises often are specifically
exempted from business taxes because of their size
or organisational form. Or tax administration may
be inadequate to monitor any but large business
enterprises.

In those cases where smaller enterprises and
unincorporated businesses are exempted by law from
income or property taxation, the exemption level
could serve as a deterrent to expansion beyond a
certain size or as a deterrent to organising as a
corporation, thereby foreclosing shareholding as a
form of business capitalisation.

In some countries municipal licence fees, other

municipal rates and fees, and transaction or stamp taxes on purchases and sales documents and contracts tend to be regressive and may constitute a significant financial burden for small enterprises.

In many cases, the most important fiscal policies affecting the competitive position of SMREs in terms of raw materials and markets may be those that do not directly apply to them. Special fiscal legislation has been enacted in a number of countries for encouraging establishment and major expansion of large-scale enterprises. Income tax and property exemptions for an establishment period, special allowances thereafter, raw materials and equipment import duty exemptions, subsidised financing, and equity or seed capital participation by the state: all have been used in developing countries to promote large-scale industrialisation. Small, rural firms often are excluded from benefiting from these fiscal incentives because of lack of knowledge or access, or as is more often the case, because such incentives are available only to a minimum scale of operation or employment.

In a study of fiscal policies in Sierra Leone, the impacts on small enterprises were found to be seriously negative. [22] There, certain large-scale firms can qualify for a package of fiscal benefits as follows:

1. Exemption from income taxes for 3 to 10 years;

2. Deferral of depreciation allowances until after the tax exemption period; and

3. Exemption from import duties on building materials for plant construction, equipment, and raw or semi-processed production materials.

Small firms cannot qualify under this legislation. They find themselves at a considerable competitive disadvantage, especially where imported production materials are used.

Similarly, the structure of import duties in some countries may work against smaller firms. Again in Sierra Leone, it was found that in many cases the kinds of imported products used by small industries often have a high duty relative to many raw materials more common to larger-scale industries.


Marketing Policy

Public policies in most developing countries impact significantly not only on the markets

27

handling many products made by smaller enterprises but also on the markets for their raw materials.

For enterprises that trade in or process agricultural products, government intervention in the marketplace, through direct buying or controlled prices, may distort prices in a way that discourages use of these products as raw materials, or weakens the incentive to trade in them. Onerous hoarding and speculation laws are major deterrents to private (including cooperative) sector entry into the field of agricultural marketing.

Perhaps one of the most effective policy areas for direct government impact on market opportunities for SMREs is in government procurement. These enterprises often can be reliable and competitive suppliers for a wide range of products purchased by government agencies. Examples include: hospital and office furniture, school equipment, tools, uniforms, and many food items.

Examples of substantial impetus to SMREs through government procurement are found in India, Botswana, and Lesotho. [23]

Policies that promote subcontracting between large and small firms have been found to be effective stimulants to the development of smaller enterprises in a number of countries. [24] Government policies to promote subcontracting include provision of brokerage services, technical assistance for quality control and design work, and skill training. It may be possible to relate certain tax incentives and import or export exemptions for large firms to their linkages with small- and medium-scale enterprises.

Some cottage industries and enterprises producing for local markets may be unable to capture demand beyond the local area. Linkage into the larger market is extremely difficult or impossible for them. Market information may be helpful to assist the enterprise to expand beyond local markets in these cases. Often, however, the lack of a marketing network to reach into rural areas and place products in the wider national and international markets limits the usefulness of market information to SMREs. The establishment of publicly owned outlets, or assistance in organising cooperative marketing networks, constitute policy options available to assist in removing these constraints. Brokerage and promotion functions to make potential urban and international wholesale buyers aware of product opportunities also can be helpful.

Perhaps the most important stimulus to develop-

ment of smaller enterprises is effective and
expanding local demand. This, of course, is
influenced primarily by general economic policies
and agricultural development policies that improve
agricultural incomes and income distribution within
rural areas. Investment in rural economic and
social infrastructure, and policies affecting the
terms of trade between agriculture and urban
consumers, are important determinants of demand
levels and the rate of increase in demand for
products produced in rural areas by small and
medium-sized firms

## Regulatory and Incentive Structures

Health and sanitary regulations, transport
regulations, controls on the movement of goods,
including municipal government licences and fees for
entry and for doing business: all tend to be
regressive in nature. Thus, they have relatively
greater negative impacts on SMREs than on larger
businesses. In many developing countries these
types of regulations do not provide the necessary
flexibility to distinguish among different scales of
enterprise and different markets for goods. Often,
enforcement is erratic or the degree of enforcement
depends upon friendships or extra-legal payments.
Paperwork required for compliance with or exemption
from certain regulations may be only an irritant to
a large business, whereas it becomes an excessive
burden for smaller enterprises.
Regulations surrounding qualification for
special incentives, such as import exemptions,
access to foreign exchange, special capital and
credit programmes, or technical assistance
programmes, even where ostensibly including smaller
enterprises, may have eligibility requirements that
discourage or make impossible participation by many
small firms. Such requirements may include things
like the availability of financial accounts and
documents, certified audits, income and sales
projections, corporate or cooperative form of
business organisation, etc.
In some countries, laws against hoarding and
speculation can be a major deterrent to enterprises
that need to store products either for resale or for
processing.
A number of observers suggest that important
incentives for the growth of SMREs are those that:
1) facilitate access to information about opportuni-

ties, raw materials and markets; 2) assist in dealing with government offices that regulate or offer potential services; and 3) provide management and technical services and training. Effective responses to these needs often are more important in promoting growth than are financial services. [25] Indirect incentives also can be effective in many situations. This may be particularly true where substantial policy constraints exist. In rural areas where basic infrastructure for economic and social development is lacking, investment in roads, electricity, schools, health, and community facilities may be a prerequisite to significant growth of small- and medium-sized enterprises.

Regardless of the particular concept or incentive instruments to be promoted, an essential condition for successfully responding to the development needs of SMREs is the establishment of an institutional framework responsive to local issues and capable of delivering the assistance at the local level.

## Industrialisation, International Trade Policy, and SMREs

The relationship of past industrialisation policies, international trade policy, and the development of rural enterprises bears analysis in this public policy overview for several reasons. First, the strategy of promoting small and medium-sized rural enterprises has emerged out of the industrialisation policies pursued by the developing countries over the last 25 years, and its place as an increasingly accepted strategy can be best appreciated when seen within this broader context. As these industrialisation policies have been, and continue to be, intimately linked with trade policies, they are presented together in order to describe adequately this broader picture. Secondly, for some activities and agribusiness projects, the external sector must be taken into account in planning or the potential success will be seriously diminished. While traditional cost-benefit analysis will take some of these trade policy factors into account, it will not consider others which will be fundamental to an effective intervention. This section first outlines the evolution of industrialisation policies in developing countries and the emerging role of SMREs and then treats some specific trade policies necessary for consideration in designing appropriate interventions.

After World War II, increased attention and
international efforts were focused on the development of the poorer nations. The developed countries
had achieved high rates of growth through the spread
of modern technology and the development of large-
scale manufacturing, so development planners argued
that the developing countries could accelerate their
own growth by doing the same. Through international
assistance and borrowing in international capital
markets, developing countries could raise the
capital for such industrialisation which would
increase productivity levels per worker, permitting
incomes to rise. Since, as people's incomes rise a
diminishing proportion is spent on food and an
increasing share on manufactured goods, demand for
industrial goods would increase as incomes rose and
agriculture would assume the marginal role of
providing food for the growing industrial work
force. Likewise, as agriculture became more
productive, the farm labour force released would
find employment in the growing industrial sector.

Industrialisation in the developing countries
presented the problem, however, that these countries
already imported manufactured goods from the
developed countries and could not hope to compete
with them. The strategy, therefore, was to produce
primarily for the domestic market by substituting
locally produced manufactures for those being
imported from the developed countries--"import substitution industrialisation." This was accomplished
by erecting high tariff walls to protect local
infant industries from outside competition and by
granting an array of subsidies to selected firms,
especially for the use of capital.

The strategy initially stimulated a fair amount
of light manufacturing which was relatively labour-
intensive and required no large-scale production to
achieve efficient levels of unit costs. There was,
however, substantial encouragement of investment in
large-scale, capital-intensive industrial activities, even in smaller developing countries with
modest domestic markets. Such production turned out
to be rather import-intensive as imported machinery,
equipment, spare parts, and even raw materials were
required. The frequent lack of competition and the
small local market size also contributed to a highly
inefficient industrial structure as manifested in
high unit costs.

SMREs played no significant role in the
strategy, nor were they intended to. Backward

linkages between large industrial firms and small, rural firms were not emphasised, as large industries were not oriented toward the natural resource base, skill levels, or production patterns of other sectors of the economy. Likewise, planners viewed SMREs as part of the backward, traditional sector which was gradually to diminish in size as the modern sector expanded, so no concrete attempts were made to subsidise them either.

Small, rural enterprises were, nevertheless, affected negatively by import substitution policies in many cases. The high level of protection of infant industrial firms, for instance, provided a monopoly power to some local industries, resulting in small firms having to pay monopoly prices for their inputs from such industries or in having to receive monopsony determined prices for their output sold to such companies. In one country, for example, it was found that the monopoly position of the domestic flour mill resulted in flour prices for small-scale bakers which were more than two times the import price. [26] Of course, the overall inefficiency of import substitution industries also contributed to increased costs for the small rural firms dealing with them.

Direct and indirect subsidies had the effect of encouraging capital-intensive and import-intensive activities and techniques to the prejudice of production by smaller firms which tends to be more intensive in the use of local resources. In one study comparing the choice of technique for textile production using automatic and semi-automatic imported and domestic looms, for example, it was found that the implicit subsidy for the more capital-intensive automatic imported looms was more than two times greater than that to automatic domestic and many times greater than to domestic semi-automatic looms, the most labour-intensive, for which there was a net negative subsidy element. [27]

Import substitution policies, in conjunction with other "equity"-motivated policies, also nega-tively affected agriculture. These effects in turn restrained both small-scale enterprises and larger agribusiness projects because of their direct links with agriculture. The whole industrialisation policy resulted in a disproportionate direct and indirect taxation of agriculture through such mecha-nisms as discriminatory subsidies, overvaluation of the exchange rate, high tariffs on imported agricul-tural inputs, taxes on agricultural exports, price controls on agricultural goods to subsidise local food consumption, etc. The stagnation of agriculture reduced demand for the products of SMREs used by farmers and farm labourers as inputs or family consumption items. Likewise, agribusinesses had difficulty in many cases in expanding production because of the unavailability of a stable and expanding supply of agricultural inputs.

In determining appropriate interventions, the distortions fostered by import substitution have traditionally been taken into account in the cost-benefit analysis of projects. Shadow pricing of the costs of labour, capital, and foreign exchange involves making adjustments for subsidies, tariffs, and wages, and wage distortions in the modern sector to determine the true costs and benefits to a country from an activity. As the method for doing this is treated in Chapter 7, its context is only noted here. A number of developing countries, however, are becoming increasingly receptive to the idea of modifying some of the mechanisms which cause these distortions, especially the exchange rate, tariffs, and subsidy policies, and it may be that some countries might be interested in an intervention based on creating more rational policies in this area.

By the mid-1960s, criticism of the import substitution strategy was widespread as it became evident that equity considerations such as employment and income distribution were little affected by the growth-oriented industrialisation approach. Out of this criticism emerged two separate strategies—that of export promotion and that of small- and medium-scale enterprise development. While the former preceded the latter, they have similar objectives, and in some cases are intimately related.

The approach based on the development of small- and medium-scale rural enterprises stands in stark contrast to that of import substitution and large-scale industrialisation. Import substitution was capital-intensive in the face of capital scarcity and widespread unemployment, and import-intensive in the use of inputs in the face of foreign exchange scarcities. SMREs, on the other hand, are labour-intensive and judicious in the use of capital, located in rural areas, and inseparably intertwined in the agricultural sector where much of the unemployment and poverty exists and from which it draws its raw materials. It has been suggested that smaller enterprises are more labour-intensive not

only because they tend to be involved in the
production of goods which are inherently labour-
intensive, but also because prices they pay for
labour and capital are not distorted by subsidised
capital and high wage rates set by labour union
negotiations.  Likewise, by providing increased
employment and income benefits in rural areas,
migration to the cities can be influenced and
employment and income distribution goals can be
achieved as small- and medium-scale rural enterprises concentrate directly on those groups in
greatest need.

A strategy of expanding the participation of
small firms in the economy depends in part on
increasing the demand for the goods and services
these firms produce.  An increase in demand for
their activities will, in turn, depend upon at least
one of the following:  1) increasing incomes of
rural families so that goods and services from small
firms are demanded in the form of farm inputs (for
example, farm implements) or farm and non-farm
family consumption items (for example, clothing);
2) by forming forward linkages with larger firms
generally located in the cities (for example, jute
sacks to a fertiliser plant in larger market
centres);  or 3) by selling the increased output of
small-scale firms in new regional markets or
exporting it to other countries.

This last area is the point where the current
export-oriented strategy and a strategy based on the
development of small enterprises link importantly.
For many products the local market does not offer
any significant opportunities to enterprises if they
want to expand their production or to new firms
wishing to start up.  To some of these firms,
exporting will offer the only viable way for
activities to grow.  As the relative importance and
potential benefit of the export market will vary
according to the type of product, size of country,
and level of development of the small-enterprise
subsector, and the country as a whole, interventions
must be tailor-made to fit the unique characteristics of the enterprises and country being assisted.

Export promotion activities are important as
part of an overall economic development effort,
especially for the smaller and/or predominantly
agricultural developing countries.  There are many
raw and processed agricultural goods for which
developing countries have a comparative advantage
because of their labour-intensity and for which the
income elasticities of demand are high   (especially

in the developed countries--for example, vegetables, certain fruits, and oilseed plants) which can be successfully exported. Agribusiness, for example, is often emphasised as a way of increasing the local value-added in agricultural developing countries. Although these increased benefits can accrue to a developing country, a substantial portion of the processed agricultural goods must be exported in order to reach economic levels of production or in order to process enough agricultural output to affect the agricultural sector favourably. If exporting can be achieved, benefits are received by the country in the form of lower prices for processed goods and the generation of additional foreign exchange, as well as increased employment in the agribusiness and agricultural sectors. These processing enterprises not only tend to be labour-intensive (a large percentage of this labour force is women) in and of themselves, but also to provide increased demand for products that can be linked to small-scale producers and/or labour-intensive agriculture. In addition, they spawn a host of labour-intensive satellite industries which provide the processing plants with such things as wooden crates, jute sacks, etc.

While the export-oriented growth strategy was also a reaction to the excesses of import substitution, there have been few attempts to link it with development of small-scale rural enterprises. As with the strategy advocated in this volume, export promotion is based on the recognition that the comparative advantage of developing countries lies in labour-intensive activities. It is likewise based on the idea that through specialisation in exportable labour-intensive production, both growth and employment objectives can be achieved.

The lack of focus on small- and medium-sized rural firms as a source of labour-intensive goods, however, can be traced in part to the practical requirements of operating in international markets. For a variety of reasons, developing countries have traditionally traded little among themselves, and the labour cost advantage exists primarily for goods shipped to developed countries, so those countries are the target of export efforts. To market goods in developed countries, however, requires that an exporter in a developing country has the capacity to fill (what are to him) large orders in short periods of time, provide products of a uniform and high quality, and ensure that the products are tailored to the tastes of consumers in the developed country

35

ordering the goods. Likewise, the exporter's
ability to market products will depend upon cultiva-
ting and maintaining contacts with importers in
developed countries, providing reliable and prompt
service, and keeping abreast of style changes and
other market information--all of which are a fixed
cost to him, regardless of the volume he exports.
Thus, exporters will be more interested in dealing
with larger companies which can supply major orders
and with whom they can make arrangements regarding
quality control and adaptation to foreign tastes.
    The entry problems for small rural firms are
obvious. Quality differences and low quality
production are common characteristics of SMREs.
Enterprises will not have access to information on
foreign markets, nor can they afford the high fixed
costs of entering the foreign market alone; and
exporters will have little interest in dealing with
only a single small firm.
    These problems are surmountable, however,
through appropriately designed interventions.
Research has shown the demand does exist in
developed countries for a large number of labour-
intensive articles produced by SMREs and that the
growth in demand for these goods in developed
countries is strong. [28] Since the small enterprises will not know, however, whether or not their
products are the ones for which external demand
exists, an appropriate intervention is that of
conducting market studies in conjunction with such
firms to determine their export potential. To overcome the lack of information, interventions can
focus on providing services which keep small enterprises informed as to market requirements for their
goods, analyse their production methods to assist in
needed adaptation to market tastes, provide
training, etc. Equally important are interventions
aimed at institution building and training in two
areas. First, a frequently needed intervention will
be the fostering of groups of small firms to coordi-
nate their production, quality levels, and adaptation to the demands of the international market.
Secondly, institution building through training will
often be needed to develop export-promotion firms
which can interact with these groups of SMREs to
funnel their production into the international
market, as well as keep them abreast of needed
market requirements, obtain export financing, and
deal with the other special exporting requirements
of smaller firms.
    This type of intervention has been accomplished

in the past through donor-provided financial
support, although it has not been directed toward
the special problems and requirements of small- and
medium-scale rural enterprises. Such interventions,
however, will be a virtual requirement for the
expansion of some type of activities on the part of
these enterprises.

NOTES

1. United Nations Industrial Development Organization, Technical Services for Small
Scale Industry (United Nations, New York, 1970),
p.7.
2. World Bank, Employment and Development of
Small Enterprises (Washington, 1978), p.74.
3. S. Daines and D. Steen, El Salvador Agroindustrial Profile (United States Agency for
International Development, El Salvador, 1977), p.66.
4. An 11-country comparison of the composition
of nonfarm rural employment shows both similarities
and some pronounced differences. See Table 2.1.
5. Milton Esman et al., The Landless and
Near Landless in Developing Countries (Cornell University, Ithaca, New York, 1977), p.2.
6. Daines, 1977, p.26.
7. See S. Daines, "Analysis of Industrial
Structure, Technology and Productivity," in The Food
Processing Sector of Brazil (Cambridge, Massachusetts, Massachusetts Institute of Technology, 1975).
8. See, for example, S. Daines, Brazil, El
Salvador, Costa Rica. Agroindustrial Profile
(United States Agency for International Development,
San Jose, Costa Rica, 1976).
9. E. Staley and R. Morse, Modern Small
Industry for Developing Countries (McGraw-Hill, New
York, 1965).
10. Ibid., pp.112-24.
11. Ibid., p.379.
12. D. Kochav et al., Financing the Development of Small Scale Industries (The World Bank,
Washington, 1974).
13. A term coined by J. D. Von Pischke for
application to the credit needs of small-scale
farmers in "A Critical Survey of Approaches to the
Role of Credit in Smallholder Development" (Paper
presented to the Eastern Africa Agricultural
Economics Society Conference in Lusaka, Zambia, May
1974).
14. See Malcolm Harper, "The Employment of

Finance in Small Business," Journal of Development
Studies, vol.11, no.4 (1975), p.367.
15.  F. J. A. Bouman, "Indigenous Savings and
Credit Societies in the Third World," Development
Digest, vol.16, no.3 (1978), p.36.
16.  Ibid., p.45.
17.  V. V. Bhatt, "Financial Innovations,
Transaction Costs and Development," Development
Digest, vol.16, no.3 (1978), p.33.
18.  Richard L. Meyer, "Financing Rural
Nonfarm Enterprises in Low Income Countries,"
Economics and Sociology Occasional Paper No.522
(Ohio State University, Columbus, Ohio, 1978), p.15.
19.  Yen-Tien Chang, "Land Reform and Its
Impact on Economic and Social Progress in Taiwan",
pp.13-16, as cited in United States Agency for
International Development, Agribusiness and Rural
Enterprise Project Analysis Manual (Washington,
1980), p.14.
20.  W. Rusch, F. Mann and E. Braun, "Rural
Cooperatives in Guatemala:  A Study of their
Development, and Evaluation of A.I.D. Projects in
their Support" (United States Agency for
International Development, Guatemala, 1975).
21.  World Bank, 1978, p.46.  Other national
and local government projects and services in rural
areas also are important employers and provide about
20 per cent of all nonfarm employment.
22.  Carl Liedholm and Enyinna Chuta, "The
Economics of Rural and Urban Small Scale Industries
in Sierra Leone," African Rural Economy Paper No.14
(Michigan State University, East Lansing, Michigan,
1976), pp.111-12.
23.  World Bank, 1978, p.25.
24.  Ibid.  Japan, Korea, India and several
countries in Latin America are cited as examples.
25.  Harper, 1975, pp.368-75; Meyer, 1978,
p.16; Von Pischke, 1974, pp.11-12.
26.  Liedholm and Chuta, 1976, p.117.
27.  Y. W. Rhee and L. E. Westphal, "A Micro-
econometric Investigation of the Choice of Technology," Journal of Development Economics, vol.4,
no.3 (1977), pp.205-37.
28.  Y. Ho and D. L. Huddle, "The Contribution
of Traditional and Small Scale Culture Goods in
International Trade and in Employment," Program of
Development Studies, Paper No.35 (Rice University,
Houston, Texas, 1972).

CHAPTER 3

DESIGNING RURAL ENTERPRISE PROJECTS TO
BENEFIT THE POOR

The fundamental issue addressed in this chapter is
how agroindustrial and rural enterprise projects can
be designed so as to maximise their benefits for the
poorer segments of rural societies.

RURAL ECONOMIES AND PLANNED CHANGE

Rural economies in developing countries are
interknit systems. Farms, small-scale enterprises,
commerce and services operate in an integrated
fashion whether or not they are guided and motivated
by a monetary economy. Growth and development in
these systems also occur in an interknit fashion.
This interrelatedness does not necessarily imply,
however, that balanced growth may stem from an
initiative in a single part of the system and then
spread evenly to other parts of the rural economy.
[1] The benefits of growth may pass outside this
economy to urban consumers or to those in both rural
and urban areas who are already relatively well off.
Interventions to assist agroindustry, agribusiness and agroservice enterprises operate at the
centre of a set of linkages which reach backward to
agriculture and forward to final consumers. Such
interventions are ideally suited to draw the parts
of the system more closely together and to pass more
evenly the benefits of growth in one segment of the
rural economy to the others by connecting producers
more effectively with final markets. [2]
If interventions are carefully designed to
benefit the poor, they can reduce the leakage of
benefits outside the rural economy and to the nonpoor, but these effects do not occur automatically.
If capital-intensive agroindustry draws its raw
materials from capital-intensive, large-scale farms,

rural production may even displace benefits and tend to isolate the poor by closing them out of the system rather than drawing them in. While interventions in these pivotal agroindustrial and rural enterprise activities have great potential to increase the welfare of the poor, the design of projects must be clearly focused on drawing the poor, with their labour resources, limited skills and entrepreneurial experience into the system.

Common sense and past experience lead to a set of a priori recommendations which can be applied to all types of projects and which constitute a check-list for designers of projects to use in testing each component and projects as a whole. The three recommendations below all have a common focus of building on the structure of existing enterprises and on maximising the involvement of the poor through the utilisation of their skills, resources and products:

i. All interventions should be designed so as to focus first on the use of the most important single resource available to the rural poor and nonfarm poor--their labour.

ii. All interventions should be designed so as to focus on the second most important resource of the nonfarm rural poor--their small-scale enterprises and the entrepreneurial skills they have developed to manage them.

iii. All agroindustrial interventions should be designed so as to draw their raw materials from the second most important resource of the agriculture-based rural poor--their small farms and the entrepreneurial skills they have developed to operate them.

As we shall see in the discussion which follows, these recommendations must be incorporated into conscious choices about project design. The nonpoor are comparatively agile in most rural and urban settings. It is they--the nonpoor--who can usually take advantage of new resources, new government programmes and incentive schemes, new market opportunities, etc. The nonpoor are the ones who by and large have the skills and mobility to shift, to adjust and to capture the benefits of most realignments in the rural economy. Perhaps the best way at least to reduce the existing advantage of the nonpoor is to involve the poor and their resources directly in the intervention itself.

FOCUSING INTERVENTIONS ON EMPLOYMENT CREATION

There are two basic ways to ensure that agribusiness and rural enterprise projects maximise their impact on employment creation. The first is to focus the project on products with a high labour intensity, that is, those which require large quantities of labour relative to capital and land. [3] The second is to utilise the technologies and techniques which are most efficient as judged by shadow prices for labour. In simpler terms, the first is to favour the production of goods which use large proportions of labour, and the second is to use techniques which utilise high proportions of labour for the production of all goods.

For example, labour represents a higher proportion of total costs in the processing of fruits and vegetables at almost all levels of technology than it does in the milling of wheat. Fruit and vegetable products may be thought of as labour-intensive products compared to wheat flour. Such labour-intensive products should be favoured in project interventions. It is possible to process either fruits and vegetables or wheat with different techniques, each having a different labour intensity. Regardless of the product involved, interventions should favour those techniques or technologies which are more labour-using or labour-intensive. The two choices--of product and technique--should be focused on maximising employment creation, and further elaboration of these choices follows.

## Favouring Labour-intensive Products

Most of the discussion in the literature on labour intensity and appropriate technology has focused on differences in the labour intensity of different techniques of production, or what has roughly been termed "labour-intensive technologies". Aside from the important issue of "how" to produce using more or less labour (which is dealt with below), there is the issue of what to produce, or more specifically, what products should be included or expanded in an agribusiness or rural enterprise project. It is argued here that this choice of product will have as much if not more impact on employment generation as will the choice of technology or how to produce. Table 3.1 presents a measure of the labour intensity of different agribusiness products. From the table it can be seen

that the two examples used above--cereal milling and
fruit and vegetable processing--are very different
in their employment intensity. Four and a half
times as many workers are utilised to produce one
dollar of output in fruit and vegetable processing
as are used in cereal milling. Table 3.1 indicates
that the choice of products for which a project will
intervene will have a fundamental influence on the
employment impact of the funds invested in the
project. With this scale of labour-intensity, the
magnitude of the range is substantial. Products
with low labour intensity create in many cases less
than one-tenth as much employment per unit of output
as do those with very high labour intensity.
Product choice is a project design issue of critical
importance for maximising employment impacts.
The labour intensity of products should be
examined in a systems context which includes the
labour intensity of both backward and forward
linkages; that is, product labour intensity should
take account of the labour intensity of the primary
agricultural product (the backward linkage) and the
labor intensity of later stages of processing (the
forward linkages). Instead of affecting only a
single product, any project will really be inter-
vening in a product chain that stretches from
primary farm production through marketing and
processing to final consumption.
Table 3.1 also provides an illustration of this
idea. While cereal milling is one of the least
labour-using of agribusiness activities, baking is
among the very highest. If a project were to select
cereal milling as a sector for intervention, the
poor labour performance of milling should be
adjusted by the high labour performance of the
baking industry, which would inevitably be affected.
But what of the backward link? From the employment
point of view, cereals generally use less labour as
compared to fruit and vegetables. The labour intensity of these different products is not difficult to
estimate, and product choice can be used as an
important design feature for increasing the employment impact of agribusiness and rural enterprise
interventions.


## Technological Choice and Labour Intensity

The same product can usually be produced in
different ways, each having a different labour
intensity. This manual is not the place for a long

Table 3.1.--Labour Intensity of Agribusiness
          Production, El Salvador

| Subsector | Index: No. of workers per $1,000 of output |
| --- | --- |
| **Very high labour intensity** | |
| Sugar | 712 |
| Wood products | 317 |
| Clothing | 276 |
| Furniture | 242 |
| Baking | 204 |
| **High labour intensity** | |
| Fruit and vegetables | 170 |
| Shoes | 143 |
| Sweets | 130 |
| **Medium labour intensity** | |
| Textiles | 93 |
| Fishing | 78 |
| Tobacco | 68 |
| Meat products | 66 |
| Coffee | 65 |
| Fish products | 62 |
| Milk | 59 |
| **Low labour intensity** | |
| Edible oils | 39 |
| Cereal milling | 38 |
| Drinks | 22 |

Source:   Industrial Census, El Salvador, 1971.

Note:     The national average labour intensity is
          100.

and/or highly technical discussion of the methods
for determining what the most appropriate technology
is in any specific case.  Where labour is substantially underutilised, its market wage rate seldom
reflects its true economic worth.  In this situation
it is usually more efficient to use more labour in
production than would be indicated by the relative

prices of capital and labour. Planners of agribusiness and rural enterprise projects should be very much aware of the need to avoid allowing distorted prices (import subsidies on capital, etc.) to encourage the use of capital at the expense of labour. The question addressed here is how can the design of agribusiness projects appropriately favour labour-intensive techniques.

Scale of operation and labour intensity of technology. The first practical suggestion is that project design may favour labour-intensive technology by choosing to intervene and support smaller-scale enterprises. Though the precise structure needs to be analysed for each country, most agribusiness and rural enterprise subsectors reveal an increasing labour intensity (for the same type of product) as scale decreases, since smaller scale enterprises tend to be more intensive. Table 3.2 shows this tendency using data from India.

The table shows that, as a general rule, firm size and labour intensity seem to be inversely related, although there are always exceptions. Importantly, we see that firms of similar sizes can themselves have substantial differences in labour intensity, and the degree to which they become less so as firm size increases can also vary according to the type of activity. This individuality of characteristics underscores the importance of actual analysis based on the country in which the project is to be undertaken.

An important issue often raised when labour-intensive technology is addressed deals with the efficiency of using labour-intensive technologies. The concern is often that, in the enthusiasm for generating employment, efficiency and profitability not be forgotten. There are valid arguments which could be made supporting the notion that in labour-surplus economies even some technologies which do not have high private profitability should be supported because they have justifiably high social profitability when the true relative economic value of resources is used to adjust factor prices. While this argument may be important, it is probably true in many if not most actual agribusiness and rural enterprise projects that such an argument is not necessary to support the viability of labour-intensive technologies simply because the private profitability of the more labour-intensive technologies is acceptably high. Table 3.3 illustrates this point for El Salvador by indicating that private profit margins are actually higher for the smaller

Table 3.2.--Labour Intensity by Scale of Operation
for Selected Industrial Groups, India

| Industrial Group | Scale of operation[a] | | |
| | Small | Medium | Large |
|---|---|---|---|
| Grain mill products | .41 | .22 | .13 |
| Miscellaneous food preparations | .45 | .24 | .11 |
| Tobacco manufacturers | .73 | .69 | .06 |
| Spinning, weaving and finishing of textiles | .41 | .39 | .29 |
| Textiles [b] | .93 | .35 | .21 |
| Sawmills and wood products (except paper and furniture) | .55 | .30 | .87 |
| Printing, publishing and allied industries | .36 | .29 | .21 |
| Basic industrial chemicals, including fertiliser | .21 | .13 | .10 |
| Paints, varnishes, lacquers, and miscellaneous chemical products | .30 | .12 | .07 |
| Nonmetallic mineral products [b] | .49 | .23 | .11 |
| Iron and steel basic industries | .39 | .33 | .15 |
| Metal products, except machinery and transport equipment | .34 | .21 | .12 |
| Machinery, except electrical machinery | .36 | .21 | .18 |
| Electrical machinery, apparatus, appliances and supplies | .34 | .18 | .15 |
| Motor vehicles repair | .41 | .37 | .42 |
| Fur products, except wearing apparel and manufacturing products [b] | .40 | .25 | .12 |

Source:  Annual Survey of Industries, Government of
India, 1965.

a       Number of employees per 1,000 rupees of
value added.

b       Not elsewhere classified.

scale, labour-intensive technologies. The table
should not be read as indicating that this is true
for all agribusiness products or all countries, but
only that the reverse presumption (that labour-
intensive technologies have lower private profitability) is not generally true.

Table 3.3.--Profit Margin by Scale of Agribusiness
Enterprise, El Salvador

| Subsector | Net income as a percentage of total value of production by number of workers per plant | | | | |
|---|---|---|---|---|---|
| | 5-9 | 10-19 | 20-49 | 50-99 | 100+ |
| | (Per cent) | | | | |
| Food products | 26 | 22 | 21 | 25 | 20 |
| Coffee | 44 | 26 | 18 | 22 | 15 |
| Drinks | 45 | 39 | 23 | 38 | 36 |
| Textiles | 25 | 22 | 27 | 14 | 25 |
| Clothing | 28 | 24 | 20 | 21 | 25 |
| Shoes | 29 | 28 | 20 | 0 | 34 |
| Wood products | 33 | 21 | 9 | 48 | 0 |
| Furniture | 29 | 18 | 18 | 27 | 10 |
| All industry | 30 | 26 | 22 | 24 | 28 |

Source: United States Agency for International
Development, Agribusiness and Rural Enterprise Project Analysis Manual (Washington,
1980), p.30.

The implication of the foregoing discussion is
that one practical project option for favouring
labour-intensive technology, and therefore increased
employment, is to select small-scale enterprises to
support. There is little evidence suggesting that
such a focus on small-scale firms will reduce the
efficiency or profitability of project investments.
Direct intervention to influence the labour
intensity of technology. A second method of
favouring labour-intensive technology is to identify
viable labour-intensive technologies and support
them directly. This alternative could be accomplished in a number of different ways. A project
could, for example, take existing labour-intensive
technologies and, using industrial extension methods

supplied through technical assistance, encourage and train enterprises to adopt them. Or, where acceptably efficient labour-intensive techniques do not already exist, research activities could be undertaken to identify and test viable options. Finally, projects could provide financial support for the installation and/or operation of labour-intensive technologies. The support could be either in money or in kind in the form of actual machinery or other inputs.

## FOCUSING PROJECT ACTIVITIES ON ENTERPRISES OWNED AND OPERATED BY THE RURAL POOR

The objective of focusing on enterprises owned and operated by the rural poor is to harness the entrepreneurial capabilities of this group in the solution of their own problems and, secondly, to reduce the proportion of project benefits which is captured by the nonpoor. Since the rural poor generally own and/or operate only small-scale enterprises, this focus also tends to concentrate project interventions on these small-scale, rural-based enterprises, although such concentration need not be completely exclusive. A second reason for emphasising those enterprises owned and operated by the rural poor is that entrepreneurial returns and profits from these enterprises are captured by the poor in addition to their income from labour. To the extent that larger-scale enterprises, not owned by the poor, are the focus of project interventions, the poor will benefit only from wages and not from entrepreneurial returns or profits.

The first part of this section outlines the implications of focusing project interventions on smaller-scale enterprises owned by the poor, or on larger-scale enterprises which may benefit the poor through employment and backward links to poor families in agriculture. The balance of the section examines optional project interventions for small-scale rural enterprises which are likely to be owned by poor rural families.

### Focusing on Scale of Operations

The major benefit of focusing on small-scale enterprises is that the poor capture both the labour and profit incomes. If larger-scale enterprises are the focus, the poor obtain only wages and earnings

arising from backward linkages from increased demand
for production from small farms.  The project choice
should therefore depend on the relative size and
profitability of these two potential income streams.
If more total income can come to the poor from added
employment in larger-scale firms and from the
increased demand which is generated for the output
of small farms than can be obtained in the form of
labour and profits in small-scale enterprises, then
the choice should be in favour of the larger-scale
intervention.  If, on the other hand, the labour
income, profits and backward linkages generated by
small-scale business are greater, the choice should
be in favour of the smaller-scale enterprises.

The backward linkage of agribusiness and rural
enterprise projects is discussed in the next
section; the balance of this section attempts to
deal with the issue of direct income and employment
potentials of projects focused on small-scale enterprises.

Benefits from employment and from profits.  It
is possible that the efficiency of larger-scale
enterprises is such that the rural poor are better
off to work in more efficient larger enterprises
than to own and operate their own less-efficient
ones.  This does not appear to be widely supported
by the available evidence and the issue should be
examined in each case.  The reasons why the opposite
appears to be the case are outlined below:

1.  Even if larger-scale enterprises are more
efficient, it is not likely that the added income
would be passed along to unskilled workers in the
form of increased wage rates as long as there is a
large pool of unemployed from which almost endless
additions could be drawn at the minimum wage.
Expanding the larger-scale operation would result
principally in expanded numbers in employment--a
critically important contribution--but not in
increased wages.

2.  Focusing on small-scale enterprises has the
advantage that all of the income, wages and profits
go to the target group.  Some empirical examples may
be helpful in illustrating this point.

The first example is shown in Table 3.4.
To interpret the table properly, it is important to
know that the productivity of labour (gross value of
output per worker) is five times as high in large-
scale agribusinesses ($6,176) as in small-scale
enterprises ($1,144).  For the food processing
sector, the per capita income from labour and
profits in small-scale enterprises is 56 per cent

48

higher than the per capita income of workers in larger-scale plants. This means that the labour productivity advantage of larger firms largely benefits the owners of the firm and is not passed along to the workers. In many sectors this is not true. In textiles, the advantage is almost reversed; workers in large firms earn more than 60 per cent more income per capita than do the owner/operators of small-scale firms. From the findings in El Salvador it would appear that labour productivity alone is not a sufficient guide to estimate potential income benefit; the actual net income potential of large- and small-scale enterprises must be examined directly for each potential project.

Table 3.4.--Comparison of Net Per Capita Incomes of Workers in Large-scale Agribusinesses and of Small-scale Owner-operators, El Salvador

| Subsector | Net income per capita | |
|---|---|---|
| | Medium and large scale | Small scale |
| | (US$) | |
| Food processing | 147 | 229 |
| Coffee processing | 271 | 215 |
| Drinks | 412 | 288 |
| Tobacco | 189 | 89 |
| Textiles | 221 | 144 |
| Clothing | 156 | 175 |
| Leather | 300 | 232 |
| Shoes | 192 | 323 |
| Wood products | 122 | 175 |
| Furniture | 222 | 230 |
| All agroindustry | 212 | 230 |

Source: Industrial Census, El Salvador, 1971.

3. Another option could involve expanding wage-earning opportunities in small-scale enterprises or expanding entrepreneurial opportunities by attempting to create additional enterprises. While incomes of owner-operators in small-scale enterprises are competitive with incomes of workers in larger ones, workers in small-scale enterprises are not comparably paid. From the data for Guatemala

presented in Table 3.5, it would appear that the
income of workers in small-scale enterprises is
substantially less than that of owner-operators.
This arises from two factors: first, the monthly
remuneration of workers is significantly less than
that of the owners (as shown in the table); and,
secondly, the number of months worked per year by
workers is less than that of the owners (not shown
in the table). While this may not be the pattern
for all activities in all countries, it does suggest
that empirical data are a necessary element to
support the choice as to whether to increase the
number of enterprises or to expand the existing
enterprises.

Table 3.5.--Comparison of Monthly Incomes of Owner-
operators of Small-scale Enterprises
with those of Wage-earning Workers in
Small-scale Enterprises

| Sector | Monthly wage rate | Net monthly income for men and women over 15 in owner-family | Superiority of owner income per month worked |
|---|---|---|---|
| | (US$) | | (Per cent) |
| Wood products | 65 | 81 | 24.6 |
| Textiles | 21 | 32 | 52.4 |
| Leather and misc. | 31 | 47 | 51.6 |
| Baking & food products | 32 | 43 | 34.4 |
| Commercial services | 28 | 60 | 114.3 |

Source: Calculated by S. R. Daines from data in the
1978 Rural Enterprise Survey by S. R.
Daines and G. Smith, Ministry of
Agriculture (Guatemala).

Harnessing Entrepreneurial Energy in Existing Small-
scale Enterprises.

Finding that incomes, profits and indicators of
output are satisfactory for very small-scale enterprises indicates that there is a vast potential for

income and employment generation within the enterprises owned and operated by the poor themselves.
There are, for example, close to 18,000 small-scale
industries in El Salvador and some 250,000 small
farms, or a ratio of one small-scale enterprise for
each 12-15 small farms.

The surprisingly large number of small-scale
industries relative to the size of the sector seems
to be the case in a number of other countries as
well. Table 3.6 shows that firms employing fewer
than 10 persons account for substantial proportions
of total employment in manufacturing in a number of
countries, and it is likely that the figures are
even higher than shown in the table because some
small-scale enterprises were omitted from censuses.

If the number of enterprises is very large, the
major problem is likely to be similar to the
problems of access encountered in projects aimed at
small farmers. From the points of view of practical
project design, administration, monitoring and

Table 3.6.--Employment in Small-scale Firms as a
Percentage of Total Employment in
Manufacturing

| | Level of employment in the firm | |
| | Fewer than 10 persons | Fewer than 50 persons |
| --- | --- | --- |
| | (Per cent) | |
| Philippines (1961) | 76 | 83 |
| Taiwan (1961) | 46 | 60 |
| South Korea (1966) | 43 | 51 |
| Thailand (1964) | 70 | 79 |
| Singapore (1966) | 45 | 65 |
| Sierra Leone (1974) | -- | 96 |
| Nigeria (1970) | 94 | -- |

Source: H. T. Oshima, "Labor-Force 'Explosion' and
the Labor-intensive Sector in Asian
Growth," Economic Development and
Cultural Change, 19, 2 (January 1971),
pp.161-83 and C. Liedholm and E. Chuta,
"The Economics of Rural and Urban Small-
scale Industries in Sierra Leone," African
Rural Economy Paper No. 14, Michigan State
University, East Lansing, 1976.

Note: The use of (--) indicates data are not
available.

institutional implications, those projects oriented toward assisting small-scale rural enterprises will be very much like projects for the small-farm subsector.

## FOCUSING PROJECTS TO ENHANCE THE BENEFITS OF BACKWARD LINKAGES TO SMALL FARMS

Agribusinesses, whatever their type and wherever their location, utilise farm and rural products as their major raw material inputs. Expansion of these industries will have important impacts on the suppliers of these inputs. This section deals with how to maximise these benefits for small-scale farmers.

### Differential Impacts from Expansion or Other Improvements

The first factor which determines whether an agribusiness project will pass on significant benefits to small farms relates to the nature of the intervention itself. If the intervention is directed at expanding the output from agribusinesses, the logical consequence will be to require more raw material input in order to produce the output. If the intervention is to change the technology used by enterprises, to change profit margins, to improve management or to make any other change which improves the business without an expansion in size, it is not likely that additional raw material will be required and hence little benefit will be passed back to suppliers. It should be noted that there are types of intervention which may actually result in a decreased requirement for raw materials. One way to increase the efficiency and profit margin of an agribusiness firm is to increase the conversion rate of raw material into final product. A feasible agribusiness project might aim to reduce the waste of raw material by the firm, and this may reduce demand for the raw material and actually reduce the incomes of suppliers of the raw material. Thus, the nature of the intervention chosen will have an important impact on the proportion of the benefit which is passed backward to suppliers, some of whom may be small farmers and part of the target group.

## Raw Material Intensity of Production

Enterprises producing different products spend varying proportions of their total expenditure on raw materials. This proportion is referred to here as the raw material intensity of production. A project will pass a larger part of its total benefit back to suppliers if it is focused on agribusinesses with a high raw material intensity. Table 3.7 presents one way of measuring raw material intensity for agribusinesses by taking raw farm products consumed as a percentage of the value of output. In enterprises producing soft drink beverages and tobacco products, the raw farm product intensity is

Table 3.7.--Raw Material Intensity and Proportion of Raw Material Utilised by Producer Subsector, El Salvador

| Subsector | Raw material intensity [a] | Per cent of output captured by small-scale farmers |
|---|---|---|
| Coffee processing | 56.9 | 6.0 |
| Drinks | 14.8 | 0.0 |
| Tobacco | 21.1 | 8.2 |
| Textiles | 44.7 | 2.8 |
| Clothing | 50.1 | 3.2 |
| Leather | 51.7 | 14.2 |
| Shoes | 41.3 | 11.2 |
| Furniture | 36.7 | 0.0 |
| Meat products | 72.0 | 19.7 |
| Milk products | 54.1 | 14.8 |
| Fruit & vegetables | 27.6 | 8.2 |
| Edible oils | 61.7b | 2.2b |
| Flour milling | 66.9b | 3.3b |
| Baking | 47.2b | 2.2b |
| Sugar | 50.5 | 7.7 |
| Sweets/candies | 38.4 | 5.8 |

Source:  S. Daines and D. Steen, El Salvador Agro-industrial Profile (San Salvador: USAID).

a        Inputs from farm products as a percentage of the value of production.
b        Imported.

less than one-fourth as large as in the food-
processing enterprises.  A project in tobacco processing, therefore, would pass a much lower benefit
back to suppliers than one in food.  Even within the
food-processing sectors the differences are large.
Choosing sectors with high raw material intensity is
important in designing projects for increasing the
backward linkages of benefits to poor, small-scale
farmers.

A related problem is the possibility that the
raw material is imported and that no benefit is
therefore passed back.  Table 3.7 presents examples
of agribusinesses which have very high raw material
intensities (edible oils and flour milling) but
which will pass on little benefit because their raw
farm product is imported.

The overall raw material intensity of small-
scale enterprises, including the proportion of
imported raw materials, can be seen in Table 3.8,
which takes India as an example.

## Proportion of Raw Product Supplied by Small Farmers

The raw material supplied to agribusinesses
does not all come from small farms operated by
members of the target group of poor.  Large farms
may supply a very large proportion of raw materials
for certain products.  In the event that the raw
materials are supplied by large farms, expanding the
demand for raw material will benefit the poor only
inasmuch as they are workers on the larger farms:
an employment benefit but not a benefit to small-
scale farmers.  There are two project alternatives
which increase the impact of projects on the welfare
of small farm families:

1.  Select agribusinesses for inclusion in
projects which process those products for which
small farms predominate in primary production.
Since there are large differences by product in the
proportion of output which is produced on small
farms, it would initially appear that a viable way
to increase the benefits accruing to small-farm
families would be to choose agribusinesses which
process traditional small-farm products.  Table 3.9
presents an example of such a computation for El
Salvador in which the small-farm share of production
for each of the raw material types is indicated.
The obvious implication for agribusiness projects in
El Salvador is that, even if small farms capture
their proportional share of demand for raw product,

Table 3.8.--Consumption of Raw Materials in Small Industrial
Units (1969-70), India

| | Raw materials consumed by reporting units | | | | |
| | Total | Indigenous | Imported | Per rupee of value added | Per rupee of output |
|---|---|---|---|---|---|
| | (Rupees '000) | | | (Rs.) | (Rs.) |
| Agricultural implements | 6,748 | 6,643 | 105 | 2.02 | 0.61 |
| Auto ancillaries | 8,627 | 6,778 | 1,277 | 2.05 | 0.59 |
| Cycles and components | 5,856 | 5,723 | 133 | 2.82 | 0.68 |
| Electricals | 20,156 | 12,808 | 378 | 1.72 | 0.60 |
| Electronics | 4,280 | 3,272 | 622 | 2.37 | 0.64 |
| Batteries | 301 | 130 | 170 | 7.37 | 0.85 |
| Light engineering | 7,772 | 6,933 | 839 | 1.23 | 0.50 |
| Hardware | 3,902 | 3,410 | 492 | 2.33 | 0.66 |
| Steel furniture | 2,786 | 2,765 | 21 | 1.48 | 0.56 |
| Utensils | 3,652 | 3,652 | -- | 1.47 | 0.54 |
| Plastics | 4,029 | 2,789 | 384 | 2.94 | 0.66 |
| Rubber products | 2,061 | 1,686 | 371 | 0.62 | 0.36 |
| Scientific instruments | 2,400 | 2,008 | 227 | 1.14 | 0.49 |
| Surgical and hospital equipment | 964 | 552 | 412 | 1.91 | 0.62 |
| Paints and varnishes | 6,525 | 4,500 | 1,537 | 4.46 | 0.75 |
| Pesticides and agrichemicals | 1,709 | 693 | 597 | 2.32 | 0.61 |
| Soap | 2,739 | 1,994 | 485 | 4.42 | 0.79 |
| Hosiery | 8,631 | 8,631 | -- | 6.80 | 0.78 |
| Printing | 3,081 | 444 | 263 | 1.96 | 0.54 |
| Food processing | 1,374 | 1,339 | 34 | 2.11 | 0.60 |
| Timber-based industries | 612 | 612 | -- | 2.62 | 0.71 |
| Sports goods | 3,010 | 2,610 | 400 | 2.37 | 0.64 |
| All industries | 101,214 | 79,972 | 8,750 | 2.00 | 0.61 |

Source:  National Council of Applied Economic Research, Study
of Selected Small Industrial Units (New Delhi, 1972),
p.62.

Table 3.9.--Small-farm Share in Primary Production,
       El Salvador

| Subsector | Small-farm share of primary production |
|---|---|
| | (Per cent) |
| Non-food processing | |
| Coffee processing | 13.1 |
| Drinks | 0.0 |
| Tobacco | 48.2 |
| Textiles | 8.0 |
| Clothing | 8.0 |
| Leather | 34.2 |
| Shoes | 34.2 |
| Furniture | 0.0 |
| Food processing | |
| Meat products | 34.2 |
| Milk products | 31.7 |
| Fruit & vegetables | 37.5a |
| Flour milling | 30.5b |
| Bakery products | 30.5b |
| Sugar | 18.9 |
| Sweets/candies | 18.9 |

Source:   Agriculture Census, El Salvador, 1970.
a         Part imported.
b         Most imported.

less than one-third of the total demand would be
supplied from their production.  The backward link,
while not unimportant, is relatively small.   This
pattern for El Salvador, of course, should not be
assumed for other countries.  It does emphasise,
however, the importance of measuring the backward
linkages for each country to determine the potential
of agribusiness projects to benefit small-scale
farmers.  It should additionally be noted
that even though the average backward linkage is
small, the differences by product are large.  Coffee
processing would pass a much smaller proportion of
its total benefit backward (less than half) than
would tobacco or meat products.
     The fact that small producers will not likely
capture their proportionate share would reduce the
impacts indicated in Table 3.9.  Large-scale farmers
are more institutionally agile, and are viewed by

processors as being more stable and capable of supplying a higher quality product. It is therefore likely that, given a choice, most agribusinesses would choose the large-scale farm suppliers.

2. Arrange the project so that part of the intervention itself structures the supply of raw materials so as to place small-scale farmers in a position to supply them, or at least raise the probability of their being in such a position. Using cooperative mechanisms for processing in which farmers actually own and operate the agribusiness is an extreme example of how a project could accomplish this restructuring of supply. A wide variety of subsidies, institutional arrangements and conditions can be envisioned which would accomplish the same thing. Locating agribusinesses in geographic areas where small farms predominate, using the agribusiness as a channel for small-farm credit, extension of technical know-how, transportation of produce to processor: all may serve this function.

## Assessing the Net Potential for Small-scale Farmers

Raw material intensity and share in supply interact to determine how much of a given expansion of an agribusiness will be passed backward to small-scale farmers. The last column of Table 3.7 illustrates the net share of the value of output from agribusiness enterprises passed on to small-scale farmers. This type of table illustrating net impact could be very useful in helping project designers choose the products to include in a project so as to maximise benefits for small farms.

## SPECIFIC TYPES OF INTERVENTIONS

The discussion so far in this chapter has dealt with a framework for choosing interventions which will maximise the benefits of agribusiness and rural enterprise projects for the rural poor. The discussion here deals with the types of interventions themselves and provides a short description of each.

1. _Training_. Short-term courses, on-the-job guidance, self-education aids and preparatory training are some of the more common means used to transfer relevant technical or managerial information. Instruction in basic accounting, marketing, production, finance and organisation can enable the manager to improve his/her operations. Short-term,

on-the-job training tends to be most useful when it is directly relevant to the entrepreneur's business problems. In addition, as small firms are often hard-pressed to release key individuals who could benefit most from training, courses which are most effective tend to be short and followed up by on-site visits.

A SMRE (small- or medium-scale rural enterprise) requires skilled labourers. Formal preparatory vocational training can contribute to the development of a more skilled labour force. In most countries, such training is accomplished through apprenticeships or the like which, although effective in transmitting skills, may perpetuate inefficient practices. Courses attuned to local employment opportunities can equip students with new or improved skills and thereby improve the performance of the SMRE.

2. <u>Research services</u>. Techno-economic services, which are often included within one or more existing government or private institutions, often include economic research, such as general statistics by industry, market surveys, and industry feasibility studies, and technical research on production processes and appropriate or modern technology. As the objective of such services is to provide the necessary knowledge for the entrepreneur to make well-informed business decisions and the government to improve policy affecting that entrepreneur, the research services must be closely attuned to the needs of the country's SMREs. It is therefore important to establish effective communication with organisations such as extension services with the specific needs of target industries and which can assist in disseminating relevant information. Some research services which have been included within organisations with wider responsibilities have suffered due to the low priority given research relative to other tasks.

3. <u>Advisory services</u>. Managerial and technical advice in all critical areas--marketing, production, accounting, management and finance--is usually offered through a variety of mechanisms. In some programmes, the government develops and supports an extension service within an existing body such as a department of industry. Unfortunately, government bodies have frequently been unable to recruit and retain highly qualified agents; civil service regulations limit salaries and promotional opportunities, and those with real business acumen usually go into business for them-

selves. In addition, many governments have been
slow in committing adequate resources to technical
assistance agencies, thereby seriously handicapping
their ability to service SMRE entrepreneurs.

To get around these problems, some programmes
have assisted in developing and/or funding both
nonprofit and profit organisations which provide
technical assistance alone or in combination with
other services. For example, technical assistance
services have been included as part of the function
of credit institutions. This arrangement can
increase the incentives for the consulting group to
provide useful and effective services so as to
improve the probability of being repaid, but it can
also reduce the credit institutions' objectivity in
reviewing loan applications.

Whether public or private institutions provide
the assistance, rural industry is not always eager
to make use of it. For a variety of reasons, there
is frequently resistance to part or all of the range
of services offered. To ensure that services are
adequately utilised, the project should be designed
to minimise these difficulties. For example,
technical assistance could be oriented toward newer
industries which tend to be more receptive to
outside advice: or credit components could be made
available to businesses which decide to use the
technical knowledge provided but which need
additional funding to do so.

When the difficulties in encouraging rural
industry to use technical assistance have been mini-
mised, those services which are specifically
tailored to the entrepreneur's operations can be
extremely useful in identifying and solving specific
constraints. Some of the more useful technical
assistance programmes have been implemented by
larger firms dependent on small suppliers under
subcontracting arrangements.

4. <u>Credit programmes</u>. Rural entrepreneurs
frequently identify credit as their primary problem.
Although in many cases credit is a major constraint,
there are often many other problems as well. Consequently, programmes offering credit alone are not
often effective in addressing the other constraints.
Hence, although credit needs clearly should be
examined, other factors should also be reviewed and
perhaps included as project components.

Facilitating the flow of credit is a multi-
faceted task. If efforts to change policy or
improve capabilities of SMRE entrepreneurs are successful, those enterprises may become more attrac-

tive customers for commercial or development banks.

Macro-level policies in particular have a significant, if not the dominant, influence on lending
activities. One of the first steps should be to
ensure that such policies do not discriminate
against the smaller, labour-intensive enterprises.
Any government intervention should direct credit and
other resource allocations in the direction of true
scarcity, although identifying the critical variables to achieve this has proven difficult.

A more direct approach provides concessional
loan funds for long-term and working capital which
allows sufficient spread to cover increased administrative costs, loan defaults and even technical
assistance. These funds can provide the lending
institution valuable experience in lending to a new
group of customers, can assist in getting certain
rural enterprises started, and can provide the badly
needed working and long-term capital often needed in
the rural sector of capital-short economies.

Provision of such funds, however, may represent
only a short-term solution. Unless the costs and
risks in lending to SMREs are reduced, the lending
institutions may not be able to maintain a viable
SMRE programme once concessional funds are no longer
available.

Another direct approach is development of guarantee schemes to make the higher risks more acceptable to lending institutions and to encourage them
to ease their collateral requirements. Experience
indicates that such schemes should minimise the time
and effort involved for credit institutions to
obtain government guarantees. While guarantees can
reduce risk, however, alone they do not always
provide adequate incentive for private lenders to
get involved in a new and still relatively unattrac-
tive area of lending. Also, if not carefully
designed, they can result in a costly review process
at two levels, that of the lending institution and
the government body providing the guarantee.

Another approach to improve the capabilities of
lending institutions which express reluctance to
move into this area because of lack of trained
personnel. Technical assistance can be directed
toward developing bankers' skills in credit analysis, monitoring and packaging to enable them to deal
effectively with smaller, rural customers.

In countries where banking facilities are
situated far from potential SMRE clients, other
mechanisms may be employed to identify customers and
establish contact between the borrower and the

lender. In addition, policy or government controlled incentives can be used to encourage movement of lending enterprises to rural areas.

5. <u>Facilitating procurement of raw materials and equipment</u>. Several approaches are possible here. First, basic policies affecting the scarcity of goods, for example those related to inflation, foreign exchange and capital formation, should be reviewed to avoid any unnecessary shortages. Second, concerted efforts to improve the efficiency and effectiveness of the purchasing and distribution system must be made. Increased availability of information on supply and demand conditions can minimise the vulnerability of smaller rural entrepreneurs. Specific training in inventory planning and control can improve distributors' and entrepreneurs' performance. Efforts can be made to encourage independent distributors to operate so as to minimise monopoly control of supply channels, although care must be given to avoid fragmenting distribution functions that require a minimum scale for efficiency. Also, purchasing organisations such as cooperatives can be formed to allow for the economies of bulk purchases. Such organisations, however, should not be regarded as panaceas; they will not remedy problems resulting from poor distribution or scarcity. Also, a cooperative-type arrangement may encounter problems in attracting trained managers.

Medium-scale operations relying on small suppliers can in particular improve purchasing through establishing incentives for a steady, adequate supply of raw material. Contracts, for instance, allow greater price stability to both supplier and purchaser and offer an assured market to the supplier, thereby encouraging his participation.

6. <u>Marketing aids</u>. Aside from training and advisory services directed toward improved marketing, other approaches include improving the flow of market information, strengthening associations and/or providing government or cooperative outlets for goods.

Better market information has often been included as part of the research service function. The government can perform market analyses or compile trade directories. In addition, efforts to encourage industrial associations or private firms to adopt such responsibilities can also be made.

Publicly owned outlets have frequently been established to purchase exclusively from small and/or rural firms. Many such efforts have met with

substantial difficulties due to poor planning and/or
to the nature of most government-run operations.
Government-operated outlets tend to be less able to
make business decisions quickly and to provide
incentives to managers to ensure aggressive selling.
In state-run economies, however, or where the
government takes on this responsibility, the
approach could be one of providing management,
technical assistance and/or training.

Another approach, somewhat similar to subcontracting, includes facilitating cooperation between
small and large firms. Large wholesale or retail
operations can provide valuable market information
and outlets for small firms and often provide
technical assistance and credit. Exchange of information through clearinghouses or other means can
enable firms with complementary needs to identify
one another.

7. Subcontracting. Subcontracting is generally used to refer to a relationship between large
and small industries where the smaller firms manu-
facture parts and components or perform processing
and finishing operations needed by larger firms.
Information exchanges on the needs of larger industries and the specific capabilities of SMREs facilitate development of these mutually beneficial relationships. Common mechanisms include development of
clearinghouses or utilisation of technical assistance agencies to channel information. A large firm
usually chooses to subcontract when it is uneconomical for it to perform the function itself (for
example, when the volume demanded for a specific
part does not justify purchase and operation of
necessary equipment) or when government legislation
prohibits its operation in specific areas.

To establish a viable relationship, the smaller
supplier must operate efficiently and produce goods
of reasonable quality. In many subcontracting relationships, the large firm provides some technical
and managerial assistance, which can be highly
effective due to its specific nature, and may also
provide credit.

Subcontracting relationships can offer the
small firm a more secure outlet and can significantly improve access to marketing information,
thereby allowing increased responsiveness. As over-
dependence on one purchaser reduces the small firm's
flexibility and limits control over price and
related factors, the smaller enterprise must evaluate the risks and returns for itself.

Given that the larger private firms can provide

product-specific assistance and have a financial
stake in ensuring adequate supply, and high quality,
it is reasonable to expect that smaller firms may
benefit more from improved commercial contacts than
from most other forms of assistance.


APPROPRIATE TECHNOLOGY

A theme which has received increasing attention
has been the need for more appropriate technologies
in development programmes. Over the past 15 years,
it has been recognised that technological options
have to be examined and chosen with greater care to
ensure that those most appropriate to local factor
endowments are selected. In terms of most developing countries, of course, this generally means
technologies should be employed which are intensive
in the use of abundant factors (labour and natural
resources) and which economise in the use of scarce
resources (capital and highly trained personnel).
Appropriate technology (AT), however, has come to
mean many things to many people, and there are
numerous issues unresolved with regard to its
practical application. This section examines some
of these issues and their relationship to small-
scale rural and agribusiness projects.


## Background to the AT Approach

Political, economic and institutional factors
have all contributed to the use of inappropriate
capital-intensive technologies in developing
countries. From the economic side, inappropriate
technologies received encouragement from both
development planners enamoured with the industrialisation and modernisation strategy as well as local
policies implemented for both political and economic
reasons. Both of these factors led to the artificial raising of the cost of labour through minimum
wage and social security laws and the artificial
lowering of capital costs through interest rate
ceilings, tariff exemptions for imported capital,
etc. Following the signals of the market place, the
private sector was encouraged to adopt capital-
intensive technologies in developing countries.
From an institutional point of view, it was
natural for international lending agencies and local
development institutions to defer to engineers and
to large companies which could deliver familiar and

tested techniques with a minimum of risk and in a short period of time with reliable servicing. Since the companies were themselves most familiar with "modern" techniques developed in the context of the industrialised countries, and since leaders in development institutions in LDCs were often educated in countries where such techniques were taught, the bias in favour of capital-intensive processes to the prejudice of local labour- and natural-resource-intensive techniques was quite natural, if somewhat irrational.

There were, however, additional factors contributing to the distortion in the choice of techniques. Certainly two important elements were the general lack of readily accessible information regarding optional technologies, in addition to the problem that no one was looking for them anyway. Also, the fact that major lending institutions in developed countries tied loans to purchases originating in their own countries encouraged a capital-intensive bias.

AT appeared to offer a way of generating beneficial impacts in terms of employment, improved income distribution and relieving migration problems by focusing production processes on labour-intensive technology. It allowed a concentration on the rural, traditional sector with links to agriculture in addition to offering a pattern of small-scale production which would not require a conglomeration of economic activities in the cities but which would allow their dispersion. And most importantly, it would maximise the positive effects on employment and income distribution through the more judicious use of scarce capital by employing more of the poor labourers and artisans per unit of capital expended, especially those who traditionally had no access to employment.

AT has been attractive not only for its economic implications but also for its applicability to other socioeconomic problems proponents have identified as arising from the industrialisation strategy. AT is seen by some as a solution to perceived ecological problems caused by large-scale industry, including the depletion of nonrenewable resources such as fossil fuels. The common suggestion of solar pumps for irrigation purposes is illustrative of this aspect. Since AT is often designed with the specific demands of a locality taken into account, it lends itself to more local influence in both the design and the decision-making processes.

## AT in Development Strategies

Difficult questions arise with regard to the practical application of AT in the development process. The emphasis of optional approaches advocated by practitioners can vary considerably.

While economic policies distorting factor costs have significantly contributed to inappropriate technologies, the removal of minimum wages, the lowering of employer contributions to social security systems, the increasing of interest rates, etc, are often politically unfeasible in order to foster more appropriate technologies through the market system, although there has been an increasing liberalisation regarding capital pricing in some developing countries in the last few years. This problem, however, points up the critical role that small-scale enterprises can play in the development and application of AT. Small-scale firms, especially rural ones, rarely have access to subsidised capital and generally pay wages which are significantly lower than those of the modern sector. We should expect, therefore, to find in at least some small-scale enterprises a variety of ATs. This is supported by evidence which shows that small-scale firms are more labour-intensive than large-scale businesses and yet can still generate attractive profits. The proposition is also supported by the premise that AT is location-specific and best developed where local participants control the decision-making process regarding the type of technology to be used. Small-scale enterprises adapt the production process to their local market conditions which they best understand and make their own technological choices, since they are relatively isolated from the modern sector and capital-intensive processes. Thus the survey of firms, including profiles of profitability and factor mix, enables planners to identify firms which apply ATs. The method permits the identification of firms which are successful and the types of technologies they employ. By comparing these technologies with those of less-profitable firms, appropriate technologies can be identified and spread.

This is not to suggest that other approaches to the development of ATs are inappropriate. It does, however, interject some irony into several basic debates which surround AT. While proponents of AT agree that the concept has application to the modern as well as the traditional sector, the traditional sector is generally targeted for priority because of

its potential for generating employment and income
for the poor. Emphasis on the traditional sector,
however, is generally directed to the need to apply
capital-saving technologies which implies the need
for "intermediate" technologies. The logical implication and actual result of this interpretation is
to focus on new and innovative research to create
new technologies which bridge this "technological
gap". A great deal of effort in institutions
working on AT is directed toward research for this
very purpose. The International Rice Research
Institute, for example, has devoted a great deal of
practical research and development in order to
design small-scale machinery and equipment--such as
power tillers and axial flow threshers--suitable for
small-scale agricultural use. Their experience has
shown however how AT must be implemented as part of
an integrated development approach or more unemployment can result from the introduction of capital-
saving techniques. While such machinery is usually
designed to alleviate the labour bottlenecks which
can constrain added output, the machinery can often
be used in other periods or more than compensate for
labour shortages at these peak periods. Thus,
unless careful planning is carried out to ensure
there is land available for new production or new
cropping patterns which increase labour demand,
unemployment can result. This illustration in part
points up the important role the survey method of
this volume provides in approaching AT. It provides
data which both permit the identification of bottlenecks and assist in integrating the required coordi-
nation of efforts.

The application of AT may also play an important role in the development of larger agribusinesses. While a number of modern food processing
technologies are already relatively labour
intensive, others are not. This difference raises
the issue of to what degree both processes might not
economically substitute more labour for capital
through the application of different technologies.
AT literature treating the modern sector commonly
tends to focus on the need either to adapt and
modify existing techniques or rediscover techniques
which used to be employed in the developed countries
at a time when relative capital and labour costs
were more similar to those in developing countries
today. This approach has led a number of AT organisations to search for older technologies among small
workshops in relatively backward regions of
developed countries, believing that this will

broaden the technological shelf of information from which developing countries can draw.

While this approach can undoubtedly be fruitful and has proven to be so in a number of cases, the survey method outlined in this volume also offers an important approach for identifying firms already applying appropriate technologies. There are many cases where agribusiness firms have little access to capital subsidies and few ties with institutions and companies which promote "modern" technologies, so they of necessity develop more labour-intensive and capital-saving technologies. The survey will allow an identification of such firms in the same way as for small-scale enterprises, allowing for dissemination of their technologies to other firms.

While it is not suggested that the approach of this volume be an exclusive one in identifying and developing appropriate technologies, it does have several advantages and should receive far greater comparative emphasis than it has in the past. One benefit of the approach is that it is relatively economical compared to the development of new technologies. Since AT is often location-specific, a machine developed for one region may not be appropriate for another. A machine might be developed which is economical when used on farms in a particular region in which the average holding size is six hectares yet be uneconomical when the average farm size is two hectares. Where existing technologies are identified within each region, they will have taken into account these very differences--that is, they will be location specific. Equally important is the fact that existing AT in use in some small-scale firms will probably incorporate and reflect local cultural and social values, so that it is likely that there will be minimum disruption of such values through wider dissemination of these techniques. Also, this method permits an analysis of the degree to which the benefits of the technology go to the target group selected for assistance. Finally, the technologies will be those which have emerged out of local participation in the development of the processes themselves. This will not only add to the probable appropriateness of the technology in economic terms but also reinforce ethnic and national pride, important elements in the development process.

NOTES

1.   An extended treatment of the dynamics of "unbalanced" growth may be found in A. O. Hirschman, The Strategy of Economic Development (Yale University Press, New Haven, Connecticut, 1958.
2.   It is increasingly argued that small-scale nonfarm rural enterprises can provide a key role in transmitting the benefits of growth to the unemployed.  See W. F. Steel and Y. Takagi, The Intermediate Sector, Unemployment and the Employment-Output Conflict:  A Multi-Sector Model (The World Bank, Washington, 1978).
3.   One review of empirical studies on employment and industrialisation concluded that "...despite the fact that there is scope for factor substitution in most activities, it seems clear that some goods can be regarded as unambiguously more labor-intensive in production than others."  D. Morawetz, "Employment Implications of Industrialisation in Developing Countries:  A Survey," The Economic Journal, vol.84, no.325 (1974), pp.491,503.  This suggests that the inherently labour-intensive activities be identified early in the project planning process to enable them to be selected for appropriate interventions.

CHAPTER 4

DEVELOPING A PROFILE OF AN AGRIBUSINESS AND RURAL
ENTERPRISE SYSTEM

The objective in constructing a profile of an agri-
business-rural enterprise system is to generate an
overview of the sector--its structure and general
level of technology--and to furnish a backdrop for
rational identification of project opportunities.
Very often, project possibilities are identified
without a sector overview, which could have provided
indications that other interventions were possible
and perhaps even preferable.

SECTORAL SUBGROUPINGS

In order to furnish project planners with a
sufficiently detailed profile, agribusiness and
rural enterprises must be broken down into component
parts which make conceptual sense in the terms used
by planners.  These components or subsectors must be
clearly defined and delimited.  It is likely that
the following categories will prove useful in disag-
gregating the sector as a whole into meaningful
subgroupings.

Types of Products

The use of product categories as a way of
grouping enterprises has a number of advantages.
First, distinctions by product category may be
reasonable proxies for other more sophisticated
distinctions such as labour-intensity; that is,
certain types of product, such as bakery goods, are
likely to be labour intensive in developing
countries when compared to other products, such as
processed edible oils.  The second advantage is that
different types of product have obvious links with

different parts of the agricultural sector; for
example, furniture-making links to forestry, fruit
and vegetable processing to intensive agriculture,
milling and baking to grain production, etc. These
links may even have regional implications which will
be easier to trace and to understand if the profile
is grouped by product types.


## Scale of Operation

Small-scale, cottage-type industry should be
distinguished from medium- and large-scale enterprises in the profile. Technology differences are
perhaps the most important reason for this distinction, yet other motives also support the division.
Small-scale enterprises exist in a unique institutional and cultural environment and require quite
distinct project instruments to access them. Small-
scale enterprises are so different from larger
enterprises that keeping them distinct is important.
Where to draw the line between the small-scale
enterprise and the larger, more complex enterprise
may be difficult in concept, but it will probably
prove to be easier in practice because the data
available leave little flexibility for the choice.
If there are data covering small-scale enterprises,
the data are usually gathered with a predetermined
breakpoint between the small and large enterprises.
It is almost always true that different data-
gathering instruments are used for small-scale or
cottage industry than for medium- and large-scale
enterprises.


## Urban and Rural Enterprises

Distinctions between urban and rural enterprises may be critical because of the tendency of
both aid agencies and governments to break programmes down into these sectoral categories and,
additionally, because of the current focus by
many development agencies on the rural poor.
For the purpose of definition in this manual,
rural includes those enterprises outside of major
metropolitan areas. Market towns and small cities
located in rural areas, serving the agricultural
sector and having strong backward links to small
farms and the rural poor would therefore be classified as rural.

Developing a Profile of an Agribusiness System

## Classification of Agribusiness

As used in this volume, the terms <u>agribusiness</u>, <u>agroindustry</u> and <u>agroservices</u> are all assumed to be included whenever the term <u>agribusiness</u> is used. Definitions should be clearly spelled out with reference to the intended coverage of the <u>sector</u>. Each country and each programme setting may require or at least imply a different definition. The definition employed here is only an example chosen to fit as many situations as possible and not to prescribe a pattern applicable everywhere.

Agribusiness enterprises are here defined as those enterprises which process, elaborate, store or market products of the primary sector--including crops, livestock, forests and fisheries--or which provide inputs to the sector.

The reader will notice that the title to this chapter, indeed the title of the manual as a whole, includes both <u>agribusiness</u> and <u>rural enterprises</u>. The use of both of these terms may at first seem redundant, yet on further reflection it should be noted that many small-scale rural enterprises are not agribusinesses according to the definition above which requires that agribusinesses process or market some agricultural product or provide farm supplies. It should also be noted that many agribusinesses are not rural. The intent in using both terms is to include even those agribusinesses which are not rural (for example, food and fibre processing in urban areas) and those <u>small- and medium-scale rural</u> enterprises which are not agribusinesses (for example, small rural shops marketing hardware or manufacturing domestic nonfood articles). The basic reason for wishing to include urban agribusinesses is their importance as links to the rural poor; they provide market outlets and supply inputs to increase rural welfare. Agribusinesses of all scales are keys to rural development even though their location may be urban. The intent of including rural small- and medium-scale enterprises of a non-agribusiness nature is their obvious direct link with income and employment of the rural poor, and more particularly the landless--the most impoverished group of rural poor.

## Geographical Dimensions

Regional differences are usually dramatic in developing countries, especially in the larger ones which display a wide range of resource endowments. Sound development programmes are likely to have strong regional orientations to fit this diversity. The sector profile should likewise preserve regional and geographical groupings to facilitate project planning and to avoid misleading generalisations which result from attempting to interpret data from widely divergent regions.

## TOPICS FOR THE SECTOR PROFILE

This section identifies and elaborates the major topics which should be included when a sector profile is prepared.

### The Subsector's Share in Total Production and Employment

This topic involves a general quantitative description of the relative size of the various subsectors defined by product type, by region, by scale, etc. It is important for project planners to start from a baseline which includes information on relative size and importance. An example is given in Table 4.1 of a profile giving shares of employment for West Malaysia.

The information contained in a simple employment or production share profile is basic to any rural enterprise planning process. In order to illustrate how other groupings of subsectors can be useful (as discussed in the definitions section above), similar employment share data for Sierra Leone are shown in Table 4.2 using urban and rural groupings. It should be noted that this simple approach could be followed for groupings by region and scale as well.

Other subtopics which might be considered under the general heading of subsectoral shares are the proportion of each subsector (defined in terms of product type, scale and region) in total production, export earnings and GNP/GDP. An example of a GNP-share table is given for Jamaica in Table 4.3, which illustrates a product-type grouping which is considerably more detailed for agroindustries than the previous one shown for Malaysia. More detailed subgroupings may assist project planners in searching for and assessing specific options for the project.

Developing a Profile of an Agribusiness System

Table 4.1.--Rural Employment by Sector, West
          Malaysia

| Subsector | Number of employees | Per cent |
|---|---|---|
| Agricultural production | 392,103 | 100 |
| Rubber | 339,943 | 86 |
| Oil palm | 22,741 | 6 |
| Vegetable oils | 23,467 | 6 |
| Tea | 1,530 | * |
| Coffee | 2,410 | * |
| Estate labour contractors | 2,012 | * |
| Commercial enterprises | 62,433 | 100 |
| Wholesale | 5,941 | 10 |
| Retail | 51,154 | 82 |
| Other commerce | 5,338 | 8 |
| Manufacturing | 52,675 | 100 |
| Food | 9,093 | 17 |
| Beverages | 502 | * |
| Tobacco | 1,531 | 3 |
| Textiles & shoes | 2,021 | 4 |
| Other clothing | 2,143 | 4 |
| Wood & cork products | 14,594 | 28 |
| Furniture | 1,614 | 3 |
| Paper & paper products | 490 | * |
| Leather & rubber | 1,700 | 3 |
| Other manufacturing (non-agroindustrial) | 18,987 | 36 |

Source:  Preliminary worksheets from Malaysian
         Population Census, 1970.  Quoted from
         Development Issues in Rural Non-Farm
         Employment (World Bank, Washington, DC,
         1977), p.13.

Note:  Use of (*) means the figure is less than
       one per cent.


Institutional Profile

    This profile should contain a description of
the major institutions which provide services to
agribusinesses and small- and medium-scale rural
enterprises.  The institutional profile should deal
with such issues as the volumes of credit for each
of the subsectors (on the basis of product type,

Table 4.2.--Employment Share Profile of Rural Enterprises, Sierra Leone [a]

| | Employment by area and size of population centre: | | | | | |
| | Rural areas | | Population | | | |
| | | | 2,000-5,000 | | over 100,000 | |
| | (no.) | (%) | (no.) | (%) | (no.) | (%) |
| Food | | | | | | |
| Baking | 3,000 | 4.4 | 206 | 5.4 | 164 | 3.3 |
| Textiles and wearing apparel | | | | | | |
| Spinning and weaving | 6,000 | 8.8 | 126 | 3.3 | 0 | 0.0 |
| Gara dyeing [b] | 9,000 | 13.2 | 380 | 10.0 | 24 | 0.5 |
| Tailoring | 20,000 | 29.4 | 1,508 | 39.9 | 2,380 | 48.5 |
| Shoemaking & repair | 1,000 | 1.5 | 18 | 0.5 | 131 | 2.7 |
| Wood | | | | | | |
| Carving | 1,500 | 2.2 | 76 | 2.0 | 14 | 0.3 |
| Carpentry | 11,500 | 17.0 | 666 | 17.6 | 345 | 7.0 |
| Metal | | | | | | |
| Goldsmithing | 2,500 | 3.7 | 32 | 0.8 | 54 | 1.1 |
| Blacksmithing | 11,500 | 17.0 | 180 | 4.8 | 37 | 0.8 |
| Welding and fitting | 0 | 0.0 | 20 | 0.5 | 86 | 1.8 |
| Repair Services | | | | | | |
| Radio | 0 | 0.0 | 12 | 0.3 | 61 | 1.2 |
| Vehicle | 0 | 0.0 | 98 | 2.6 | 578 | 11.8 |
| Watch | 0 | 0.0 | 16 | 0.4 | 76 | 1.6 |
| Others [c] | 2,000 | 2.9 | 446 | 11.8 | 963 | 19.6 |
| Total | 68,000 | 100 | 3,784 | 100 | 4,913 | 100 |

Source:  Enyinna Chuta and Carl Liedholm, "The Role of Small Scale Industry in Employment Generation and Rural Development:  Initial Research Results from Sierra Leone," African Rural Employment Paper No. 11 (Department of Agricultural Economics, Michigan State University, East Lansing, Michigan, 1975).

a    Estimates, omitting centres with populations from 5,000 to 100,000.
b    Gara is a local cloth.
c    Although none is listed for rural areas, the other items include watch and bicycle repair, as well as hammock- and basket-making.

scale and region) by institutional source. Technical assistance provisions should be outlined. The
role of industrial associations, cooperatives, craft
and trade organisations, etc. should be discussed
and their relative contributions to various financial and technical services estimated. The institutional section will often be the least quantified
but among the most important sections of a profile;
for it is at this point that limits on the ability
of external interventions to play a useful role will
begin to surface and areas of need will begin to
take shape.

## Employment Potential and Labour Intensity

The profile should contain an assessment of the
employment potential of the sector and its subcompo-
nents. The cost of generating additional employment
is a vital issue to which a profile can direct
attention by presenting an outline of the labour
intensity of each subgrouping. With this information, project planners can assess the relative
potential of different product types, different
scales of operation and for different regions.

Table 4.4 presents examples of employment costs
in terms of capital costs per employee for India and
El Salvador. For a discussion of the data required
to compute these labour-intensity figures, see
Chapter 8; for methodology see Chapter 5.

## Profitability

Profitability is an important concept because
it relates to the financial feasibility of expansion
of, or indeed starting up of, an enterprise. It
contains information on the efficiency of technical
and managerial processes, the market demand for
products and the necessity for technical and managerial assistance. A profile setting out the likely
profitability of a project gives the planner a broad
understanding of many factors at once. It is particularly important to utilise all of the groupings
mentioned in the previous discussion of basic definitions. Product type, scale and regional distinctions in profitability profiles will illuminate
important project design issues.

Tables 4.5 and 4.6 set out profitability
profiles as examples of two subsectoral groupings:
by scale--for Brazil, and by product type--for El

Developing a Profile of an Agribusiness System

Table 4.3.--Value Added for Agroindustries with 10
or More Workers, Jamaica

| Agroindustry | Value added | Percentage of all value added in manufacturing |
|---|---|---|
| | (J$'000) | |
| Meat | 33,533 | 3.3 |
| Dairy products | 48,356 | 4.8 |
| Edible oils and fats | 21,428 | 2.1 |
| Bakery products | 61,019 | 5.4 |
| Sugar and molasses | 104,984 | 10.4 |
| Drinks | 80,239 | 8.0 |
| Animal feeds | 40,087 | 4.0 |
| Tobacco products | 58,641 | 5.8 |
| Textiles | 13,156 | 1.3 |
| Clothing | 27,522 | 2.7 |
| Canning/preserving | 13,769 | 1.4 |
| fruits/vegetables | 17,531 | 1.7 |
| Grain mill products | 27,512 | 2.7 |
| Wood & wood products | 17,633 | 1.8 |
| Other food and drink | 27,326 | 2.7 |
| Total | 592,736 | 58.1 |

Share of Value Added of Manufacturing by Selected
Food Processing Subsectors

| | (J$'000) | (Percentage) |
|---|---|---|
| Poultry meat | 25,176 | 2.51 |
| Ham and bacon | 4,787 | 0.48 |
| Processed meat | 1,370 | 0.14 |
| Condensed milk | 22,869 | 2.28 |
| Ice cream | 4,118 | 0.41 |
| Preserving of fish | 2,132 | 0.21 |
| Flour and cornmeal | 21,659 | 2.16 |
| Bread and cakes | 39,360 | 3.92 |
| Rum | 7,637 | 0.76 |
| Alcohol | 1,771 | 0.18 |
| Beer and stout | 51,575 | 5.13 |
| Aerated waters | 19,256 | 1.92 |
| Poultry feed | 25,365 | 2.52 |
| Pig feed | 10,863 | 1.08 |
| Cattle feed | 3,331 | 0.33 |
| Cigarettes | 54,522 | 5.42 |
| Cigars | 4,119 | 0.41 |
| Total | 424,551 | 42.26 |

Source:   Jamaica Department of Statistics,
          Production Statistics, 1977.

Salvador.

The combination of profitability and labour-intensity findings in Table 4.6 indicates how the topics in a profile may be interrelated. For example, in El Salvador, subsectors using the most labour (highest labour intensity) were also the most profitable (39.4 per cent return), while those using the least labour (highest capital intensity) had the lowest profitability (20.1 per cent). Simple comparisons like this in the profile can suggest important project emphases and directions.

Table 4.4.--Capital Costs of Employment, India and El Salvador

### India

| Subsector: | Small | Medium | Large |
|---|---|---|---|
| ('000 Rupees/employee) | | | |
| Grain mills | 2.1 | 8.4 | 11.7 |
| Misc. food | 2.1 | 5.9 | 8.5 |
| Tobacco | 0.3 | 1.1 | 3.4 |
| Textiles | 1.3 | 2.8 | 3.8 |
| Wood products | 1.5 | 4.4 | 5.3 |
| Fertiliser | 4.3 | 8.2 | 41.4 |

### El Salvador

| Subsector: | Medium and large |
|---|---|
| (US $/employee) | |
| Fishing | 4,700 |
| Food processing | 1,720 |
| Coffee and misc. | 20,072 |
| Drinks | 4,852 |
| Tobacco | 2,288 |
| Textiles | 9,145 |
| Clothing manufacture | 768 |
| Shoes and leather | 1,920 |
| Wood products | 1,004 |

Source: India, Annual Survey of Industries, 1965; El Salvador, Industrial Census, 1971.

# Developing a Profile of an Agribusiness System

While profiles indicating profitability will have a high degree of utility in project planning, the most likely case is that the unavailability of appropriate data (as explained below) will prevent the computation of profitability and require capital productivity measures to be substituted instead.

Table 4.5.--Profitability by Scale of Employment and Sector, Brazil

| Sector | Number of employees | | | | |
|---|---|---|---|---|---|
| | 1-4 | 10-19 | 70-99 | 150-249 | 500-999 |
| | (Net income/fixed + working capital, in percent) | | | | |
| Food products | 26 | 19 | 17 | 25 | 23 |
| Clothing and shoes | 21 | 10 | 24 | 27 | 33 |
| Textiles | 27 | 19 | 23 | 25 | 31 |

Source: Based on the 1970 Censo Industrial, Fundacao Instituto Brasileiro de Geografia Estatistica; quoted from S. R. Daines, Analysis of Industrial Structure, Technology and Productivity in the Food Processing Sector of Brazil (Massachusetts Institute of Technology, Cambridge, Mass., 1975), p.96.

## Capital Productivity

In almost all situations in developing countries, capital is among the most scarce of resources; and therefore the output per unit of capital used in production can be regarded for our purposes here as the best single indicator of "efficiency". While capital productivity may be a good indicator of efficiency in the broad sense of the best use of capital in the economy as a whole, it does not indicate financial feasibility or that a project deserves to attract funding. A profile of the capital productivity of each of the subsectors by product type, region and scale provides insights into the advisability, from an efficiency perspective, of expanding individual types of enterprise. Table 4.7 presents a sample productivity profile by

Developing a Profile of an Agribusiness System

scale and by selected subsectors for India. [1]

Table 4.6.--Profile of Profitability in Agroindustries, El Salvador

| Subsector | Net return to capital | Relative net return to capital by category of labour intensity | |
|---|---|---|---|
| | | Relative return* | Category |
| | (Per cent) | | |
| Coffee | 0.1 | 0 | Median |
| Drinks | 12.9 | 0 | Low |
| Tobacco | 67.1 | 851 | Median |
| Textiles | 75.4 | 945 | Median |
| Clothing | 13.1 | 165 | High |
| Shoes | 19.3 | 242 | High |
| Wood products | 9.2 | 115 | High |
| Furniture | 2.8 | 34 | High |
| Agroindustry average | 34.7 | 435 | High |
| Food processing in detail | | | |
|   Meat products | 34.5 | 432 | Median |
|   Milk products | 26.4 | 331 | Median |
|   Fruit & vegetables | 58.5 | 733 | High |
|   Fish products | 41.9 | 525 | Median |
|   Edible oils | 17.7 | 222 | Low |
|   Flour milling | 22.4 | 280 | Low |
|   Bakery products | 32.2 | 404 | High |
|   Sugar products | 48.4 | 606 | High |
|   Sweets | 18.3 | 229 | High |
| Average: all food | 35.1 | 440 | High |
|   High labour | 39.4 | 493 | High |
|   Median labour | 34.2 | 429 | Median |
|   Low labour | 20.1 | 251 | Low |

Source: S. R. Daines and D. Steen, El Salvador
Agroindustrial Profile (United States
Agency for International Development, San
Salvador, 1977), p.16.

Note: Manufacturing equals 100.

Developing a Profile of an Agribusiness System

## Labour Productivity

The use of labour productivity figures as a
guide to project choice is very difficult in developing countries due to the prevalence of unemployment.  Labour is not the most scarce factor, and
labour-saving technologies (which usually also have
high output-labour ratios) are not therefore the
most indicative.  It may nonetheless be useful to
profile the labour productivity of the industries in
question where appropriate data can be obtained for
this purpose. [2]

Table 4.7.--Profile of Capital Productivity in
Selected Agroindustries, India

| Subsector | Scale | | |
| | Small | Medium | Large |
| --- | --- | --- | --- |
| | (Output/capital in value terms) | | |
| Grain mill products | 1.19 | 0.55 | 0.67 |
| Misc. food products | 1.09 | 0.70 | 1.03 |
| Tobacco | 4.17 | 1.27 | 4.76 |
| Textiles | 1.85 | 0.93 | 0.92 |
| Wood products | 1.22 | 0.74 | 0.22 |
| Clothing & textiles | 0.64 | 0.56 | 0.32 |
| Fertilisers | 1.15 | 0.97 | 0.24 |

Source:  Annual Survey of Industries, 1965, India.
Quoted from Employment Creation and Small
Scale Enterprise Development (World Bank,
Washington, DC, 1977), annex 1, p.10.

## Income

Since increasing the incomes of poor households
is the principal aim of most rural enterprise
projects, the profile on income generation is
perhaps the most important one generated to assist
in project selection.  The income profile also
assists in laying the basis for the selection of a
project target group by indicating the types of
households that fall into the category "the rural
poor".  Table 4.8 illustrates an income profile by
product type and scale. [3]   In this example, the
incomes for medium- and large-scale enterprises
include only income to workers; incomes to share-

holders and owners are not included since these groups are assumed to be outside the potential target group. For small-scale enterprises (with less than five workers), all owner-worker incomes are included.

Table 4.8.--Income Profile by Scale and Type of Product, El Salvador

| Subsector | Net income per capita by scale | |
|---|---|---|
| | Medium and large | Small |
| | (US dollars) | |
| Food processing | 147 | 229 |
| Coffee processing | 271 | 215 |
| Drinks | 412 | 288 |
| Tobacco | 189 | 89 |
| Textiles | 221 | 144 |
| Clothing | 156 | 175 |
| Leather | 300 | 232 |
| Shoes | 192 | 323 |
| Wood products | 122 | 175 |
| Furniture | 222 | 230 |
| All agroindustry | 212 | 190 |

Source:   S. R. Daines and D. Steen, El Salvador Agroindustrial Profile (United States Agency for International Development, San Salvador, 1977), p.26.

Agribusiness Linkages

One of the principal interests in agribusinesses and small-scale rural enterprises is the indirect effect these activities have on small-farm agriculture by stimulating demand for agricultural products and providing institutional linkages for increasing farm production. The profile should contain information on these important backward linkages. Different types of product draw more heavily on agricultural production and more importantly on production from small farms. Table 4.9 illustrates some sample profiles of backward linkages which would be useful to project planners in attempting to assess the potential for creating indirect impacts from optional investments in agribusiness and small-scale rural enterprises.

# Developing a Profile of an Agribusiness System

Many optional modes of computation may be used; any will serve reasonably well to illustrate the linkage between the enterprise sector and production from small farms.

Table 4.9.--Agroindustrial Impact on Production from Small Farms, El Salvador

| Subsector | Raw material intensity [a] | Proportion of output captured by small farms |
|---|---|---|
| | (Per cent) | (Per cent) |
| Coffee processing | 56.9 | 6.0 |
| Drinks | 14.8 | 0.0 |
| Tobacco | 21.1 | 8.2 |
| Textiles | 44.7 | 2.8 |
| Clothing | 50.1 | 3.2 |
| Leather | 51.7 | 14.2 |
| Shoes | 41.3 | 11.2 |
| Furniture | 36.7 | 11.2 |
| Food industry: | | |
| Meat products | 72.0 | 19.7 |
| Milk products | 54.1 | 14.8 |
| Fruit & vegetables | 27.6 | 8.2 |
| Edible oils | 61.7 | 2.2b |
| Flour milling | 66.9 | 3.3b |
| Baking | 47.2 | 2.2b |
| Sugar products | 50.5 | 7.7 |
| Sweets | 38.4 | 5.8 |

Source:  S. R. Daines and D. Steen, El Salvador Agroindustrial Profile (United States Agency for International Development, San Salvador, 1977), p.264.

a       Farm product as a percentage of the value of production.
b       Mostly imported goods with little domestic production linkage.

Developing a Profile of an Agribusiness System

## Growth Trends and Product Demand

Where statistics permit, a time trend should be included in the profile to depict the sectoral growth patterns of output. While demand and growth rate estimates are useful in the sector profile, they are much more important in the project identification and analysis of constraints which follow in Chapter 5. Examples and a fuller discussion are given there. [4]

## Women in Agribusiness and Rural Enterprises

In most developing countries, rural enterprises employ large numbers of women in worker and managerial roles. Rural enterprises have the potential of being the most important avenue for improving the status and welfare of rural women, and it is important therefore that the profile includes information on the nature and magnitudes of these roles. Table 4.10 illustrates one possible profile showing the employment share of women by scale and sector.

Table 4.10.--Women's Share in Employment in Small- and Large-scale Manufacturing, Ghana

| Industry | Share of all workers | | | Share of sector | |
|---|---|---|---|---|---|
| | Large scale | Small scale* | Women | Large scale | Small scale |
| | (Per cent) | | | | |
| Food | 3.4 | 96.6 | 85.8 | 7.5 | 37.3 |
| Beverages | 7.9 | 92.1 | 57.0 | 5.1 | 10.3 |
| Tobacco | 96.2 | 3.8 | 13.9 | 2.2 | 0.0 |
| Textiles | 41.5 | 58.5 | 14.6 | 20.1 | 4.9 |
| Wearing apparel | 3.7 | 96.3 | 64.5 | 6.3 | 28.1 |
| Furniture | 6.9 | 93.0 | 2.2 | 3.0 | 7.0 |
| Total for all industries | 14.1 | 85.9 | 54.0 | 100.0 | 100.0 |

Source: W. F Steel, Small-Scale Employment and Production in Developing Countries, Evidence from Ghana (Praeger, New York, 1977), p.190.

Note: Employment in the small-scale sector is calculated as a residual (100 per cent minus the percentage employed in the large-scale sector).

83

DATA FOR AN AGRIBUSINESS AND RURAL ENTERPRISE SECTOR
PROFILE

## Use of Existing Data or Generation of New Data

An agribusiness and rural enterprise profile is
best used as a prelude to more specific project
identification and project analysis. In this role,
it is important that constructing the profile not
take an excessively long time or compete with
resources needed for the project analysis process
itself. These two factors imply that a profile
should be based on existing data sources; to mount
special surveys to provide the data required would
take unwarranted time and resources and compete with
the task of analysing the target group and project
which normally follows preparation of a sector
profile.

The required data may appear not to exist, yet
careful search of ministries, trade and industrial
organisation files, lending institution records and
census information will usually provide information
to complete the profile for most of the topics
discussed above. Often sources of information are
not readily apparent because data are still in their
raw form and have not been processed to the stage
necessary to complete a profile. It is often
possible and usually worthwhile to process and
analyse selected data from census, ministry or
credit agency files. What is not usually possible
or advisable, however, is to generate special
surveys or primary data collection efforts to
generate the information simply for the purpose of a
profile.

## Sources of Data

Industrial census files. Most developing
countries conduct periodic industrial and commercial
censuses. Over the past decade, the influence of
the United Nations statistical assistance effort has
been substantial. The formats recommended by the UN
are excellent from the point of view of providing
data for a rural enterprise profile. Almost all of
the topics mentioned in this chapter can be completed where a UN-type industrial census has been
conducted. Considerable reprocessing of these data
files may be necessary to cast the census data in
the form necessary to complete a profile, but even
if the original census questionnaires must be repro-

cessed, the task is a manageable one. Profiles based on census files should be possible in roughly half of the developing countries, and this proportion is constantly increasing.

Existing surveys. As a part of the UN statistical system, countries are encouraged to update their census activities with interim samples which cover only a small proportion of the enterprises. Individual ministries and in some cases universities or trade and industrial organisations may conduct surveys. These sources are generally more detailed and consequently more useful than census data for constructing a profile. Unfortunately, these surveys often cover only a limited geographical area or a limited range of product types, and may thus prove inadequate as a basis for constructing a sector-wide profile.

Institutional files and records. Credit institutions, industrial associations and other organisations gather data in their normal course of business which may be drawn upon to support a profile. Only careful reviews of the files themselves will reveal the existence of such sources. It is extremely difficult to describe the data needs of a profile in such a way that officials in charge of institutional files can determine whether their data fit the description. It is much more efficient to proceed by making a complete inventory of all data collected by the institution in the course of carrying out its main activities and then determine independently if the data are suitable for the profile. Confidentiality is usually not a problem if data are summarised to some minimum level of aggregation and if the sensitive parts of the information never leave the institution. For example, if enterprise files which are useful for a profile are kept in a credit institution, names, addresses and cash-flow information should be masked when forms are photocopied. Alternatively, nonsensitive data may be copied onto coding sheets by personnel of the institution itself. In these ways, confidential information is never obtained, and thus the issue of maintaining confidentiality does not actually arise.

## ANALYTICAL METHODS FOR AN AGROINDUSTRIAL AND RURAL ENTERPRISE PROFILE

Analytical methods should be limited to simple statistical comparisons and accounting methods. Profitability and productivity ratios represent the

most difficult methods feasible, given the time and
resource limitations imposed on the construction of
most profiles. Since the methodologies for enterprise accounting, profitability and productivity
analysis are the same for the profile and the more
detailed project analysis, these methods will be
discussed in Chapter 5.


NOTES

1.   For purposes of valuation, capital is often
divided into four categories:  working capital,
equipment, buildings and land, and human capital
(although the last is commonly omitted).
     For comparative analysis, capital is frequently
valued in two alternative ways.  One method is to
use the capital stock, that is, the gross value of
capital at the time of purchase.  This measurement
suffers from the fact that depreciation rates vary
among industries, as does the extent of obsolescence
of existing equipment.  Also, in an inflationary
setting, the replacement cost of capital can be very
significantly different from its original purchase
value.  This is sometimes remedied by using replacement values where available.  Additionally, since
many small-scale enterprises rent rather than own
their buildings and land, the value of these items
will frequently be omitted and thus distort comparisons of capital stock.
     An alternative approach is to use capital
service, that is, the value of capital which is used
up in the production process.  With this method, the
capital stock is frequently discounted to take into
account depreciation and the opportunity cost of
capital.  This method also has difficulties since it
generally assumes that the rental price of capital
and the rate of depreciation are the same in each
industry compared.
     Given the limitations of each method, it is not
clear that one approach is decidedly preferable to
the other in practice, although the second is more
theoretically appealing. The method selected will
generally be determined by the availability of data
in addition to constraints of time and finance.
2.   It might be pointed out that in some cases
labour-intensive processes have yielded lower
output-capital ratios than less labour-intensive
techniques.  See A. S. Bhalla, "Choosing Techniques:
Handpounding v. Machine Milling of Rice:  An Indian
Case", Oxford Economic Papers, vol.17, no.1 (1965),

pp.147-57.

3.    A common characteristic relevant to income and agroindustrial linkages (the next section) is the fact that small-scale enterprises are often a secondary yet significant source of income for farm workers.

4.    The issue is sometimes raised as to whether or not there is sufficient demand for their products to warrant small-scale enterprises increasing their output.  It has been estimated that in Sierra Leone, at least, rural expenditure elasticities of demand for the products of small-scale industries are sufficiently high to expect moderate potential for growth through increased demand.  See R. P. King and D. Byerlee, "Income Distribution, Consumption Patterns and Consumption Linkages in Rural Sierra Leone", African Rural Economy Paper No. 16 (Michigan State University, East Lansing, 1977).

# CHAPTER 5

## PRELIMINARY ANALYSIS AND PROJECT IDENTIFICATION

This chapter continues with the overview of project
analysis techniques by outlining approaches which
ultimately enable more detailed specifications of
activities and components to be developed and
included in the design of projects. A major purpose
of the chapter is to further elaborate the use of
various profiles as part of a general format for
examining and ranking constraints.

## TABULAR PRESENTATION OF CONSTRAINTS BY SUBSECTOR

The diversity of the agribusiness and rural
enterprise sector must be kept in mind when
proceeding to examine apparent constraints which
limit welfare of poor families. Factors which
constrain large-scale food processing industries are
not likely to be the same as those factors which
limit small-scale tailoring shops. The lack of data
and detail in a typical sectoral profile implies
that much of this complexity will be unseen in the
preliminary analysis of constraints and must be left
to the later, more complete examination of
constraints during the preparation of the project
document. In order to direct attention to the
diverse situations of the various subsectors or
groupings, the tabular format illustrated in Table
5.1 is suggested. The listing of constraints is
discussed further below.

Constraints limit expansion or improvement in
an enterprise. In order to understand the concept
of constraints as used in the tabular format, and in
later discussion, it may help to explore the types
of expansions or improvements an entrepreneur could
make. Each possible improvement or expansion
suggests corresponding factors which are limiting.

Table 5.1.—Tabular Format for Preliminary Ranking of Constraints Based on the Sector Profile and Expert Judgment

| | Constraints on: | | | |
| | Resource use | | Resource availability | |
| | Efficiency constraints | Price constraints | Resource constraints | Marketing constraints |
| | Process technology Management Product mix Training | Input prices | | |
| **Region I** | | | | |
| Small-scale | | | | |
| Product a | | | | |
| Product b | | | | |
| ... | | | | |
| Product n | | | | |
| Medium- and large-scale | | | | |
| Product a | | | | |
| ... | | | | |
| Product n | | | | |
| **Region II** | | | | |
| Small-scale | | | | |
| Product a | | | | |
| ... | | | | |
| Product n | | | | |
| ... | | | | |
| **Region N** | | | | |

An entrepreneur in an agribusiness or rural enterprise may increase his income in two basic ways: (1) by increasing the resources he utilises, or (2) by changing the way resources are used. He may increase the size of his operation by acquiring additional resources, or may increase the efficiency with which the resources he has are used. Of course, both changes may be made at the same time. These two basic possibilities for increasing income at the level of the enterprise provide a useful way of organising the analysis of constraints.

Constraints may be grouped into those factors which limit the efficiency with which the enterprise utilises resources and those factors or conditions which limit the quantity of resources the enterprise has available to it. It should be noted that all of these constraints operate at the level of the firm and that no assertion is implied as to final or principal cause in the economy as a whole. There are secondary and tertiary institutional, cultural, political and other constraints which influence or cause these enterprise-level constraints. These institutional or secondary constraints must be identified before projects can be adequately designed. Even though these secondary constraints exist, it is useful to begin by examining the alternatives and constraints at the level of the firm in order to make more orderly and accurate the process of examining contributory or causative factors at public or institutional levels. An example of this constraint "chain" is provided by liquidity. Assume that the data indicate that small-scale enterprises are profitable and could expand if they had additional liquidity. Credit would be identified as a constraint at the level of the firm. A wide variety of secondary causative or contributory factors might then be identified. It may be that government policy restricts credit entities from recovering the added costs of making small-scale loans by charging higher interest rates or fees. This might be a constraint at the policy level. In the format of Table 5.1, no assertion is made as to ultimate cause; only factors which limit the enterprise itself are identified.

While the organisation of constraints as described above may assist in clarifying what factors limit increased welfare in the rural enterprise sector, the utility of the format does not depend on this particular classification of types of constraints. Each analyst may have an individual perspective on how to organise and classify the factors which limit the improvement of welfare in target enterprises. All that is necessary for the tabular format to be useful is that the analyst has a list of these factors, and that he or she recognise that they are not equally limiting or important for all regions, scales of production and types of enterprise. The analyst should simply substitute a new list for the constraint column headings in Table 5.1 and proceed to assign a priority to each type of constraint for the major enterprise groups considered.

## Preliminary Ranking of Constraints

The hope of the project designer is that some factors or limiting conditions are more important than others, since the underlying assumption is that altering some elements in the environment will cause a positive change. If all elements or factors are simultaneously and equally binding and all must be attacked equally at once for any improvement to result, then the very hypothesis of projects as feasible instruments of change must be rejected since they cannot hope ever to affect all of these factors at once. The process of assigning priorities to the constraints may take place explicitly in some tabular format or implicitly in the minds of project planners. Using a record-keeping system like the tabular format has three advantages:

- Others can follow the process which led to the selection of particular project activities;
- The use of evidence from the sector profile in the identification and ranking of constraints is facilitated; and
- Expert judgments may be explicitly compared with the sketchy quantitative evidence.

At the stage of project identification, only the roughest level of precision is expected from this exercise. It may be useful to submit a blank table like Table 5.1 to each of the officials concerned with identification of the project, and then compare these first results with the evidence drawn from the profile. In some cases one might conclude that the limited statistical evidence and the expert judgments are leading in identical directions. In others there may be conflicts and inconsistencies between the profile and the expert opinion, or perhaps even differences between different experts. The tabular format provides a way to keep track of these contradictions and to add up the implications of whatever consensuses emerge. If there is sufficient agreement on what the problem is (what is constraining improvement), there is ample reason to proceed to decide what to do about it. If no consensus exists on even the roughest definition of what the problem is, agreement on how to solve it is impossible. Project identification should not be overburdened with pressure for certainty, detailed evidence or clarity; and there is little danger that such pressure will be excessive given typically short programming cycles. Project identification has been properly viewed as a stage for raising reasonable hypotheses for confirmation during the project approval process. It is unfortunate, however, that few project identification documents even state the underlying hypotheses about the problems or constraints which are to be attacked. Without clearly stated hypotheses about the problem at the level of the firm and connecting hypotheses about the way the project hopes to change the problem, it is impossible to design a rational evaluation and monitoring system.

Assigning priorities, however tentative, to the constraints indicated in the tabular format may be an effective way of structuring project identification and of stating project hypotheses.


## A Typology of Constraints at the Enterprise Level

A wide variety of typologies may be developed to classify the factors constraining the increasing of incomes earned by families operating rural enterprises. The classification which follows serves the double purpose of suggesting a scheme where an analyst may not have a better one and provides a basis for discussing the analytical process of connecting the data in a sector profile with the analysis of constraints and selection of projects.

The discussion which follows explains the concept of specific constraints and then illustrates how data from a sector profile could be used to assign a preliminary priority to each constraint. It should be remembered that expert judgment should be used to supplement and adjust profile findings and may substitute for such findings in the absence of any data.

## Constraints on Resource Use

Constraints on resource use are those factors which limit income by impeding the efficiency with which resources are utilised in the enterprise. Two general classes of "use" constraints are defined: those which relate to how resources are combined in the production process, and those which relate to the prices paid for outputs and inputs.

Technological constraints on production processes. An entrepreneur could increase his income if he could use more efficient physical techniques to process the materials used in production. If such a change is feasible, and if his current technology is very inefficient, then this constraint should be given a high priority.

The sector profile may be examined to see if it contains data on this constraint. If profitability varies widely with scale, and if larger firms have significantly higher profitability rates, one would suspect that perhaps inefficient technologies could be a major constraint. It should be noted that most engineers simply assume without examination that production technology is obviously the most important constraint. Without the more detailed type of enterprise accounting data generated for later project analysis, it is impossible to distinguish this constraint from other "resource use" constraints through the use of profitability ratios.

Constraints on administration and technical management. Differences in accounting know-how or technical management ability may cause two entrepreneurs to obtain different incomes even though they are using the same technology in the production process. This constraint needs to be tackled through training and technical assistance.

The same data are used here as for the analysis of the constraints on production technologies. If profitability and/or capital productivity is much higher for firms of similar type and size in areas where entrepreneurs have had different levels of education, this constraint may be important.

Product mix. Similar resources (wood for example) may be used in the same process technology (gluing, shaping, etc.) but in different proportions to produce very different products (chairs or packing cases). Two enterprises may have different incomes from similar levels of process technology and management simply because the mix of products is more efficient in producing income.

This constraint can only be identified with

data on product mix which are not likely to be available during the process of identifying the project. [1]

Constraints on input prices. An entrepreneur can increase his income by reducing the prices he pays for inputs without changing anything else in his enterprise. Large differences in profitability among cooperative enterprises (if they purchase inputs) would tend to indicate this is an important constraint which it is feasible to alter.

Constraints on output prices. Income can be increased if output prices can be increased with no reduction in physical volume of sales. They might be increased by increasing quality of product or the way in which the product is marketed. The goods may be cooperatively marketed, sold at a different location, or sold at retail instead of wholesale.

Large differences in profitability or capital productivity among similar enterprises in different physical proximity to markets indicates that constraints may well be operating on output prices.

## Constraints on Resource Availability

Constraints on resource availability affect the quantities of resources available to the enterprise. In a certain sense, all of these "availability" constraints are critical only if efficiency is not. If the technology used in the enterprise is inefficient (that is, has a profitability ratio less than zero), then resource availability should not be considered a priority constraint since it will not increase income to put added resources into a process which cannot turn a profit. Some technological, or price, relationship must be altered, some nonresource constraint must be attacked, before the availability of resources becomes a concern. Additional liquidity is not a constraint if current financial resources are not profitable, additional labour is not a constraint if current labour productivity is less than the going wage rate.

It is important to use profitability, capital and labour productivity measures as an indication of the limiting nature of resource supplies. If profitability is high but incomes are low, this is strong evidence that additional resources would increase income and therefore resource availability is the critical constraint. If income is determined more by the size of the enterprise than differences in profitability and productivity ratios, resource

constraints would be suspected to be binding. To
determine which resources (capital goods, raw
materials, labour, and/or other inputs) are limiting
income is difficult. It is therefore convenient to
view untied credit (or liquidity) as a general limi-
tation, since it is fungible across a wide variety
of resources--that is to say, credit can be used to
lessen or eliminate any of these constraints. If
the profitability and productivity ratios of small
enterprises are high, and these enterprises also use
low levels of credit per unit of output, liquidity
and resource availability should be suspected as
constraints.

## Constraints on the Marketing System

Roads, transport facilities and storage and
handling facilities may be important constraints on
incomes. These constraints manifest themselves as
price constraints which force an enterprise to
accept lower prices for its products--and in many
cases the existence or nonexistence of these facilities may make such a price difference that no
production of particular products is feasible.
Where roads are poor, transporters may effectively
control producer prices. These are essentially
constraints which exist external to the firm but
which exert a strong influence on the firm.

There will be differences in profitability and
productivity among firms with different proximities
to marketing facilities and transport networks. The
analysis of constraints will help to identify a
project by pointing to problems and stimulating
thought about what solutions are feasible.

## SELECTING A TARGET GROUP

One of the major purposes of the sector profile
and the preliminary analysis is to facilitate the
selection of a target group for a particular project
or an integrated set of projects. Two separate
steps in selecting a target group are facilitated:

- The sector profile facilitates the process of
  determining what subpopulations or subgroups of
  households qualify as poor by accepted definitions, and
- The preliminary analysis of constraints should
  suggest which subgroups have a high potential

for improvement with interventions of the type donor agencies can provide.

These two steps, first determining qualifying subgroups and second identifying subgroups with potential for improvement with external interventions, set the stage for the identification of an appropriate target group. In many cases the groups qualifying for assistance and amenable to improvement may be so diverse (both geographically and in other ways) that it is not practical to implement a project to access them. The last stage in identification of target groups is therefore to search for practical groupings around which a single project mechanism or institution could reasonably implement an intervention.

## Determining Which Subgroups Qualify for Assistance

The sector profile attempts to estimate income for the various subgroups. This is important for, without it, it is impossible to determine which subgroups would qualify as "poor" for project assistance. In defining poverty, some accepted standard of income needs to be used to determine where assistance is appropriate. The linkage section of the sector profile is particularly important since many enterprises in urban areas or larger-scale rural industries may qualify due to their strong impact on the income of small-scale farmers.

Since it is not practical to measure the income of households or enterprises before admitting them to participation in a project, it is necessary to look for proxies for income which can be used easily and fairly. The sector profile should assist in making first approximations of these admission criteria. For example, it may be that scale of operation is closely related to income, and all (or almost all) of those enterprises with fewer than 10 workers qualify as poor. Size of enterprise is a practical criterion for use in the field. Firms with over 10 workers could be identified and excluded with relative ease, while it would be impossible to measure income each time. Regional and product-based groupings will also be helpful in defining groups that qualify in such a way that it will be practical to use the definitions in actual projects.

Preliminary Analysis and Project Identification

## Identifying a Target Group with the Potential to Benefit from Projects

Using the analysis of preliminary constraints to identify groups with potential for improvement will suggest a wide variety of project options which in turn imply the selection of different target groups.

## Using the Target Group Selection Process to Identify Specific Projects

There is an obvious interaction between determining which groups can be positively affected by a project and identifying a project. The most important element which must be added and which is missing from the process of identifying target groups is the addition of an institutional mechanism. Project planners must identify an existing or feasible institutional structure to make the needed intervention. It should be remembered that most often project planners begin with an institution and a more-or-less completely hatched project idea before any target group identification or sector profile is undertaken. In this more common case, the information generated should not be used to justify that conception but rather to refine it within the boundaries imposed by the institution selected. The more advisable course is to begin with an overview of the sector in the form of a profile, add to that an examination of the constraints which limit improvement for different groups in the sector, define a target group based on level of poverty and potential for improvement, and last of all select mechanisms to attack some critical set of constraints.

## DETAILED PROFILES OF FAMILIES IN THE TARGET GROUP

The preparation of the target group profile assumes the existence of a set of data which has been gathered for the purposes of project development. The data-gathering process necessary to prepare a target group profile is described in Chapter 8.

The reason for constructing profiles of families in the target group is to provide planners with a comprehensive view of those to be benefited by project interventions. Three major dimensions of family welfare are important in the profile:

- family income and economic activities;
- family employment patterns; and
- other dimensions of family welfare, such as housing, health, nutrition and education.

A short description of these elements of profiles is given below with examples drawn from actual project documents.

## Profile of Income and Economic Activities Among Target Group Families

The income profile should include families of workers as well as those owning/operating rural enterprises. Subgroupings should of course include only those enterprises and types of families selected as the focus of the project. In most cases, the choice can be represented by a certain region, scale and class of enterprise. Table 5.2 presents an example of an income and economic activity profile for a target group of small-scale enterprises. The target group was selected as follows:

Region--Central Highlands
Scale--Fewer than 10 workers
Product types--As indicated in Table 5.2.

Both enterprise-owning families and hired workers are included in the profile.

## Profile of Employment Patterns

The employment profile of target families should include content on the role of women in the enterprises, as well as employment in non-enterprise activities such as work on family or other farms. Table 5.3 illustrates the concept of an employment profile.

Employment patterns can indicate to the project planner the existence and seriousness of labour constraints. For example, in the food and leather sectors additional labour would probably have to be hired from outside the family. In the other sectors significant slack exists.

Preliminary Analysis and Project Identification

## Creating Profiles of Other Welfare Dimensions

Information on housing, health and nutrition, while useful, may be too costly to generate. If data already exist they should certainly be included in the profile. Educational and cultural information may be extremely useful in building a more complete picture of the target group.

## DETAILED PROFILES OF TARGET GROUP ENTERPRISES

The second segment of the target group profile shifts from the family to focus on the economic and technical characteristics of the enterprise itself. The enterprise is the vehicle for increasing welfare and it is important to examine its principal characteristics in an adequately structured profile.

The first general topic for the profile of the target group enterprise is the concept of efficiency. Efficiency should be broken down into financial efficiency (or profitability), economic efficiency with capital productivity as the primary indicator and labour efficiency using labour productivity as the indicator. The second general area for a profile is the structure of the enterprise, its output patterns, resource endowments, etc.

## Efficiency Profile

Efficiency is an important concept to profile since it will help to sort project options into two general classes: those which seek to increase the efficiency of the enterprise, and those which seek to expand the enterprise. If efficiency is low, then increasing efficiency should be the focus of project activities. If efficiency is relatively high and expansion looks possible, then expansion should be the focus.

Profitability profile. Profitability is an indicator of financial efficiency. It is a measure of the value of profits earned divided by the value of assets (including working capital to finance variable costs) required to produce the profit. The concept is identical to that already described in the sector profile sections. In the sector profile, the data will not often permit computation of the profitability of enterprises, and it is unlikely to be worth the time and effort to gather the necessary data at that stage to do so. While the omission of

Table 5.2.--Income and Economic Activity Profile for Small-scale Rural Enterprises, Guatemala

**A. Small-scale rural entrepreneurs**

| Sector | No. of families | Net income per family from family enterprises (US$) | Net income per capita from family enterprises (US$) |
|---|---|---|---|
| Wood products | 4,037 | 886 | 132 |
| Textiles | 17,944 | 500 | 73 |
| Leather and miscellaneous | 6,729 | 744 | 130 |
| Baking and food products | 7,626 | 735 | 113 |
| Commercial and services | 8,523 | 993 | 226 |

**B. Workers in small-scale rural enterprises**

| Sector | Monthly wage rate (US$) | Net income/month for adults in owner-family (US$) | Superiority of owner-income per month worked (per cent) | Net income per capita for worker-family (US$) |
|---|---|---|---|---|
| Wood products | 65 | 81 | 24.6 | 139 |
| Textiles | 21 | 32 | 52.4 | 45 |
| Leather and miscellaneous | 31 | 47 | 51.6 | 66 |
| Baking and food products | 32 | 43 | 34.4 | 69 |
| Commercial and services | 28 | 60 | 114.3 | 50 |

Source: United States Agency for International Development, Agribusiness and Rural Enterprise Project Analysis Manual (Washington, 1980), p.75.

Table 5.3.--Employment Profiles of Families in Rural Enterprises, Guatemala

|  | Number of workers in family | Person-months family labour in enterprise* | Per cent of family labour available used in enterprise | Women as per cent of total employment |
|---|---|---|---|---|
| Wood products | 1.58 | 12.9 | 68 | 8 |
| Textiles | 2.01 | 18.8 | 75 | 50 |
| Leather and miscellaneous | 1.71 | 18.8 | 92 | 17 |
| Baking and food products | 2.01 | 23.2 | 96 | 47 |
| Commercial and services | 2.28 | 19.7 | 72 | 65 |

Source: United States Agency for International Development, Agribusiness and Rural Enterprise Project Analysis Manual (Washington, 1980), p.75.

Note: It should be noted that the recall-based surveys on which this table was constructed perform less well in providing estimates of actual family labour input in person-months or in person-days than with almost any other type of data included in the manual.

profitability analysis is permissible at the stages of profiling the sector and identifying the project, to fail to include it in preparation for the project document would be a serious shortcoming. The data for an analysis of profitability are required not just to construct a profile of enterprises in the target group but also for the cost-benefit analysis and determination of financial feasibility. Table 5.4 provides an example of a profitability profile for a target group of rural enterprises.

In most countries the cost of capital goods will have changed significantly between the time enterprises purchased them and today's cost of expansion and purchasing additional equipment. It is important, therefore, to compute not just what current profitability is but what profitability would be after expansion and at today's prices.

Table 5.4.--Profitability Profile of a Target Group of Rural Enterprises, Guatemala

| | Current profitability [a] | Profitability after expansion [b] | Value of equipment per firm | |
|---|---|---|---|---|
| | | | Cost | Replacement |
| | (per cent) | | (US$) | (US$) |
| Wood products | 67 | 32 | 823 | 1,892 |
| Textiles | 54 | 36 | 615 | 968 |
| Leather and miscellaneous | 64 | 34 | 750 | 1,490 |
| Baking and food products | 79 | 50 | 324 | 760 |
| Commercial and services | 78 | 50 | 848 | 1,409 |

Source: United States Agency for International Development, Agribusiness and Rural Enterprise Project Analysis Manual (Washington, 1980), p.77.

a       Rate of return to total capital value at cost including working capital.
b       Based on replacement values for equipment.

Economic efficiency and capital productivity.
If capital is the scarcest resource in a developing
country, it follows that the productivity of capital
is the best measure of economic efficiency.  There
are many measures more satisfying in an elegant and
sophisticated sense in that resources are given
shadow or opportunity prices, but all these methods
are complex and require time and data not usually
available for the preparation of a project document.
Estimating the productivity of capital in simple
terms is, however, a simple computation to make and
captures much of the meaning of economic efficiency
since it tells us what society is getting in terms
of output per unit of its scarcest resource.  There
may be situations in which other resources (such as
materials, skilled craftsmen, etc.) may be even more
scarce than capital, and in these cases capital
productivity would be replaced by, for example, "raw
material" productivity as the best measure of
economic efficiency.  Those sectors or target group
enterprises with high financial profitability may
not be the same as those with the highest capital
productivity since prices may distort private
returns away from the socially most productive
sectors.  Table 5.5 illustrates a set of computations for capital productivity (value added per unit
of fixed and working capital).  [2]

Table 5.5.--Capital Productivity for Small-scale
Target Group Enterprises

| Target group subsectors | Value added divided by the value of fixed and working capital |
|---|---|
| Wood products | 1.30 |
| Textiles | 0.92 |
| Leather, ceramics and fibre products | 0.98 |
| Baking and food products | 1.44 |
| Commercial enterprises | 1.56 |
| Services | 0.31 |

Source:  United States Agency for International
Development, Agribusiness and Rural
Enterprise Project Analysis Manual
(Washington, 1980), p.78.

Labour productivity. Labour productivity is not a good measure of efficiency in developing countries because it does not measure output per unit of scarce resource; labour is not usually scarce. An exception is seasonal labour in those regions where it can become an acute problem. It is, however, useful as a welfare measure since it does indicate incremental additions to welfare per person. Table 5.6 illustrates a profile of labour productivity for India.

Table 5.6.--Labour Productivity Profile for Selected Agroindustries, India

| Sector | Scale of enterprise | | |
|--------|-------|--------|-------|
|        | Small | Medium | Large |
| (value added per employee in rupees) | | | |
| Grain milling | 2,426 | 4,590 | 7,806 |
| Food preparation | 2,243 | 4,145 | 8,705 |
| Tobacco | 1,369 | 1,441 | 16,486 |
| Spinning and weaving | 2,423 | 2,549 | 3,444 |
| Wood products | 1,802 | 3,279 | 1,149 |

Source: Government of India, Annual Survey of Industries, 1965, as cited in Employment Creation and Small-Scale Enterprise Development (World Bank, Washington, DC, 1977) Annex 1, p.10.

Labour productivity and labour efficiency are two different concepts. For example, the value added per employee in tobacco from small-scale to large-scale increases by a factor of 10, but this may be due simply to the fact that in the larger plant there is 10 times as much capital per labourer (that is, capital has been substituted for labour) rather than that labour is working more efficiently.

## Profile of Enterprise Structure

In designing projects to improve the performance of enterprises, it is useful to have a profile of a wide variety of financial and technical characteristics of the firms in the target group. The types of information used are simple, and examples of each type are not necessary in order to visualise

them. A single example is presented in Table 5.7.
The list which follows, while not comprehensive,
covers those which are of the most use to project
planners:

- Patterns of credit use;
- Wage bill for hired labour;
- Use of family labour;
- Patterns of savings;
- Value of capital assets; and
- Type of energy used and patterns of use.

As is indicated in the chapters which follow, there
are many other items of data not listed above which
are needed to conduct various parts of the project
analysis. The topics noted here are the ones which
would appropriately appear under the general heading
of "enterprise profile".

Table 5.7.--Sources of Finance for Small
Manufacturing Businesses in an Urban
Area, Accra, Ghana

| Source of finance | No waged employees | No. of waged employees | | All firms |
|---|---|---|---|---|
| | | 1-9 | 10-29 | |
| | (percentage of firms in each category) | | | |
| Personal savings or money from relatives | 91.7 | 96.9 | 80.9 | 90.8 |
| Derived in part from farming | 16.7 | 19.4 | 10.0 | 15.9 |
| Personal savings only | 41.7 | 78.1 | 28.6 | 55.4 |
| Personal savings plus some other source | 25.0 | 9.4 | 42.9 | 23.0 |
| Bank loans | 8.3 | 3.1 | 23.8 | 19.8 |
| Number of respondents | 12 | 32 | 21 | 65 |

Source: Accra Manufacturing Survey, 1973, from W.
F. Steel, Small-scale Employment and Production in Developing Countries: Evidence
from Ghana (Praeger, New York, 1977).

Note: Percentages may add to more than 100
because some firms use multiple sources of
financing.

NOTES

1. The ability of firms to increase income through more efficient mixes of products will vary considerably among types of industries. Also, taking advantage of such a strategy requires a level of accounting sophistication not always found among small-scale firms. Even firms producing multiple product lines in industrialised countries will not always have the accounting records necessary to determine the relative profitability of each product. Provision of assistance in analysing and/or improving accounts may be of substantial benefit in some cases.

2. It has been argued that ratios depicting the productivity of a single resource are inappropriate because they exclude other important "causes" of the desired outcome and therefore depend upon subjective assessments of resource scarcity. This argument suggests that all resources are scarce to some extent and should therefore be included in the ratio. All that is needed to construct a composite ratio of productivity is a set of shadow prices with which to value each of the resources consumed. Benefit-cost ratios are the commonest of this variety. Composite productivity ratios are not without their weaknesses however, as their very comprehensiveness implies a loss of detail. With a composite ratio, the analyst cannot see the influence of one factor of production--land, for example--separate from that of others--for example, capital--or of different categories of the same factor--arable, cultivated and total land area for instance. This loss of detail can obscure important interactions.

While the disadvantage of the composite ratio is that it obscures the contribution of each separate resource to the outcome, the parallel weakness of the single resource ratio is that it attributes all of the outcome to a single resource. Unless carefully used, either ratio can be misleading. Two solutions to this quandary have been used with varying degrees of success. The first is to compute both single and composite productivity ratios and use them together, accepting the limitations of each. The second technique is to calculate a production function, which is a rather complex method for assigning or attributing a proportionate share of production to each major resource. This approach however suffers from a number of drawbacks, both conceptual and logistical, which weakens its

potential application to the process of project
formulation. The productivity ratio, with all its
difficulties, remains in practice perhaps the most
useful technique for project analysis. Much of this
usefulness stems from its conceptual simplicity, its
relative ease and cost of implementation and its
reduced requirement for data.

CHAPTER 6

EXAMINING PROJECT POTENTIAL AND FEASIBILITY

In the context of this manual, agribusiness and rural enterprise projects are undertaken to improve the welfare of the poorer members of a community. This chapter, together with Chapter 7, deals with three basic project-related issues:

- What will the project benefits be? (What are the magnitude and probability of improvements in target group welfare if the project is implemented as designed?)
- Can the project be implemented as designed? (What is the probability that the project is feasible?)
- Do the likely benefits of a project justify its costs?

In this and the next chapter, an attempt is made to explore the possible methods of analysis which can focus data and judgment on each of these issues. Project analysts familiar with the procedures used by many donors will recognise the last two issues as the traditional topics of feasibility and cost-benefit analysis. One of the intentions of this manual is to highlight the common neglect and emphasise the importance of adequate analysis of the first issue, which relates to estimating the potential of the project to create improvements in target group welfare. The most common inadequacy in project analysis is the weak basis for estimating benefits for the target group arising from the project's activities. Very often projects contain extensive benefit-cost analysis but lack any systematic evidence that the assumed benefits will actually happen. This chapter begins by presenting methods for estimating the potential of a project for creating benefits for the target groups.

The methods for estimating project potential may be divided into two general categories based on the data required. The first methods require some type of systematically gathered and statistically representative accounting information on enterprises in the target group. These methods are treated in the first half of this chapter. The other methods range from those requiring no data at all (expert judgment) to methods requiring accounting data which are not statistically representative of target group enterprises as a whole (micro or case study estimates). These methods are discussed in Chapter 8. The fact that this chapter is devoted to formal or relatively structured methods does not imply that other methods are not important. In current practice informal methods make up the bulk of project analysis and in many cases use logic and reasoning equal in complexity to the more conventional and structured methods. The reason for the relative lack of attention to nonformal methods in this manual stems from two problems with these methods--the first is a problem of substance, the second one of presentation:

- Given the lack of serious evaluation of impacts for projects using informal estimates of project potential, it is difficult as yet to test the validity of these methods.
- The informal methods tend to be highly personal; that is, the procedure, logical reasoning, and analytical processes are as varied and numerous as are the analysts or officials who use them. There is little which is standard or generalised which could be presented in a manual of this type. These methods depend on the analyst and his/her experience.

The purpose of the second half of the chapter is to explore methods for examining the feasibility of agribusiness and rural enterprise projects.

## ACCOUNTING METHODS FOR ANALYSIS OF PROJECT POTENTIAL

Common to all of the data-based methods of estimating project potential is the requirement for simple accounting information for a more-or-less representative group of target group enterprises. This section outlines the accounting procedures necessary to provide this information but does not discuss the methods for obtaining the raw information from the enterprises; that topic is dealt with in Chapter 8. The discussion here deals with how to manipulate the raw data into simple accounting concepts required by the analysis of constraints and the estimation of a project's potential.

## Welfare and Efficiency Accounting Concepts

Care must be taken to make certain that the accounting definitions fit the intended analysis. Two basic goals of project analysis dealt with in this section require different types of accounting information. The first is the need for accounting information to measure the change in families' welfare resulting from enterprise activities. The second measures the efficiency of the enterprise. From an accounting point of view, welfare results depend on who owns the resources (labour, land, capital goods), whereas efficiency does not. Efficiency depends on how much of some output is produced per unit of resource utilised regardless of who owns that resource. An example may serve to sharpen the difference between these two types of accounting. If we wish to measure welfare in terms of changes in family income resulting from the enterprise, we would not treat the labour which the family provided as a cost; yet if we wish to measure the efficiency of the enterprise, this family labour would need to be counted as a cost, or as a utilised resource.

Efficiency and welfare are not unrelated concepts; both must be addressed in estimating project potential and feasibility. There is no need to discuss which is superior as they do not compete. Each serves a different analytical function and both are needed to address different issues.

Defining income to allow measurement of welfare and efficiency. Definitions of income for estimating welfare and efficiency are given below.

- A welfare definition of net income: Value of enterprise output (sold, traded, or consumed) minus cash or expenses in kind, and depreciation on durable goods outlasting the production period.
- An efficiency definition of net income: Value of output (sold, traded, or consumed) minus actual or imputed costs of all labour and resources used in production and depreciation on durable goods outlasting the production

period.

   In the efficiency definition <u>all</u> resources used
in the production process must be treated as costs
regardless of who owns them.
   <u>Imputed costs for efficiency accounting</u>.  Where
a resource is owned by the operating family, such as
family labour, machinery or circulating capital
funds, a value must be imputed to the cost of utilising this resource even though no actual out-of-
pocket expenditure is made.  The normal convention
used to establish a price for an owned resource is
replacement cost.  For example, in the case of
family labour an estimate would be required of the
number of person-days worked by adult males in the
family;  this total quantity would then be multiplied by the average daily wage which would have had
to be paid to "replace" this family input with
purchased labour services.  In some cases, adjustments should be made for skill level and age factors
so that comparable wages are imputed for comparable
types of labour services.  Since an owner/operator
performs managerial as well as labour services, it
may be difficult to account adequately for the replacement value of the managerial services.  Most
computations are for the purpose of comparison, and
as long as most comparisons are between similarly
managed owner/operator firms, no distortion should
result.
   Imputed returns must also be calculated for the
value of fixed capital goods and for the value of
circulating capital tied up in paying for annual
costs.  These imputed cost items are usually called
imputed interest or imputed return to capital.  The
method for this computation involves estimating the
book value of owned assets utilised in the enterprise.  An estimate of the value of circulating
capital required to operate the firm may be made by
taking the average cash expenditure level during the
year, or it may be estimated by taking the total
annual value of non-durable expenditures and multi-
plying that figure by a turnover ratio which is used
to approximate the rate at which circulating capital
expenditures would be replaced out of receipts.
This figure varies widely by enterprise type and is
related to the seasonality of the production cycle.
For most rural enterprises it will be from 60 to 90
days.  The value of circulating capital is then
added to the total value of assets utilised in the
production process to approximate the total value of
fixed and working capital.  This total value of

capital is then multiplied by an imputed interest rate which is taken to be the interest rate at which a similar enterprise with acceptable credit standing could borrow. This imputed interest constitutes an assumed reasonable return to owner's capital.

Efficiency accounting for income results in a figure similar to that which is called "pure profit" by economists in that reasonable returns to all factors have been subtracted from gross value of production. When reasonable returns have been removed for owner's labour, management and capital, the residual even in attractive businesses may be negative. These negative numbers need not surprise or discourage the analyst, since their use should be as comparisons, not as absolutes. The difference between efficiency and welfare measures can be seen in the case where the efficiency measure of income-- pure profit--is negative, but the entrepreneur is making a good return on his effort and investment.

An illustration of these methods of accounting for a rural enterprise project can be seen in Table 6.1.

The efficiency rate of return measure in Table 6.1 is the pure profit divided by the total value of fixed and circulating capital. The welfare rate of return is the net income to the family divided by the total of fixed and circulating capital.

## Capital and Inventory Accounts

Even though rural enterprises and most agri-businesses in developing countries are small, they are nonetheless complete businesses using capital goods, accumulating inventories, making expenditures in one period for production in another, producing a varied bill of products, etc. In order to obtain reasonable estimates of net income, all of the normal accounting conventions used for large busi-nesses must be applied to the small-scale rural enterprise as well.

Valuation of capital goods at original cost or replacement. Valuing capital goods at their ori-ginal cost or at replacement cost may make a size-able difference in the rate of return expected in a project. The choice of method depends largely on the project's goals. If the project intends to provide advice to entrepreneurs, but not to provide funding for new equipment, it may be that the rele-vant valuation is at original cost since the project intervention should not result in the introduction

Table 6.1.—Welfare and Efficiency Measures of Income for Small-scale Rural Enterprises, Guatemala

| Type of Enterprise | Net income to family (welfare measure) | Efficiency measures of income and imputed costs | | | Rate of return | |
|---|---|---|---|---|---|---|
| | | Imputed family labour and management | Imputed return to capital | Pure profit | Welfare | Efficiency |
| | (US$ per enterprise-family/year) | | | | (Per cent) | |
| Wood products | $797 | $791 | $111 | $-111 | 67 | -9.4 |
| Textiles | 445 | 338 | 82 | - 25 | 54 | -3.0 |
| Leather and miscellaneous | 664 | 577 | 105 | - 18 | 64 | -1.7 |
| Bakery and cereal products | 656 | 670 | 83 | - 97 | 79 | -11.7 |
| Commercial enterprises | 887 | 552 | 114 | +221 | 78 | +19.4 |

Source: S. R. Daines et al., Guatemala Rural Enterprises (United States Agency for International Development, Guatemala, 1978).

of new capital. If the project aims at expanding credit availability to the entrepreneur with the intent of updating or replacing his equipment or expanding the capital goods base of the business, it would be well to examine profitability using both valuations. The rate of return calculated at original capital cost would tell the analyst how efficient the enterprises are currently, while the replacement value computation would indicate probable efficiency with project funds. Table 6.2 presents an example of a "welfare" rate of return computation using both original and replacement valuations of capital.

Table 6.2.--Rate of Return (Welfare Measure) Using Original Cost and Replacement Cost Valuations of Capital in Small-scale Enterprises, Guatemala

| Type of enterprise | Rate of return ($ of net income/value of capital) Fixed capital at: | |
|---|---|---|
| | Original cost | Replacement cost |
| Wood products | 67 | 32 |
| Textiles | 54 | 36 |
| Leather, ceramics, miscellaneous | 64 | 34 |
| Baking and food products | 79 | 50 |
| Commercial enterprises | 78 | 19 |

Source: S. R. Daines et al., Guatemala Rural Enterprises (United States Agency for International Development, Guatemala, 1978), p. 53.

Amortisation of capital goods. Capital goods represent a surprisingly large proportion of the costs of small-scale rural enterprises. [1] To disregard capital goods as an annual cost would be a critical mistake. The composition and value of capital must be estimated, and simple depreciation schemes must be used to charge an annual allowance

against the income accounts. The method for depreciation (straight line, declining balance, etc.) and
the estimates used for useful life are less important in themselves than that they be used consistently across all enterprises studied so that compa-
rability of data is assured.

## Analysis of Constraints at the Level of the Firm

The potential of a project to improve welfare
depends directly on whether the intervention
addresses an important and correctable need in the
targeted enterprises. Identification of critical
constraints at the level of the firm must be an
integral part of project design and estimation of
project potential. This section discusses ways of
using enterprise-level data to examine what factors
most severely constrain improvement in target enterprises.

Accounting information. A careful review of
accounting indicators may point to critical needs in
the target enterprises. For example, a review of
absolute and comparative profitability may provide
insight into the need of the enterprise to improve
its financial efficiency. In reviewing profitability as well as the other accounting indicators, a
list of potential ways in which the small-scale
enterprise may increase its net income should be
kept in mind. Income improvement may be achieved
by:

- Increasing the quantity and/or value of output
  per unit
  - by changing technology or practices,
  - by improving management practices, and/or
  - by changing the mix of products produced;
- Increasing the quantity of output with added
  inputs
  - by expanding all inputs through additional
    liquidity; and/or
- Increasing the prices for outputs or reducing
  prices for inputs
  - by improving product quality and/or
  - by changing marketing practices for inputs
    or outputs.

The process of linking accounting indicators
with constraints was discussed in Chapter 5 and need
not be repeated here. It is important to note,
however, that there may be considerable variation in

the needs of different types of enterprise. Some
may have favourable market situations and room to
expand, while others may require fundamental
internal managerial and technological restructuring
before income can be increased. Data from the level
of the firm will assist in identifying both the
commonalities and differences in such a way that
project interventions can be tailored to actual
needs.

## Entrepreneurial Perceptions of Constraints

A second way to explore the relative importance
of constraints at firm level is to ask entrepreneurs
themselves in large enough numbers that the results
can be expected to be representative. Given the
subjective nature of questions about constraints,
the method for interviewing is fraught with possibilities of misunderstanding and inaccurate reporting.
It is, however, useful since it gives the project
designer a reasonably representative view of how
entrepreneurs respond to questions about their businesses and what factors are holding them back. How
the entrepreneur perceives his problem is important
even if it is later decided from more objective data
that his perception is incorrect. Over the last two
decades there has been a growing consensus that
small farmers are rational economic men and very
often have correct perceptions about how to manage
and improve their businesses. While there is less
concrete evidence available on small-scale, nonagri-
cultural enterprises, what there is supports the
idea that the small-scale entrepreneur is rational
and that his opinions about constraints should be
considered seriously.

One method for obtaining opinions on constraints is to ask a representative sample of entrepreneurs a question phrased as follows: "What are
the most important reasons you do not expand your
production in the coming year above your planned
level?"

The entrepreneur may then be allowed to respond
freely or may be given a series of options from
which to choose with allowance made for open-ended
and unstructured responses. He may also be asked to
indicate which reasons are first, second, or third
in order of importance. Where the question is open-
ended, the interviewer may have a precoded list of
options among which he classifies the response and
may add to the list if the entrepreneur suggests

other reasons. Wide experience with such surveys indicates that entrepreneurs respond almost universally with little hesitation and most are able to grasp the concept of ranking and seldom appear uncertain about priorities. Additionally, open-ended responses do not significantly increase the complexity of coding, since almost all responses fit easily into a preset list of less than ten major reasons. To be sure, there is much overlapping in concept between different factors. Credit as a constraint, for example, may overlap with increased supplies of raw material or scarcity of labour, since credit is fungible and may be used to purchase increased raw material or hire additional labour. While entrepreneurial opinion is not definitive, it can be very useful, as shown by Table 6.3 which presents results from a sample of small-scale rural enterprises in Guatemala.

## ESTIMATING THE POTENTIAL FOR BENEFICIAL IMPACTS ON TARGET GROUP FAMILIES

Estimating the potential of the project to increase income, employment or some other form of welfare will require a different technique for each type of intervention. There are, however, some general principles which may apply to most of the common types of project.

Most projects aim to provide some added service, input or infrastructure to enterprises. Each project operates on the hypothesis that the chosen intervention will cause additional welfare. At this stage we are not asking questions about project feasibility; we assume that the project intervention is feasible. The issue addressed in this discussion is: if accomplished, what will be the impact on income or employment

## Comparisons of Enterprises With and Without Project Intervention

The first method of obtaining evidence indicative of the potential impact of projects on income, employment or other welfare dimensions is to compare the incomes, etc., of enterprises with and without projects. If the intervention is credit, then the comparison should be between those enterprises with and without credit services, but of similar size and cultural setting as the targeted enterprises. This

Table 6.3.—Reported Reasons for Entrepreneurs' Not Expanding Production of Small-scale Rural Enterprises in Guatemala

| Type of enterprise | Percentage of entrepreneurs responding by reason and priority | | | | | | | |
|---|---|---|---|---|---|---|---|---|
| | Lack of market | | Lack of credit | | Lack of raw material | | Lack of labour | |
| | 1st | 2nd | 1st | 2nd | 1st | 2nd | 1st | 2nd |
| Wood products | 17 | 3 | 55 | 10 | 3 | 41 | 7 | 7 |
| Textiles | 7 | 4 | 69 | 13 | 7 | 19 | 5 | 23 |
| Leather and misc. | 4 | 17 | 75 | 8 | 6 | 17 | 13 | 13 |
| Bakery and food products | 8 | 17 | 63 | 21 | 8 | 25 | 4 | 4 |
| Commercial enterprises | 6 | 13 | 67 | 14 | 3 | 11 | 3 | 8 |

Source: S. R. Daines et al., Guatemala Rural Enterprises (United States Agency for International Development, Guatemala, 1978), p.113.

comparison could also be drawn from a before-and-after measurement following a similar intervention, but the probable non-existence of any systematic before-and-after comparison of similar enterprises in comparable settings usually rules out this approach. It should be noted that adequate post hoc evaluation of the proposed project will provide a before-and-after comparison for future projects.

Setting aside then the use of before-and-after comparisons because they are rarely possible, we now discuss the method and limitations of cross-sectional comparisons. The idea of a cross-sectional comparison is to find enterprises with and without the proposed intervention to identify what the actual differences in income, employment, etc., are, with the implication that if the project provides the intervention to those enterprises without in the comparison they would achieve the income levels of those enterprises with in the survey. This approach has a number of strengths and weaknesses, and the discussion which follows attempts to examine both.

Can with-and-without enterprises be easily found in the area? The first difficulty with cross-sectional comparisons arises from the fact that the proposed intervention may in fact be new to the target area, and in fact may be new to the country as a whole. Indeed, one might argue that, if the intervention is common, there is no justification for a project to introduce it. Careful examination of the proposed intervention will reveal in most cases, however, that the project will extend or expand a service or resource rather than actually introduce it. While there may be strong reasons for aid agencies wanting to present the project as something "new", the specific intervention is almost always something which already exists but only on a limited scale. If we take the major project options as examples, the lack of newness in most cases may be more obvious. Usually the element which is new in the project is the method of delivering or organising the intervention, not the intervention itself. More concern has typically been directed to the feasibility of the delivery rather than to the potential impact if delivery is feasible.

The above discussion may be clearer if examples from each of the major project interventions are examined. The potential of credit as an intervention could be estimated by measuring the income of enterprises with different levels of credit. If those enterprises with credit had incomes double or triple those of similar enterprises without credit, that could be evidence that a credit intervention would have an impact on income. It is unlikely that there are so few enterprises with any credit that such a comparison would be impractical. Credit may not have been delivered the way the project proposes to deliver it (in most cases enough of the basics of the proposed delivery system can be found to make comparison viable), but in almost all situations the proposed intervention (i.e. increased credit) operates widely enough in the target or similar areas to permit a comparison.

Technical assistance may be more difficult to analyse, but is in many ways similar to the credit example in that it is usually the delivery mechanism which is novel and not the intervention itself. Ascertaining the potential of technical assistance requires an examination at the level of firms in case similar technical assistance has not been extended to enough enterprises to provide a viable comparison. In the case of technical assistance, there are two possibilities. First is where a sufficient number of enterprises have already received the proposed service so that a comparison of performance with those not receiving the service is possible. Second is situations in which the service is entirely untried. Where there is experience, the comparison is direct and relatively easy to make between those enterprises receiving none and those receiving varying amounts of the assistance. Table 6.4 illustrates this type of comparison.

If technical assistance of the type the project proposes has never been tried, an attempt can be made to determine what the changes in served enterprises will be, that is, what is the "package" that the assistance will attempt to get adopted. If the objective of the assistance is to get a certain type of enterprise to change its practices, to use a new input or type of equipment, then that practice or input or equipment is the intervention and firms currently using the recommended practice, input or equipment could be compared with those which are not to estimate the potential impact of the intervention. Field assessments are strongly preferred to engineering estimates since they have the substantial advantage of realism if they are taken in the same general environment as the proposed project. Project designers should seek to learn what actually happens in project areas when enterprises adopt the proposed practices, inputs or equipment.

Table 6.4.--Income Comparison of Small Farms with
Different Levels of Technical
Assistance, Guatemala

| Level of technical assistance (TA) | Farms with TA linked to other services | Farms with TA but without other services |
|---|---|---|
| | (US$ of net income per hectare) | |
| None | 45 | 76 |
| 1-4 visits | 53 | 105 |
| 5-9 visits | 68 | 89 |
| 10+ visits | 86 | 123 |

Source:   S. R. Daines et al., Guatemala Farm Policy
Analysis (United States Agency for International Development, Washington, 1975), p.
106.


        Such evidence is, of course, not conclusive.
One might argue that the observed intervention was
not as well organised or not as well oriented as the
one the project plans.  However, such assessments
provide a baseline from which intelligent discussion
can proceed.  It is unfortunately true that the
project development environment creates an atmos-
phere in which project designers are cast at a very
early stage as defenders and not analysts.  They may
choose not to undertake comparisons such as those
described above simply because they would rather not
have to explain away negative findings; they know
that in the project review cycle an assertion of
potential is given roughly equal weight to firm
evidence of project potential.  Having the evidence
also has the significant disadvantage in the project
selection process that it almost inevitably leads
discussion by project opponents into the weakness of
measurement procedures; it is easier to cast doubt
on a quantitative comparison (for example, the
groups were not similar enough, the sample not
representative enough, all other factors were not
equal, etc.) than it is to attack a bald assertion
of potential.

## Accounting Projections

The second method of estimating project potential using data from the level of the firm involves
using accounts as a basis for making projections of
impact. These projections may use expert judgment
about what will happen if the project intervention
is implemented, or may be based on the expressed
intentions of surveyed entrepreneurs. It is important to note that the judgments or intentions do not
refer to final impact, but rather specific changes
in the firm. The simplest case would be a project
with the aim of expanding production in targeted
firms without changing technology, practices or
efficiency. In this case the analyst would use
firm-level data to estimate first how much expansion
could be obtained per unit of project-supplied input
and then, by using income accounts for each type of
enterprise, how much net income would result. Such
accounting projections are much less reliable than
comparisons based on an observed intervention
because there are so many assumptions involved.
Assume, for example, that the input provided by the
project is credit and the intent is to increase
production without changing technology. To add
reliability to the projections, the interest and
intent of entrepreneurs can be assessed and compared
with the project designer's assumption that they
would take additional loans and use them to expand
production. Each additional assessment adds further
evidence and reduces reliance on the analyst's
guesswork. Every project intervention presents a
different problem of how to estimate potential
welfare and how to increase the reliability of that
estimate.

Table 6.5 presents an estimate of impact based
on a sample of entrepreneurs indicating the quantities of project input they would want, and what
they would do with it if free to choose. The estimates in Table 6.5 illustrate the use of enterprise
accounting data (net income accounts, credit/output
ratios, etc.) and data on entrepreneurial intentions
(size of loan desired and use of funds) to estimate
the total income-generating potential of a proposed
rural enterprise project.

## A CHECKLIST FOR ASSESSING PROJECT FEASIBILITY

A project may have excellent potential for
improving the welfare of the target group and yet

Table 6.5.--Estimated Impact on Income of a Rural
            Enterprise Project [a]

| Sector | Average size loan re- quested | Number of fami- lies benefited | Net in- crease in income [b] | Increase in family income |
|--------|------|------|------|------|
| | (US$) | | (US$) | (Per cent) |
| Wood products | 2,380 | 504 | 701 | 79 |
| Textiles | 800 | 1,500 | 265 | 53 |
| Leather | 2,133 | 609 | 670 | 90 |
| Baking/foods | 1,939 | 619 | 892 | 121 |
| Commercial services | 1,290 | 930 | 593 | 60 |
| All small-scale enterprises | -- | 4,162 | 544 | 75 |

Source: United States Agency for International
        Development, Agribusiness and Rural
        Enterprise Project Analysis Manual
        (Washington, 1980), p.89.
a       With US$8.5 million in credit disbursed.
        The table includes owner-families only.
b       The net increase in income is per family
        per year.

not be implementable because the institutional
structure is inadequate, because the would-be participants are not willing to participate in the
project as designed and presented and/or market
conditions are such as to make the project unfeasible. This remainder of this chapter provides an
overview of those items which need to be considered
in examining the feasibility of projects.

INSTITUTIONAL CAPACITY

     A wide variety of institutional capacities
ought to be subjected to an analysis of feasibility.
In many cases, this analysis is complicated by the
fact that one of the common project objectives is to
strengthen particularly weak aspects of the institutional structure. Where institution-building is one
of the central objectives of the project, the
analyst must first assess the feasibility of this

component (that is, is the institution capable of absorbing and internalising the proposed improvement?) and then proceed to analyse whether the institution as improved will be capable of sustaining the other project responsibilities.

Methods for examining institutional capacity are not standardised or systematic enough to permit extensive exposition. Some factors can of course be quantified, yet in the main the subject is more one of judgment than of statistics. What can be done is to suggest a series of topics which should be examined and to present examples of the types of information which have been used.

## Outreach Capability

Most agribusiness and rural enterprise projects involve the delivery of some kind of input or service to a large number of enterprises. The geographic dispersion of these enterprises often complicates the delivery problem. The capability of the institution to service large numbers of small-scale enterprises and interact with clients whose business and accounting experience is very limited is usually a vital issue.

## Financial Capability

Funds and resources will usually be channelled through an existing institution. The financial integrity and performance of the institution are of utmost concern and should comprise a large part of the institutional analysis. Such factors as the proportion of current loans delinquent are useful indicators for credit institutions. The capacity of the institution to commit funds necessary for the operation of the project should also be examined in terms of both the availability of the funds and the commitment of institutional personnel to the allocation of funds for project-related purposes.

## Technical Capability

Where projects involve technical expertise, which includes almost all conceivable rural enterprise projects, an assessment of industrial engineering, enterprise management and technical assistance personnel and systems should be an integral

Examining Project Potential and Feasibility

part of a review of institutional capacity.

FINANCIAL FEASIBILITY

There are two important aspects of financial feasibility: first and foremost is the issue of the profitability to the entrepreneur of the intervention, and secondly the financial viability for the institutions involved.

Profitability at the level of the firm. Profitability is never a more useful indicator in project analysis than in assessing feasibility. If an intervention does not have a very high probability of increasing profits to the entrepreneur, it should not pass the financial feasibility test. This seems so obvious as not to need restatement, yet very few project analyses provide satisfactory evidence of this potential beyond the assertion that the intervention will be profitable. Data indicating levels of profit of enterprises in the target area, or at least in similar areas where the proposed intervention has already been tried, should be presented to support the assertion that the intervention is financially feasible.

An additional difficulty related to profitability is the fact that entrepreneurs may not appreciate the potential of a workable and profitable intervention and may not, therefore, be willing to participate. While this may be treated as an issue relating to financial feasibility, this manual deals with it under the heading of demand for project services.

Financial feasibility at the institutional level. In addition to concern about the capability of an implementing institution, there is also concern that the proposed project will not return sufficient funds to allow the institution to retain its financial viability. This is particularly true of credit operations, but may also apply to technical assistance and research programmes in that project activities may drain institutional resources without proper allowance for their replacement. Interest rate policies, public commitment to institutional budget allocations and the like are all topics of concern when examining the question of institutional financial feasibility.

125

ESTIMATING THE DEMAND FOR THE PROPOSED INTERVENTION

While some interventions may be less sensitive
to the level of demand for the service or input, it
is usually true that target group interest in and
acceptance of the project concept are crucial feasibility issues. It is important, therefore, to be
able to estimate the magnitude of interest and willingness to participate in the project among the
intended beneficiaries. The method for estimating
the demand for the project intervention varies by
type of intervention. Estimating the demand for
credit allows a variety of analytical methods to be
used, while there are only a few, relatively
imprecise methods for estimating the demand for
technical assistance and research services.

## Estimating the Potential Demand for Credit and Financial Assistance

Credit interventions depend centrally on the
willingness of entrepreneurs to assume additional
liability, and there may be concern that small-scale
rural entrepreneurs will be overly cautious in
avoiding risks and avoid even wise borrowing. An
important issue for credit projects or credit components of broader projects is whether there is sufficient interest and willingness to borrow among
target group enterprises. There are at least four
methods which might be used to estimate that demand,
and each is given a short description below.
1. The most obvious, and probably the best,
method is to ask the entrepreneurs themselves if
they are willing to participate. It is necessary
only to ask a sample of firms, as described in
Chapter 8. The manner in which the questions
relating to possible interest are phrased may
provide different perspectives which may be of considerable use to planners. Three approaches are
described here, each providing a different measure
of interest.
General interest in credit. Entrepreneurs can
be asked about their general interest in credit in
order to assess their perception of its importance.
This may be done either by an open-ended question
about what they need to improve their business, or a
list of potential constraints may be named and the
entrepreneur asked to comment on the relative importance of each. Both these alternatives were
described and illustrated in Chapter 5. The entre-

preneur may additionally be queried about the availability of credit and asked if there is sufficient
already available for his needs.  This general
approach is quite different from more specific
methods, but may give a better idea of the
"promotable" level of demand, or the level of demand
which may be accessed with adequate promotion.

Interest in borrowing and possible uses of
credit funds.  Many entrepreneurs may be interested
in credit in general and sense its importance to the
improvement of their enterprises, but may still be
unwilling to undertake the added responsibility and
risk of borrowing.  It can be seen from Table 6.6,
based on a survey of small-scale rural enterprises
in Guatemala, that an average of 77 per cent of
respondents indicated that credit was a priority
need, yet only 61 per cent indicated that they
actually wanted to borrow additional money during
the coming year.

In order to ascertain willingness to take additional risk, three elements should be added to the
questions of general interest.  The first element is
the description of terms and conditions under which
credit could be extended through a question such as:
would you be interested to borrow additional money
at 10 per cent interest with a mortgage or other
security, for repayment on a monthly basis beginning
in 6 months, for a 12-month period?  The very specificity of the question will help sort out responses
which are not grounded in actual interest.  The
second element which can be added is what the entrepreneur would use the credit for.  If he/she has
specific ideas already in mind with reasons for
thinking such investments would return the money
necessary for repayment, one gets the feeling that
the estimated demand is closer to effective demand.
The last element which has been effective in
reaching a more realistic estimate of demand is to
ask the entrepreneur how much he or she would be
interested in borrowing for each intended use.  Not
only does this financial element make the estimate
of "effective" demand more reliable, but it also
assists in estimating the quantity of demand.

Table 6.6 indicates the responses of small-
scale entrepreneurs in rural Guatemala to both
general questions and the more specific willingness-
to-borrow formulation.

Interest in the specific project.  The third
level of specificity which may be used to estimate
demand is to mention the proposed project by institutional name, stating the project terms, conditions

Table 6.6.--Responses to Credit-related Questions
by Small-scale Rural Enterprises,
Guatemala

| Type of enterprise | Firms indicating that credit is their main problem | Firms requesting added loans under stated terms and conditions | Average amount of added loan requested per firm |
|---|---|---|---|
| | (Per cent of firms) | | (US$) |
| Wood products | 65 | 72 | 2,380 |
| Textiles | 82 | 58 | 800 |
| Leather and miscellaneous | 83 | 73 | 2,133 |
| Baking and food products | 84 | 57 | 1,939 |
| Commercial enterprises | 81 | 60 | 1,290 |
| Average per cent | 77 | 61 | |

Source:  S. R. Daines et al., Guatemala Rural Enterprises (United States Agency for International Development, Guatemala, 1978), p.42.

and qualification requirements, and then asking
about the interest of the respondent in participating during the coming year.  It must be clear that
the survey does not imply any kind of a commitment
either way so that subsequent problems are not
created by the survey.
By using these methods with a soundly chosen
sample, a reasonably realistic estimate of the
demand for credit may be made.  The responses of the
individual firms may be extrapolated to the target
population of enterprises and the total credit
increment may be used as an estimate of effective
demand, subject to the crosschecks outlined below.
2.  An alternative to the survey approach in
estimating credit demand, and a crosscheck on such
an estimate if made, is to estimate the demand for
products which would be produced by the target
enterprises and then, working backward, estimate the
additional credit which could be absorbed in order
to meet the estimated demand for the product.  This
method may be an important crosscheck since individual entrepreneurs may each perceive a favourable

demand situation, yet if all expand at once the
demand may rapidly be met and exceeded. Each firm
may perceive correctly, yet the sum of the
perceptions is incorrect.

Projecting demand for products of small-scale
enterprises may be very difficult to do, both
because of conceptual problems and lack of data. If
reliable statistics are available, such as price or
income elasticities, income growth rates, etc.,
demand may be approached directly. Since these data
are seldom available, however, demand must be estimated indirectly from extrapolated trends in production. Credit supply can then be projected, and
assuming a constant credit-output ratio, a credit
shortfall or credit demand can be estimated. Table
6.7 illustrates this approach for medium- and large-
scale agribusinesses. From the table it can be seen
that only in food products is there a credit shortfall, hence this method indicates a demand for additional credit only for enterprises in the food subsector.

3. A third method for estimating the demand
for credit is based on a microeconomic analysis of
the accounting relationships within the firm. This
method attempts to measure the net income productivity of credit for the last unit of credit obtained
by the average firm for many types of firm represen-
ting the target group. If the estimated marginal
revenue product of the last unit of credit supplied
to the firm is significantly above the cost of
credit (interest and related costs), then it would
be assumed that a rational entrepreneur would desire
more credit. Assuming a profit-maximising businessperson, the analysis could estimate the total amount
of credit which the firm could absorb before the
benefit (net revenue produced) by the credit
equalled the cost of the credit.

While this method is conceptually interesting,
it requires a data base and time frame for analysis
normally not available for project design work. In
addition, it ignores the fact that most small-scale
entrepreneurs have practical problems which may make
this simple model inaccurate.

4. Many interventions are based on the notion
that small enterprises are discriminated against in
the distribution of credit. A method of estimating
demand for credit would be to find a measure of the
magnitude of this discrimination and assume that the
demand would be that amount of credit required to
put the small enterprise on a comparable footing
with a larger enterprise. The difficulty in this

Table 6.7.--Demand for Credit Estimated from Growth Rates in

Output and Credit Supply in Medium- and Large-

scale Agribusiness Enterprises, Guatemala

| Subsector | Values for 1975 | | | Annual growth rate in: | | Annual short-fall in credit |
|-----------|--------|--------|--------------------------|--------|--------|--------|
| | Output | Credit | Credit/ output ratio | Credit | Output | |
| | (US$000,000) | | | (Per cent) | | (US$) |
| Food products | 333 | 20.0 | .06 | -4.4 | 6.7 | 889,000 |
| Textiles | 51 | 12.1 | .24 | 8.8 | 2.8 | -0- |
| Clothing | 18 | 5.8 | .31 | 6.6 | 3.9 | -0- |
| Wood products | 34 | 2.4 | .07 | 12.9 | 4.8 | -0- |

Source: Direccion General Estadistica, Encuesta Trimestral de la Industria Manufacturera Fabril and Banco de Guatemala, Prestamos Concedidos por el Sistema Bancario a la Industria, Guatemala, 1976.

approach lies in defining the measure. Acceptable
alternatives have been found in estimating credit
operating ratios by sector or product type. A
credit operating ratio would be computed either by
dividing the value of credit carried by a firm by
the value of its assets or by the value of its
production. The first measure would be aimed at the
creditworthiness of the firm, the second at the more
technical question of the amount of credit required
or utilised to produce a unit of output. If these
ratios are much lower for target firms than they are
for firms with freer access to credit, it indicates
that discrimination exists and that there ought to
be a level of demand approximately equal to the
magnitude of difference in the operating ratio.
Note that the example of this type of computation
presented in Table 6.8 is not for agribusiness but
rather for farms, although the methodology is the
same. From the table it can be observed that credit
per cropped hectare on small farms under 2 hectares
is less than 10 per cent of the national average.
It can also be seen that the credit operating ratio
rises from less than $10 per hectare to over $200
and then fluctuates between $250-400. It might be
suggested that $200 should be the expected or
minimum level for efficient production in El
Salvador based on the observed credit operating
ratios. The difference in the actual supply and
this expected operating ratio level could be used as
an estimate of the latent credit demand on small-
holdings.

## Estimating Demand for Technical Assistance and Advisory Services

The process of estimating demand for a service
such as technical assistance or advice is more difficult than it is with credit. The first part of
the problem is that it is much more difficult for
the entrepreneur to sense a direct need and benefit
which may come from technical advice. It is therefore possible that negative responses from entrepreneurs, when asked about their interest in receiving
technical assistance, may not be conclusive evidence
that they do not need or would not benefit from such
advice. While negative responses may not be accurate perceptions, they are indicative of an acceptance problem which may affect the ability of the
project to succeed. An alternative approach is to
base the estimate on the acceptance and rejection

Table 6.8.--Credit Operating Ratios for Farms, El
         Salvador

| Farm size | Credit per cropped hectare | Credit per cropped ha. as a per cent of the national average |
|---|---|---|
| (Hectares) | (US$/ha.) | |
| 0.0 to 0.49 | 7.53 | 4.3 |
| 0.5 to 0.99 | 7.78 | 4.6 |
| 1.0 to 1.99 | 14.25 | 8.2 |
| 2.0 to 2.99 | 21.31 | 12.2 |
| 3.0 to 3.99 | 26.48 | 15.1 |
| 4.0 to 4.99 | 34.99 | 20.0 |
| 5.0 to 9.99 | 48.10 | 27.5 |
| 10.0 to 19.99 | 73.24 | 41.9 |
| 20.0 to 49.99 | 195.21 | 111.7 |
| 50.0 to 99.99 | 396.82 | 227.0 |
| 100.0 to 199.99 | 344.25 | 196.9 |
| 200.0 to 499.99 | 275.45 | 157.6 |
| 500.0 to 999.99 | 350.05 | 200.2 |
| 1,000 to 2,499 | 237.58 | 135.9 |
| 2,500 and over | 383.12 | 219.2 |
| Average for all farms | 174.82 | 100.0 |

Source:  United States Agency for International
         Development, Agribusiness and Rural
         Enterprise Project Analysis Manual
         (Washington, 1980), p.93.

rates of existing technical assistance services.  In
addition to rejection or acceptance rates, client
perceptions about the benefits derived from existing
technical assistance services may add realism to the
estimates of demand.
    Another approach is to attempt to define the
specific technical package or set of recommendations
which the technical assistance service intends to
carry to enterprises.  A short description of this
service could be given to a sample of target entrepreneurs and they could be asked:
    1. How important would such advice be to them?
    2. Would they be interested in having a competent
       technician come to explain the following, or
       how to operate the following machinery, etc?
    3. Would they be willing to pay for such advice?

The results of such a survey could assist not only in estimating the demand for the service, but also in planning the content of the technical assistance effort.

## Estimating the Demand for Infrastructural Projects to Benefit Agribusiness and Rural Enterprises

If the intended intervention is the establishment of a marketing facility, access roads, improved marketing services or other infrastructure aimed at improving the operating environment for rural enterprises, the estimation of demand may proceed in much the same way as was outlined above for credit. Entrepreneurs may be asked how important they think the new facility is, if they would be willing to participate somehow in the costs of its installation (donate labour, for example) or other questions formulated to elicit their perception of the importance and expected use of the facility.

Estimates should be made of the demand for products to be marketed through the facility, for use of the road etc. The increased profitability of participating enterprises might be used as evidence of demand based on the assumption that affected entrepreneurs are profit maximisers and therefore utilise an added input or service as long as its marginal revenue exceeds its cost.

Each of the approaches mentioned above attempts to estimate demand as derived from the benefit conferred by the facility and not directly based on the perceptions of those who will use or presumably benefit from the infrastructure. While this may appear to be risky, it should be remembered that infrastructural projects do not depend upon entrepreneurial acceptance in order to be implemented in the same way that technical assistance and credit projects do. In the case of a credit project, if no one wants to borrow, the project cannot even be implemented. It is, of course, true that a project may be implemented and not have the desired final impacts on the welfare of the poor. Yet the question of final impact is one of advisability, not feasibility. Since this section deals with feasibility, it should be noted that fewer problems to do with entrepreneurial interest and willingness need be addressed in the feasibility stage of analysis for infrastructural projects; these issues should however be intensively analysed when the project's potential impacts are estimated.

## ANALYSIS OF COMPARATIVE COSTS

Even if there is interest in and demand for project inputs, and there appears to be demand for project outputs, there remains the important issue of competitive production from other sources which may satisfy that demand and prevent participants from even implementing the interventions contemplated by the project. In order to examine this possibility, some analysis of comparative costs needs to be undertaken to establish the feasibility of project activities' competing with other possible sources of production.

Comparative cost analysis is conducted through an examination of resource costs and the quantities utilised in the productive process. Possible national, and indeed international, competitors should be examined to ascertain their resource costs and amounts of resources used to produce and market the product in question.

If the conclusion is negative, that is, the project participants cannot compete on a cost basis with other sources of production, there may still be reason to think that the project may under certain conditions be feasible. The first of these conditions is the traditional case of protection or public subsidy. The protective measures may come in the form of trade restrictions, input cost subsidies, or special marketing arrangements. There are, however, serious costs which must be considered before such market distorting arrangements are made. One must be certain that such interventions are in the long-term best interest of the target group. In many cases the use of such protection measures encourages small-scale entrepreneurs into productive activities which later become unprofitable after considerable investment has been made.

In some cases the small-scale entrepreneur can compete in terms of price if his labour is regarded as a resource obtained at a price below that prevailing in the market. In this situation he can sell a product for a price below that of the competition and still benefit because the opportunity cost for family labour is substantially below the actual wage rate paid by competing larger-scale enterprises. A finding that at current wage rates the small-scale entrepreneur cannot compete is not sufficient evidence that the project is not feasible. The market wage may be appropriate for the competing firm's calculation of labour cost, but for the small-scale entrepreneur the opportunity cost of family labour should be substituted for the hired wage rate. When comparative costs are computed in this way, a realistic view of competitive feasibility will emerge from the analysis.


NOTE

1.　For example, in 561 rural enterprises surveyed in Guatemala (which averaged only two workers per firm), the average value of capital goods was $940 at original cost and $1,569 at replacement cost. See S. R. Daines et al., Guatemala Rural Enterprises (United States Agency for International Development, Guatemala, 1978).

CHAPTER 7

BENEFIT-COST ANALYSIS OF AGRIBUSINESS AND RURAL
ENTERPRISE PROJECTS

This chapter deals with the process of comparing
potential benefits (discussed in Chapter 6) with the
costs of undertaking an agribusiness or rural enterprise project.

ESTIMATING THE BENEFITS:  HOW MUCH AND FOR WHOM

One of the purposes of Chapter 6 was to explore
ways of estimating the potential benefits of agribusiness and rural enterprise projects.  The most
important failing of most benefit-cost analyses lies
in the inadequate data and methodology used to estimate the size and probability of expected benefits.
It should be remembered that the methodology of
benefit-cost analysis does not assist in estimating
the probable benefits, but only provides a way of
comparing the benefits, once known or estimated by
other means, with project costs.  Little added work
is necessary to transform a well-developed estimate
of potential project benefits into a benefit-cost
ratio; almost all the work, effort, time and intel-
lectual energy is consumed in making the original
estimate of expected benefits.  It is unfortunately
true that in most benefit-cost analyses, little
effort has been expended and few data have been used
in measurement of benefits; the time and work have
been focused on the arithmetic of benefit-cost
methodology.  While Chapter 6 contains the discussion on how to estimate the expected potential benefits of a proposed project, it is worth summarising
the main options discussed there as an introduction
to benefit-cost analysis.

## Comparing Global Results vs. Projecting from Firm-level Changes

In a general sense there are two broad avenues of approach to estimating the probable benefits which would flow from an agribusiness and rural enterprise intervention. The first is to compare actual with-and-without situations and measure the final difference in terms of resulting benefit to family incomes, health and nutrition, and other indicators of welfare. The second is to describe the assumed changes at the level of the individual firms which will generate the final impacts and, using any of several types of data, attempt to relate each of the probable changes to the magnitude of the final result.

Each of these approaches has advantages and disadvantages; their accuracy and feasibility depend on different factors. The accuracy and feasibility of the first (with-and-without comparison) depend on the possibility of making comparisons which satisfactorily isolate the intervention and control other factors which may influence final results. To the degree that such control is possible, this technique is useful.

The accuracy and feasibility of the second technique (projecting the impact of each probable change contributing to a chain of causality) depends on our abilities to understand all of the ways the intervention may cause a final result and to predict how individual entrepreneurs in a particular cultural and economic setting will react in each of these causative chains. The degree to which the system is simple—if there are only a very few ways in which the intervention can affect final welfare (income, employment, health, etc.) and the degree of confidence in our ability to predict how the enterprise system will react in each of these chains of causation—will determine the usefulness of the "projection" technique.

In the project planner's world, it is obvious that neither of these assumptions holds very well. We cannot normally control adequately all of the factors which could affect welfare in a with-and-without comparison, nor is it likely that we understand how enterprises and households operate in diverse cultural and economic situations and how each possible cause will finally affect the complex enterprise and household system. The planner is left with a choice between two approaches, both of which are questionable. It is difficult for the

project planner to make judgments about the relative inaccuracy of methods, and the tendency therefore is simply to reject all methods which require
time. The approach most often taken is simply to
sum the best official guesses as to expected benefits and spend what little time and money are available on manipulating these best guesses inside the
internally consistent and easily controllable arithmetic of benefit-cost calculations. A confused
planner or manager can always defend himself by
making reference to discussion such as that outlined
in the last paragraph and saying "even the experts
admit that the best methods for estimating benefits
are questionable at best; if even the experts
disagree on how to do it, it is probably best not to
gather data at all."

A better alternative would be to review carefully the relative confidence which analysts have in
the factors which determine the accuracy of the two
techniques and choose one of these approaches for
estimating potential benefits. Table 7.1 should
help to structure that review by organising the
questions to be asked. The two alternatives in
terms of analytical approach will be termed comparisons and projections. Definitions of the two terms
follow:

Comparisons: Comparisons, with and without the
intervention, of existing enterprises and households. The items
compared are final welfare indicators such as income, employment,
health and nutrition, housing, sanitation and education--what are often
termed basic needs.

Projections: Accounting projections, with and
without the intervention, based on
what is expected to happen at the
level of individual firms as a
result of the intervention. The
attempt is to show the expected
magnitudes of final welfare impacts
in relation to the different changes
arising from the project intervention.

These methods were described in more detail in
Chapter 6.

The answer suggested by the method review
questions in Table 7.1 will vary from situation to

situation depending on many factors: the type of
intervention, cultural diversity inside the target
group, availability of data of different types, and
others. Yet the questions themselves are not likely
to be answered with equal confidence. It is interesting to note that the two methods are not equally
flexible in the kind of data required. The comparison method requires data on enterprises and households collected from the target group in the field;
there is little possibility of conducting this type
of analysis based on expert opinion or judgment.
The projections method is much more flexible; it can

Table 7.1.--Review of Methods for Estimating
Benefits of Agribusiness and Rural
Enterprise Project Interventions

| Question: Which can we do better? | Better method to choose |
|---|---|
| 1. Identify the ways this set of project interventions will change enterprises and households, how they will react to these changes and how the changes will in sum affect household income, employment, health, nutrition, housing, sanitation, etc. | Projections |
| 2. Identify households and enterprises with and without the kind of interventions proposed but from similar cultural and economic situations. | Comparisons |

be conducted at almost any point along a continuum
from extensive field data collection to office-bound
best guesses, and while the results may vary tremen-
dously in quality depending on the reliability of
the data sources, the results do not vary in form.
By looking at the final result of the analysis, one
cannot tell in the projection method the difference
between a careful and reliable estimate and a "seat

of the pants" guess. It is probably the result of this flexibility and not of a systematic review of the alternative which leads most project analysts to choose projections as the method for estimating benefits. Where analysts could answer question two in the review table with more confidence than they could question one, they have typically chosen comparisons as the more appropriate method. There is also the additional concern that comparisons may indicate that the intervention does not create sufficient benefits to justify the costs of the project. In the case of projections, simple adjustments to the projections themselves can easily improve the expected benefits to a sufficient level to justify costs.

## Benefits...for Whom?

Traditional benefit-cost analysis is concerned with total benefits and does not focus on any special group in the economy. In the first half of the 1970s, many international aid agencies redirected some or all of their activities towards an explicit focus on the poor and disadvantaged. Integrating considerations relating to particular population groups, such as the poor, into benefit-cost analysis is not easy because this approach departs immediately from one of the attractive properties of the benefit-cost ratio; that is, if properly calculated, projects with ratios greater than one are acceptable investments while those with ratios less than one do not generate sufficient benefits to justify their cost. If only a part of the benefits is included in the numerator of the ratio, the unity value of the ratio loses its significance as a simple cut-off point. As comparative tools, the ratios would retain their utility if adjusted to account only for income benefits to the poor, but the significance of the absolute ratio and the extent of its departure from unity would disappear.

For direct benefits and reasonably immediate indirect benefits, it may be possible to keep track of the income levels of the beneficiaries in accounting terms so that they can be classified as poor or nonpoor. For truly indirect benefits, it is virtually impossible without fairly elaborate "input-output" models to make such a distinction. The poor who benefit from agribusiness and rural enterprise projects in a reasonably direct fashion fall into the following groups [1]:

- Poor entrepreneurs or owners of enterprises
  (benefits come in the form of increased
  profits, returns to invested capital, or
  returns to management and labour).
- Poor wage- or salary-earning labourers who work
  in affected enterprises (benefits come from
  increased employment or increased wage rates).
- Poor farm families who own and operate farms
  supplying raw materials to the affected enterprises (benefits come as increased farm
  profits, returns to invested capital or returns
  to management and labour).
- Poor farm labourers who work for wages on farms
  (both poor and nonpoor) which supply raw materials to the affected enterprises (benefits come
  from increased employment and/or wage rates).

If it is possible to measure the proportion of each
affected group which lies below an acceptably
defined poverty line, it will be possible to use one
of the three methods described below to make
benefit-cost ratios reflect a direct concern for
income to the poor.

Include in the numerator of the ratio only
benefits to the poor. The first approach is to
enter benefits in the numerator only if they are
benefits to the poor. Income benefits to households
above the poverty line are simply ignored. This
treatment results in a ratio reflecting income
benefits to the rural poor divided by total project
costs. Using such a ratio, projects are ranked
according to how much income to the poor is
generated for each unit of investment cost. As a
comparative device to evaluate optional projects
aimed at benefiting the poor, ratios computed in
this way should provide very useful results.

Include in the numerator income to all households. The second approach is to include income to
all households (poor and nonpoor) in the numerator,
but weight the income of each income stratum dif-
ferently to reflect a preference for income to the
poor. For example, added income earned from the
project by families with pre-project annual incomes
over US$1,000 could be given a weight of 0.1,
families from $150-999 a weight of 0.5 and families
with an income of less than $150 (the "target
group") a weight of 1.0. Each income benefit would
then be multiplied by the appropriate weight
depending on the income of the family to whom the
income accrued before the benefit was added into the
benefit-cost numerator. Many different weighting
schemes could be envisaged, each with its explicit

relative valuation of the income to different income classes. [2] The advantage of this approach is that it avoids the intellectually unsettling notion of a fixed line dividing rich and poor; it allows for a much more flexible valuation of relative poverty. The disadvantage of the weighting approach is that there is little concrete basis for choosing the weights themselves.

Separate calculations of benefits to the poor. The third approach is to calculate the benefit-cost ratios including any income to all households, and then eliminate separately the proportion of income accruing to each stratum. This approach results in a percentage distribution of income across the various income strata which could be used as a separate consideration for project selection.

## COSTS IN BENEFIT-COST ANALYSIS

The denominator in benefit-cost ratios is considerably less troublesome than the numerator; except for a few adjustments, the cost side of the ledger can be generated from existing data. The adjustments required are discussed in later sections of this chapter and will not be examined here. Costs are the sum of project investments, added costs to entrepreneurs and indirect costs created outside the enterprises involved but not paid for out of project revenues.

## THE TREATMENT OF TIME IN BENEFIT-COST PROJECTIONS

Time is a vital factor in benefit-cost analysis. It is therefore important that time-related estimates and choices be made with some care. There are four principal time-related issues in benefit-cost analysis of agribusiness and rural enterprise projects: first, the selection of a time horizon for counting project costs and benefits; second, the estimation of start-up times, lags and repayment periods; third, the choice of a discount rate; and, last, the choice of social discount rates.

## Selecting a Time Horizon for a Project Accounting Period

Benefits from a successful agribusiness or rural enterprise project should continue in some

form almost without end; costs will continue to be
present in direct and indirect forms for at least a
generation or two. It might appear that the time
horizon for accounting for benefits and costs ought
to be likewise very long. Three important reasons
make such accounting periods inadvisable or
unnecessary. First, discount rates used in all
benefit-cost analyses, especially those over 10 per
cent, imply an insensitivity to long-run impacts.
Even if it were possible to project the benefits
which would result from the intervention as far as
30 to 50 years into the future with any accuracy,
benefits occurring so far away in time would be
reduced to insignificance by the simple arithmetic
operation of the discount rate. At a 15 per cent
discount rate, a dollar of every benefit 30 years
from now is worth only one cent in the numerator of
the benefit-cost ratio.

The second reason for choosing shorter time
periods is the obvious difficulty of making reliable
projections far into a future we obviously know
little about.

The third reason for choosing shorter time
horizons is that most agribusiness and rural
enterprise projects usually put in place some
specific combination of inputs, equipment, plant or
technical assistance system which has a useful life;
and that useful life defines a natural time period
over which to consider the costs and--with some
stretching of the concept--also the benefits of the
project. At the end of that period, if there is
little hope that benefits will have had a chance to
mature, then two of these "useful-life" periods may
be taken as the appropriate time horizon for
accounting of benefits or costs. If the
intervention is to install a processing plant, a
marketing facility or supply improved machinery to
rural enterprises, the useful life of those
installations provides a convenient and appropriate
accounting period. Where no physical installation
is contemplated, as in the case of technical assistance or an institution-building project, it is more
appropriate to choose a time horizon during which
final welfare benefits are expected to mature.
Costs in these cases are annually recurring, since
no physical installations are likely to need to be
amortised over a useful life, and there are fewer
logical points to assist in choosing the proper
accounting period.

## Estimating Start-up Times and Lags

Another important time-related problem in
benefit-cost analysis is the estimation of time lags
in project costs and benefits. Because of the
operation of the discount rate, the point in time at
which benefits and costs occur will affect fundamentally the magnitude of the ratio. It takes time to
get a project moving; disbursements take time; there
are inevitable lags in construction, installation,
etc. Good benefit-cost analysis should allow realistically for much of this expected delay in the flow
of projected costs. Likewise, benefits will not
occur instantaneously; it will take time for enterprises to accept project interventions and to make
the necessary adjustments before benefits will be
forthcoming. Credit projects aimed at expanding
production without capital investment have perhaps
the fewest lags, although projecting disbursements
may still involve time-phasing the anticipated take-
up rate of loans.

## Choosing a Discount Rate

In order to put costs and benefits which occur
at different times on an equivalent footing, a
discount rate is used in benefit-cost analysis. The
discount rate chosen will have an important impact
on the final benefit-cost ratios, and it is
therefore important to understand the basis on which
one is to be chosen. Different projects will get
different scores, both absolutely and relatively, on
benefit-cost ratios using different discount rates.
A high discount rate will not simply reduce the
ratios of all competing projects equally; it may
also cause their relative positions to change. A
project which at a lower discount rate had the most
attractive benefit-cost ratio among the options may
become the least attractive using a higher discount
rate.
Higher discount rates tend to favour projects
with shorter start-up times and benefits that
materialise early in the life of the project; lower
discount rates favour those with larger benefits
arising further away in time. Two concepts may be
used to select a discount rate. First, a time-
horizon criterion which focuses on the length of
time over which a planner or project designer wishes
to observe benefits. Using the time horizon
employed by a country's planners results in what is

normally termed a social discount rate. A social discount rate is usually the product of a policy decision made in a national planning office. Most social discount rates vary in the range of three to six per cent. Second, an opportunity-cost criterion focuses on the return to the same amount of capital in optional investments. The opportunity cost of capital is usually taken to be the average interest rate which a relatively riskless investment would earn in the country where the project is to be based. The rate most often used is the market rate of capital.

## COMPUTATION OF BASIC BENEFIT-COST RATIOS

Three major computations are normally carried out for benefit-cost analysis and should be computed for agribusiness and rural enterprise projects. These are: a present value for costs and benefits (PV), a benefit-cost ratio (BCR) and an internal rate of return (IRR). The project analyst should not use this manual as a guide to the arithmetic of these computations; the examples presented below are not explained in sufficient detail for this, but are included to give the project planner an overview of the general methodological processes which lead to the ratios. [3]

## Present Value of Benefits and Costs

Table 7.2 illustrates the calculation of present values of benefits and costs using a 15 per cent discount rate for a rural enterprise project in Guatemala. If a benefit or cost occurs in the future, it is worth less than if it occurred today if it is a benefit and, if a cost, is less expensive than if the expenditure occurred today. For example, the total incremental value of project output in Table 7.2 would be $7,333 for the first year and $11,112 for each of 14 years; the total sum of values is $162,901. This sum is referred to as the undiscounted value of benefits or output. Since much of that benefit occurs in the future, it is worth less than if it took place today. The rate at which we reduce future values so that they are comparable in terms of today's values is the discount rate—in the example 15 per cent.

Benefit-cost Analysis of Projects

Table 7.2.--Present Value and Benefit-cost Ratios
for Small-scale, Rural Enterprises,
Guatemala

|  | Year 1 | Years 2-15 | Present value at discount rate of 15 per cent | Benefit-cost ratio |
|---|---|---|---|---|
| Incremental project output ($'000) | 7,333 | 11,112 | 54,678 | |
| Incremental project costs ($) | | | | |
| Hired labour* | 462 | 666 | | |
| Family labour* | 1,046 | 1,396 | | |
| Other annual costs | 5,514 | 5,514 | | |
| Investment | 3,275 | -- | | |
| Total incremental costs | 10,297 | 7,576 | 41,746 | 1.310 |

Source: Derived from S. R. Daines and G. Smith,
Guatemala Rural Enterprise Sample Survey
(Guatemala: United States Agency for
International Development, 1978).

Note: Family and hired labour are valued at 42
per cent of the market wage rate to reflect
the opportunity cost of labour estimated by
the average employment rate in rural
Guatemala.

Discounted (reduced) 15 per cent each year, the
value today of $162,901 is $54,673, or less than
one-third. This discounted value is called the
present value of benefits. Costs are likewise
discounted to their present value. In the example
in Table 7.2, the present value of costs is $41,746.
The net present value of the project is equal to the
present value of benefits ($54,678) minus the
present value of costs ($41,746), which equals
$12,932.

146

Benefit-cost Analysis of Projects

## Benefit-cost Ratio

The benefit-cost ratio is simply the present value of benefits divided by the present value of costs. In the example, it is $54,678 divided by $41,746, or 1.310.

## Internal Rate of Return

The internal rate of return approaches the issue of a discount rate from the opposite direction and asks what the discount rate would have to be to set the net present value of the project equal to zero. The IRR is a measure of the breakeven discount rate at which the project is justified as an investment. Where only benefits to the poor have been included in the numerator, there are conceptual problems with the IRR since there is no longer any significance to a BCR of 1.0, and the IRR implies a BCR of 1.0.

If the IRR is lower than the market opportunity cost of capital, then the project would be inadvisable. Table 7.3 presents a sensitivity analysis (an analysis showing the consequences of using different assumptions) of the IRR for a rural enterprise project in Guatemala. The IRR is computed by successively calculating the net present value using different discount rates in a trial-and-error search for the discount rate at which the net present value equals zero. Relatively inexpensive pocket calculators increasingly include a preprogrammed IRR function, which eliminates the need to use a trial-and-error search.

## SHADOW-PRICING PROJECT LABOUR

Underutilisation of unskilled labour is characteristic of most developing economies. In many areas, some or all rural wages are institutionally fixed and do not fall even in the face of considerable unemployment. Rural wages may not therefore realistically reflect the supply of and demand for unskilled labour.

A project should not be charged the full cost of the labour it utilises, since society does not really forego the value of alternative production because a large part of the labour is or could be drawn from the unemployed. It should be remembered that in some cases seasonal peaks of labour demand

147

Benefit-cost Analysis of Projects

in rural areas imply that, even though labour is
unemployed much of the year, the market wage rate
may still be an accurate representation of the
opportunity cost of labour if the project will need
labour during the peak periods.

Table 7.3.--Internal Rate of Return Analysis for a
Rural Enterprise Project in Guatemala

| | Internal Rate of Return |
|---|---|
| | (Per cent) |
| Assumptions: | |
| Option 1 | |
| 1. Labour at market wage rate | |
| 2. No start-up period | 25.0 |
| Option 2 | |
| 1. Labour at shadow wage of 42 per cent of market rate | 59.6 |
| 2. Two-year start-up period | |
| Option 3 | |
| 1. Hired labour at a shadow wage of 42 per cent of market rate | |
| 2. Family labour at a shadow wage rate of zero | 64.8 |
| 3. Two-year start-up period | |
| 4. Technical assistance at 8 per cent of the loan | |

Source: Derived from S. R. Daines and G. Smith,
Guatemala Rural Enterprise Sample Survey
(United States Agency for International
Development, Guatemala, 1978).

The computation of the shadow wage rate used
for valuing project labour may be done in many ways.
Perhaps the most practical is to use the unemployment rate as a weighting factor; that is, if the
general unemployment rate among workers who would be
drawn into project labour is 50 per cent, then the
shadow wage ought to be 50 per cent of the market
wage. The theory for this calculation is that on
average only 50 per cent of the labour diverted to

the project will be employed and hence no more than
50 per cent of alternative production, measured by
the wage rate, will be foregone. Table 7.2, for
example, values project labour at 42 per cent of the
market wage rate.

Using a shadow wage rate increases the benefit-
cost ratio of project options in direct proportion
to their labour intensity, and it therefore automatically biases project choice in the direction of
favouring those projects which productively utilise
more labour in situations characterised by high
unemployment.

An alternative method for computation of agribusiness shadow wages is summarised below. To use
this method, three assumptions are required:

1. The probability that workers for the
   project will be drawn from the ranks of the
   unemployed will be higher the higher the
   level of unemployment;
2. The market wage rate can be accepted as
   approximating the worth of previously
   employed workers; and
3. The market cost of obtaining a subsistence
   diet is a fair approximation of the economic value of a previously unemployed and
   unskilled person.

The shadow wage is then a weighted sum of the market
wage rate and the market cost of a subsistence diet,
the weights being the probability that workers are
previously employed (in the case of the market wage
rate) or unemployed (in the case of the cost of a
subsistence diet). [4] The market cost of
obtaining a subsistence diet is used to avoid some
of the complex issues involved in the valuation of
subsistence consumption; however, farm-gate prices
for food commodities could also be used to value the
subsistence diet for some sectors of the population.


SHADOW-PRICING PROJECT INPUTS AND OUTPUTS

Aside from revaluing labour, there may be sound
reasons for altering the prices of other items which
enter as either project inputs or outputs. A few
specific cases will be given below to illustrate the
general idea. The basis on which market prices are
rejected as a way of valuing inputs or outputs for
an agribusiness or rural enterprise project is that
the market does not reflect the true value or cost

of the item. Three examples are agricultural
produce which embodies labour in its production,
imported goods, and products which have subsidies or
price supports.

## Farm Produce Consumed by the Agribusiness Subsector

The discussions in Chapters 2 and 3 treat the
importance of the backward linkages of agribusiness
and rural enterprise projects to farm production.
Increasing the demand for agricultural products will
increase employment opportunities and also increase
incomes of small-scale farms when they supply
products to meet the new demand. These desirable
backward linkages may be treated in two ways. The
first is to include in the numerator as an indirect
effect the incremental gross income of the poor
farmers and include in the denominator the costs of
that incremental production, with the labour costs
properly shadow-priced as discussed above. The
second method is to shadow price the raw material
input when it enters as a cost item in the denominator. Shadow-pricing the raw farm input may be
done by reducing the market price of these products
by the labour shadow price (as described above).
For example, if the assumed unemployment rate is 40
per cent, the shadow wage may be estimated at 60 per
cent of the market rate. If $1,000,000 worth of
agricultural produce at market prices is to be
purchased by the project, and if the labour cost of
production of that raw product was $400,000, then
the market value might be reduced from $1,000,000 to
$840,000 (the labour cost would be reduced from
$400,000 to $240,000, or 60 per cent, which would
reduce the total cost by $160,000).
A difficulty with this approach is that agricultural production will usually demand added labour
during the normal peak times in a region's employment cycle, and it may be that there is almost no
unemployment during those peaks. Very careful consideration must be given to the timing of the labour
requirements of the products to be included in the
project.

## Shadow-pricing Imported Goods and Subsidised Inputs

It is often the case that public policy has
resulted in making imported capital goods cheap
relative to other goods. It is important to correct

this distortion when conducting benefit-cost analysis in order that the true cost of these goods is reflected. An overvalued exchange rate may cause such a distortion for all imported goods, and specific types of capital goods may be the subject of particular regulations which result in an import subsidy. A more realistic exchange rate (shadow price of foreign exchange) which can be used for this adjustment will usually have been calculated by the planning office of the central bank or other central planning unit.

Certain domestic products used as project inputs may also be subsidised such that their prices are not indicative of their true economic worth. It may be, for example, that price controls or subsidies are applied to flour to keep the price of bread down for poor urban consumers. A bakery using this subsidised input should be charged with a more realistic shadow price to reflect the real costs of the goods in question. It is not always easy to identify those goods which should be shadow-priced, but a review ought to be made of all major inputs utilised to see if their prices are distorted in any important way by public policy or regulations.

## Shadow-pricing Project Outputs

Many agribusiness enterprises are involved with products which are destined for export or which compete with imports. These two cases present problems for benefit-cost analysis because of the potential for price distortions which affect the measurement of the value of project outputs.

In the case where the output of a project is to be exported, it is not uncommon for a country to provide a set of direct and indirect incentives. These incentives can be in the form of direct subsidies on the price of the output which operate by allowing the exporters access to a more favourable exchange rate for their financial transactions. The subsidy may be indirect in the sense that exporters are given soft loans, exempted preferentially from certain taxes, given special transport rebates from public railways, reduced costs at public ports, etc. All of these measures may be beneficial and wisely designed, yet their impact on benefit-cost analysis is to underestimate the costs and overvalue the product of the project. [5] Most of these subsidies can be adjusted by properly shadow-pricing the value of the output and reducing the actual price received by the value of the subsidies.

A second important problem may be that the price of the output is not subsidised, but competing imports are charged tariffs to protect the local agribusiness enterprise. When assessing project potential, the issue of competing imports and comparative costs needs to be discussed; and it is probably more important to deal with this problem at the assessment stage rather than including it in the arithmetic of benefit-cost analysis. There is a simple way to include such a consideration in the calculation of the ratios: merely use the lower international price rather than the internal protected price to value the output of the project.

## ESTIMATING INDIRECT BENEFITS AND COSTS

Where the project is such that backward linkages to small farms and the rural poor are assured by their integration into the project, then the problem of estimating indirect benefits to these producers does not arise since they should simply be included in the accounting as if they were direct beneficiaries. This treatment implies that all of their incremental costs as well as benefits must be included.

If the raw products of the agribusiness or rural enterprise are purchased without preference to small farms, it will be necessary to estimate the backward linkage in a different way. The major difficulty arises in attempting to identify the added costs as well as benefits which are created for indirect beneficiaries. The practical result of this problem is that only in rare cases will adequate data be available to integrate indirect beneficiaries into the ratios. A better approach is to estimate the project's indirect benefits in a separate analysis. If an adequate input-output model exists, totals may be estimated for indirect benefits throughout the economy. Since such models are rare, most agribusiness projects must be analysed with only the crudest estimates of backward-and-forward-linkage impacts beyond the direct producers of raw material inputs. For examples of the measurement of backward linkages to small-scale farmers, see the discussion in Chapter 3.

Examples of the indirect impact estimates possible when input-output coefficients are used are

Benefit-cost Analysis of Projects

contained in Tables 7.4 and 7.5.

NOTES

1.    Different approaches to groupings are possible.
See, for example, UNIDO, Guide to Practical Project
Appraisal:  Social Benefit-Cost Analysis in
Developing Countries  (United Nations, New York,
1978), pp.53-4.
2.    The UNIDO guidelines cited above also set out a
methodology for estimating distribution weights.
3.    There is a huge literature on benefit-cost
analysis and a number of practically oriented
manuals, of which some of the better known are:
UNIDO, Guidelines for Project Evaluation (United
Nations, New York, 1972); J. R. Hanson, Guide to
Practical Project Appraisal, Social Benefit-Cost
Analysis in Developing Countries (United Nations,
New York, 1978); I. M. D. Little and J. A. Mirrlees,
Project Appraisal and Planning for Developing
Countries (Heinemann, London, 1974); J. Price
Gittinger, Economic Analysis of Agricultural
Projects (Johns Hopkins, Baltimore, 1972); and
Maxwell L. Brown, Farm Budgets:  From Farm Income
Analysis to Agricultural Project Analysis (The World
Bank, Washington, 1979).  A broader approach is
contained in Dennis A. Rondinelli, Development
Projects as Policy Experiments (Methuen, London,
1983).
4.    On the social pricing of labour, see A. C.
Harberger, "On Measuring the Social Opportunities
Cost of Labour," International Labour Review,
vol.103, no.6, pp.559-79 and D. Mazumdar, "The
Rural-Urban Wage Gap, Migration, and the Shadow
Wage," Oxford Economic Papers, vol.28, no.3, pp.406-
25.
5.    It was found in Pakistan, for example, that the
cost of using electric pumps to deliver an acre-foot
of water was 50 per cent more when done by diesel
pumps rather than electric pumps.  When, however,
the alternative systems were costed on the basis of
social prices, it was found that the social cost of
diesel pumps was a third less than that of electric
pumps.  See F. C. Child and H. Kaneda, "Links to the
Green Revolution:  A Study of Small-Scale,
Agriculturally Related Industry in the Pakistan
Punjab," Economic Development and Cultural Change,
vol.23, no.2, pp.249-75.

# Benefit-cost Analysis of Projects

Table 7.4.--Indirect Income Impact of a Rural Enterprise
Project on Low-income Households, Guatemala

| Sector | Additional output caused by project | Income to poor households | | |
|---|---|---|---|---|
| | | Per dollar value of output | Direct | Indirect | Total |
| | | (US $) | | | |
| Wood products | 1,210 | 0.678 | 497 | 323 | 820 |
| Textiles | 1,360 | 1.068 | 672 | 780 | 1,452 |
| Leather | 1,380 | 1.019 | 816 | 590 | 1,406 |
| Baking, foods | 2,540 | 0.909 | 695 | 1,615 | 2,310 |
| Commercial | 1,800 | 1.082 | 693 | 1,251 | 1,944 |
| Small-scale | 8,290 | -- | 2,768 | 4,559 | 7,327 |

Source: United States Agency for International Development,
Agribusiness and Rural Enterprise Project
Analysis Manual (Washington, 1980), p.110.


Table 7.5.--Impact of a Rural Enterprise Project on On-farm
Employment, Guatemala

| Sector | Farm employment multiplier* | Person-years of additional on-farm employment created by the project |
|---|---|---|
| | (US $) | |
| Wood products | 0.059 | 211 |
| Textiles | 0.090 | 363 |
| Leather | 0.092 | 378 |
| Baking, food | 0.141 | 1,066 |
| Commercial | 0.075 | 402 |
| Small-scale | -- | 2,420 |
| Medium-scale | 0.048 | 339 |
| Project total | -- | 2,759 |

Source: Derived from S. R. Daines and G. Smith, Guatemala
Rural Enterprise Sample Survey (United States Agency
for International Development, Guatemala, 1978) and
S. R. Daines, Columbia Agriculture Sector Analysis
(Washington, 1972).

Note: The farm employment multiplier is the dollar value of
unskilled farm labour per dollar of added enterprise
output.

154

CHAPTER 8

DATA COLLECTION FOR PROJECT ANALYSIS

The first section of this chapter characterises the
types of data used in various stages of analysing
agribusiness and rural enterprise projects and
inventories briefly optional sources for data. The
second and third sections elaborate in far greater
detail the types of data to be collected and data-
gathering methods available for use.

OPTIONS FOR DATA-COLLECTING BY TYPE OF DATA

Sector-wide Data

General economic trends. At various stages in
project analysis, general economic data will be
required. The major use of this type of data is in
the preparation of a general study or assessment of
one or more sectors of the economy. This type of
data exists in a number of secondary sources, such
as those shown in Table 8.1. Given typical cost and
time constraints, it would be impossible to generate
these data if they did not already exist in
secondary sources, and it would be prohibitive even
to process original data which may exist but which
have not yet been analysed. Project planners are
therefore dependent on secondary documents in which
these data have already been processed and appear in
final form.
Sector profile data and sectoral trends.
Chapter 4 contains a description of the types and
sources of data needed for sector profiles. The
discussion there concludes that industrial and commercial censuses provide the best possible source of
such data. Institutional files and records (industrial associations, credit institutions with port-
folios covering appropriate enterprises, etc.) and

existing surveys of industrial or small-scale enterprise activities may also be possible sources.

Table 8.1.--Types of General Economic Data and Possible Sources

| Type of data | Possible sources |
| --- | --- |
| GDP, GNP, trade balances, agricultural and industrial output | Central bank reports, UN regional statistics, national statistical office, national accounts, industrial census, agricultural census |
| International trade and foreign exchange balances, international borrowing | IMF International Financial Statistics, central bank reports, national accounts |
| Population, education, housing, health, etc. | Population census, appropriate ministry documents for particular subjects |

## Data from Enterprises in the Target Group

Many types of data are required which have to be obtained from enterprises in the target group. These types of data constitute the core of adequate project analysis. Possible sources for such data are inventoried below.

Sample surveys of enterprises. Since the concern of project analysis is to obtain a representative view of enterprises in the target group, a sample survey of the target enterprises is probably the most appropriate source of data. It is unlikely that such an exercise will already have been carried out, and it is difficult to get the necessary depth and statistical breadth from the data sources which are listed below. A more complete discussion of sample surveys is reserved for later in this chapter.

Case studies. Case studies, or in-depth analyses at the level of the firm, provide a viable alternative to sample surveys. Such studies may be conducted on a limited number of enterprises and place a much-reduced organisational burden on the institution involved. Some studies of this type may already exist, yet it is unlikely that these contain the particular focus needed for comprehensive project design. The principal disadvantage of these studies is that they can be conducted only by highly trained personnel (economists, sociologists, industrial engineers, anthropologists, etc.), whereas sample surveys--due to their scale--are usually conducted using a high proportion of trained but non-expert personnel. The case study can contain a depth and richness in concept and coverage impossible in sample surveys, and the quality of the resulting data is often very much higher. If properly designed to test project-related hypotheses, they can provide a remarkably complete picture upon which to base project design.

The weakness of case studies is, of course, that their representativeness is impossible to judge. If enterprises in the target group are very homogeneous, the reliability of case studies should be very high. If there are identifiable types of enterprises which are different yet which vary little within each type, the case study is very appropriate since a few cases can provide representative information on a large number of enterprises. The precise difficulty however is that in most cases the degree of homogeneity of the enterprises is not known; it is usually not even known how the different types of enterprise are distributed in the target population. The case study is unable to answer preliminary questions of distribution of types of enterprises, incidence of credit use, sources of credit, etc. What the case study does very well is investigate project-related issues in depth at the level of the enterprise.

Case studies are much more manageable data-gathering efforts than sample surveys because there are fewer people involved, less transportation needed and simply less logistical support required. That is not to say that they are less costly. The skill levels of the manpower involved are usually so much higher in case-study efforts that the added cost of the manpower compared with the relatively low cost of interviewers used for sample surveys results in similar overall costs for the two different approaches. A case study using economists, sociologists or other experts and based on 10 to 20 enterprises will ordinarily cost roughly the same as a sample survey of 500-1,000 enterprises. What is gained in depth and richness in the case study is

traded for the statistical breadth and reliability
of the sample survey; the costs cannot be expected
to differ significantly.

Institutional files and records. A third possible source of information on enterprises may be
the files and records of institutions serving agribusinesses, agroindustries and rural enterprises.
Industrial associations, rural cooperatives, banks
and public credit institutions are the most probable
sources. Credit applications containing information
from the balance sheets prepared by enterprises are
a common example. Coffee and certain other com-
modity-focused associations commonly maintain rather
sophisticated accounting information on their member
enterprises. While these sources ought to be
reviewed, it is unlikely that they will have either
the product breadth or conceptual coverage necessary
for a useful project analysis. In the event the
planned project is product-focused, for example on
coffee processing, these institutional sources may
in rare cases have adequate and very reliable data.

Industrial censuses, surveys and other public
sources. The last two decades of UN-advised industrial, economic and commercial census efforts has
created a large source of data for analysis of
agribusinesses and rural enterprises. In addition,
interim surveys have been set up in many countries
under the auspices of national statistical offices
to update the results of the periodic censuses. The
detail in these interim surveys is usually as good
as or better than in the censuses themselves, and
the size of the surveys is such that they can often
be more easily accessed and utilised to carry out a
project analysis. In many cases, the coverage of
these census efforts is such that they can provide
data not just for sector profiles but also for
project identification, testing hypotheses relevant
to project design and describing in detail the
target group. The disadvantage of these censuses
and interim surveys as data sources is that the
quality of the interviewing and supervision may be
spotty, particularly in those countries where the
1970 census was the first industrial census. A
second disadvantage is that in many cases small-
scale rural enterprises (under five workers) are
excluded from census coverage. Under the UN scheme,
these small-scale enterprises should be the focus of
a separate questionnaire, simplified in concept but
administered in the same year as the general, or
large-scale industrial census. In many countries,
however, such efforts focused on small-scale firms

were not undertaken, or were done with such poor
control that the results were either not processed
or were processed but presented such inconsistencies
that they were not released. In the past several
years, ILO has commissioned a number of studies of
small enterprises in the informal sector, and these
may provide useful characterisation of such firms
missing in other sources.

Further discussion of the use of and problems
related to census and interim survey data follows
later.


## Data from Households in the Target Group

It is unfortunately true that most of the
sources which may be relied upon to provide data for
the analysis of enterprises fail to provide the kind
of information necessary for satisfactory project
analysis. Agribusiness and rural enterprise
projects may be important contributors to household
welfare, but they are only part of the system which
impacts on households, which are increasingly the
focal point for many aid-funded projects. Household
members often have more than one type of employment,
and farm employment and non-agricultural employment
may be important complements. To analyse only employment in the enterprise without information on
other household employment activities would be too
partial an approach for project analysis.

Of the four mentioned possible sources for
enterprise-level data, only two offer significant
hope of providing the necessary household data for
project analysis. These two are sample surveys and
the case-study method. Existing censuses, surveys,
institutional and other secondary data sources are
unlikely to contain the information on household
welfare required to link the analysis of agribusiness and rural enterprises to benefits at the household level.

Data on health, nutrition, education, housing,
sanitation and participation at the household level
are most adequately elicited in a case-study format
where both the time and expertise on the part of the
interviewer permit the necessary depth useful for
these issues. Project analysis requires a con-
nection between the welfare dimensions and data on
enterprises, and it is therefore unlikely that
existing case studies of these non-economic indicators will suffice.

Sample surveys face a significant disadvantage

in these areas because of the lack of time for interviewing and the lack of training on the part of interviewers. The most striking disadvantage is in the case of nutrition where nutrient intake, a common nutrition indicator, is simply beyond the reach of virtually all feasible survey efforts.

Data on employment are among the most difficult to obtain with single surveys or case studies. The seasonality and complexity of employment patterns make it difficult to rely on annual or even monthly recall. If detailed data on employment are desired, it is usually necessary to conduct case studies or sample surveys on a weekly basis during a complete year. General employment indicators may be gathered in case studies or sample surveys using recall over a 12-month period, but they should be used only for broad comparative purposes. The same case study or sample survey which is designed to gather data at the enterprise level may be harnessed also to provide the added household data for project analysis. It is therefore possible to mount a general data-gathering effort focused on households and enterprises without incurring the double administrative and cost burdens which would be implied by two separate efforts.

## Data on Credit and Rural Financial Markets

Credit supply and demand. Data on the supply of credit to agribusiness and rural enterprises are normally easily obtained for that portion of credit which comes from established institutional sources. It is likely that the files and accounts of fewer than ten credit sources will cover more than 95 per cent of all institutional credit to the sector. The more difficult credit supply to quantify is obviously informal credit provided from a wide variety of rural lenders from the traditional "moneylender" to local input suppliers and product purchaser/marketers. The easiest viable way to gather information on credit supply from these informal sources is to survey or carry out case studies on the enterprises themselves.

Information on the demand for credit may be obtained indirectly through credit institutions, but adequate treatment will only be possible when firm-level demand can be based on data derived from the firms themselves.

Rural savings. Information on rural savings may be obtained by gathering data from the rural

institutions which mobilise savings. Postal
savings, cooperatives and other rural savings institutions are possible sources for useful data, but
household savings held as cash or other forms of
investment will not be accounted for by institutional data. Again case study or survey alternatives appear to be the best methods, but even with
these approaches it is notoriously difficult to
obtain reliable and representative data on savings.

## Data on Demand and Comparative Costs

Data on production trends. Trends in output
may be used to estimate demand in the absence of any
direct data indicating levels of demand. Data on
trends in production levels are not likely to be
available for the target group as a separate system,
yet the general production trends captured in the
sector-wide sources discussed at the beginning of
this chapter should provide adequate data for this
purpose. It is unlikely that the case study or
survey alternatives will provide adequate data for
this purpose; secondary and existing census sources
are the only viable possibilities.

Projections of consumer demand. The principal
data required for rational demand projections come
from household surveys of a different type than
would be contemplated for project analysis. This
type of data is a good example of what could not be
easily included in a multipurpose case study or
sample survey of target households and enterprises.
To elaborate demand estimates, price or income elasticities are needed. These coefficients originate
normally from household consumption surveys but, as
explained above, it is not usually possible to
collect reliable consumption data in the type of
sample survey efforts which would be fielded in
preparation for analysing rural enterprises.

Import and export data. For projecting demand,
it is usually very important to have adequate import
and export data. The ultimate source of these data
is almost always the public entity which controls
international trade. Their annual publications, if
available, usually suffice for the level of analysis
required. Such data are also normally processed
fairly quickly by national statistical offices,
which often issue periodic reports containing annual
series.

Comparative cost data. The costs of production
in optional project areas, or even different

countries, may be important information to have, as described in Chapter 6. The sources for this type of data are almost always existing case studies or other micro-level studies. Some data can be obtained on comparative resource costs by accessing information on regional or international wage rates, but the richest data will likely come from scattered estimates of the costs of production for the products in question. The sources for this type of information are very spotty, and cost prohibits the project analyst from generating primary data for this purpose.

## Data on Institutions and Infrastructure

Institutional data. Data covering institutional aspects such as outreach capacity, financial and technical capability and management potential must usually be gleaned directly from institutional accounts. The adequacy of these data is always a discomforting reality, yet the process of gathering such of it as exists is neither time consuming nor methodologically difficult.

Data on infrastructure and marketing. There are likely to be few existing sources of data to cover the interface between infrastructure and marketing facilities and the project. Data on marketing margins may be gathered at substantial cost, and these data seldom exist in any secondary form. If marketing is a central component of the project, both case studies and sample surveys of marketing enterprises will be justified and should provide the necessary information. If non-marketing enterprises are the major focus of the project, then a module can be added to the survey/case-study questionnaires to allow these data to be collected from the enterprises.

There may be isolated cases in which adequate marketing studies already exist upon which the project analyst may draw.

## OPTIONAL APPROACHES TO DATA-GATHERING: RECALL, RECORD-KEEPING AND DIRECT OBSERVATION

This section deals with the ways in which data are obtained at the level of the household or enterprise. These approaches may be used regardless of the method employed to sample or select the units to be interviewed or observed, and they apply equally well in situations requiring either case studies or sample surveys.

## Recall

"Recall" refers to the use of methods which depend on the memory of the respondent for the data. The extent to which reliance can be placed on data obtained through recall has been the subject of much discussion, but in the fields relevant to this manual there has been little research which provides a concrete basis for judging the advisability of using recall or other methods in particular situations. In general, it is true that direct observation, where the researchers actually measure or observe the phenomena of interest themselves, produces superior quality data. Recall should only be used where the subject does not permit direct observation or measurement, or where direct measurement would be too costly.

While there are no overall guiding principles to govern the choice among different techniques, there are a few general rules which apply and which can be used to help in making the choice between techniques using recall and those which do not.

1. The number of events influences accuracy of recall. It is obvious that the number of events one is asked to recall will have an effect on the accuracy of memory. Few would question that the small-scale entrepreneur can recall with a high degree of accuracy the location of his business establishment, the type of product he produces, or whether he produces during the summer or not. If, however, he is asked to specify the number of days the business operated last year, the recall may be questionable unless the number of periods it operated is small. It may be, for example, that it operated only in the summer, in which case he may simply be able to multiply the summer months times 22 days to arrive at the figure. In this case, the number of events for recall purposes is only two, a beginning and an ending time for the summer operation. The larger the number of events the entrepreneur is asked to recall, the less accurate will be the response.

Each time a data item is inserted in a questionnaire to be completed from recalled information, the planner of the study should identify the approximate number of items which will be required, or the level of detail to be recalled. If the number

is large, the item should be carefully examined to
see if direct measurement or record-keeping could be
used instead.

2. The time elapsed influences accuracy of
recall. The distance in time from the point at
which the question is asked to the event which the
respondent is expected to remember will also affect
the quality of data. If it is deemed necessary to
have good estimates of what people do with their
time, it is probably necessary to ask only about the
last few days. To obtain a reliable view of time
allocation over a year, daily or weekly visits are
probably necessary if recall is used.

3. The importance of the event to the respondent will affect recall. Different events enter
memory with different force, and that force may be a
function of many cultural, social and economic
factors. For example, deaths in the family are
usually exceptions to the "time elapsed" rule of
recall; if a respondent is asked to recall the
number over the last 10 years, the importance of the
events will probably overcome the tendency of time
to erode memory.

4. Types of information inappropriate for
recall. It should be obvious that the timing of
interviews is a factor that can be adjusted to
reduce both the number of events to be recalled and
the time elapsed since those events. While employment data, for example, are generally impossible to
obtain on an annual recall basis, weekly or bi-
weekly visits can reduce the time elapsed and the
number of employment "events" to be recalled so that
reasonable data can be obtained. Multiple visits
are very costly, however, and most project planning
cycles preclude such observations. Therefore, while
the comments which follow identify certain types of
data as appropriate for recall and others as inappropriate, it should be remembered that this discussion assumes that weekly visits over a one-year
period are not likely to be feasible. In certain
cases, intensive interviewing may be possible, and
these comments should be adjusted accordingly.

a. Employment information organised on a man-
day basis. Employment events are large in number
even for a small firm if the unit of accounting is
man-days-worked. Even if there are only two or
three workers, the respondent may be attempting to
remember many hundreds of events or days. Since
man-day figures are particularly useful in analysis,
it is tempting to try to arrive at employment in
man-day terms, but it is unlikely that recall will

be useful even for the month preceding the interview. Without reducing the time interval since the
employment events, the analyst can reduce the number
of events to be recalled and obtain less-detailed
data for the same period. This may be accomplished
by asking for employment figures in terms of months
or seasons for each employee. For example, the
entrepreneur may be asked to recall the names of
workers who worked in his enterprise during the last
year. For each worker (if there are fewer than,
say, five), he may be asked if this person worked
more-or-less full time and for how many months.
This approach may reduce the number of events to a
manageable level. Even so, the data would probably
only be safe if used for comparative purposes (that
is, to make comparisons with other firms where the
data had been gathered in the same fashion) rather
than to indicate absolute levels of employment.

   b.   Data on nutrient intake. Agribusiness and
rural enterprise projects often have improved nutrition as one of their central objectives. Nutrition
may be assessed either in terms of improved diet or
better health as indicated by physical growth
patterns or patterns of nutrition-related illnesses.
Improved food intake is virtually impossible to
measure reliably using recall, even for the day
prior to the interview, and therefore should not be
attempted. Because food intake is so difficult to
quantify reliably, even with a high intensity of
visits, it will normally be preferable to use either
health or physical measures as an indicator. (See
discussion of direct-observation techniques below.)

   c.   Costs of production. Costs of production
for enterprises may be gathered if the scale of
operations is small (that is, if few inputs are
purchased) and if no attempt is made to obtain
information on input use as opposed to purchases of
inputs. It is also generally impossible to
construct product-by-product costs of production
based on recall methods. Total enterprise costs and
output may be obtained with reasonable reliability
if the volume of sales and purchases is small. If
the volume is very large, and if the business is
nonseasonal, sales estimates for the preceding week
or month may be used and then expanded. The dangers
of unrepresentative weeks or months in the observations will be reduced if the number of observations
is large. Seasonality may be addressed by conducting repeated visits in the principal seasons to
obtain weekly or monthly recall data on sales. The
association of particular inputs with particular

products is a task of very substantial proportions and should only be attempted through multiple-visit surveys or detailed case studies.

5. Types of data appropriate for recall-based methods. Much of the data useful in project analysis can be adequately obtained using methods based on recall. Among these items are purchases of inputs (if the firms are small and the volume of inputs is small), credit information (where there are few sources and the importance of credit is great), and equipment inventories and original costs. Replacement values may not be known but, if the respondent claims to know, the data are usually reasonably reliable. It is also reasonable to gather information on housing, sanitation, family education and mortality on a recall basis.

## Record Keeping

A familiar method for obtaining data is to obtain them from records kept by the enterprise, household or other respondent. If records are normally kept, this may facilitate the process, but it also brings problems of its own, especially in the case of agribusiness and rural enterprise projects. If income is to be estimated, it is important that all enterprises are subject to the same accounting conventions, similar depreciation methods, definitions of income, etc. It is unlikely that even if records are kept they will be similar enough to be used for anything more than logs of purchases and sales.

Where records are not kept, the survey process may introduce them for the purpose of gathering accurate data. The difficulties are many: illiteracy biases the type of entrepreneur who is able to use these systems and compliance is difficult to enforce between visits. Where accounting data are concerned, there are few situations in which record-keeping as a method of obtaining data is of much help. There are limited situations in which it may be useful. For example, if the central problem is the recall of a series of events which are too numerous for memory to cope with reliably over a year, simple record-keeping systems which overcome the literacy problem have been used. A small box may be put in a prominent place in the enterprise to receive small sticks (or other tokens provided by the interviewer) each day the owner works close to a full day in the shop. This approach may also be extended to workers, and in fact to the recording of many types of data for which recall may be inaccurate due to the number of events to be remembered.

## Direct Observation

Nutrition is a classic case where direct observation is the only reliable method of obtaining accurate data. Height, weight and arm circumference measurements are common indicators of nutritional status in children. It is reasonably simple and inexpensive to obtain these data by having survey personnel actually weigh and measure the children in the sample households. The age of the child is the only recall data needed, but poor recall here can seriously bias the results. Since measurement in children over six years of age is sensitive only to differences in ages on an annual basis, recall presents more serious problems in the case of younger children, where both the month and year of birth are required. For children under five, however, monthly ages are necessary and there is considerable evidence that recall at this level of detail is generally quite poor.

Direct observation or measurement of accounting data for enterprises is not usually practical because of the number of multiple visits which would be required to obtain the data. In the event that highly technical data on production rates, labour productivity on different machines or other technical phenomena are needed, direct measurement is likely to be the only acceptable method of gathering data.

## DATA-GATHERING METHODS

The discussion here focuses in more detail on the methodology of data collection.

## Case-study Approaches

Selection of cases. Two major compromises are involved in selecting the case-study approach to generating data on enterprises and/or households. The first is that the statistical reliability of the data is uncertain. The second is that with a limited number of cases, the richness of comparisons is very limited. Both weaknesses draw attention to

the method by which cases are selected for inclusion
in the study.
1. Selecting for maximum representation. If
some survey or census information is available, it
should be used to help select the cases to be
studied. Even if the data available help only to
clarify the geographical concentration of firms, the
distribution of firms by scale and/or sector of
activity, this information can increase substantially the chance that the cases will be drawn to
represent at least the most important classes of
enterprises. The strongest case-study design is one
which subsamples a small number of cases from representative samples in order to provide data of
increased depth and detail in conjunction with a
larger sample survey effort.

By utilising a census or survey to classify (or
stratify) the enterprises into classes, the case
study can draw one firm from each general type with
some confidence that the resulting cases bear some
desired relationship to the sector or target group
as a whole. With some overall data to use as a
weighting scheme, the relative importance of the
findings of different enterprise case studies can be
roughly estimated. For example, if small baking
enterprises represent only four per cent of the
target group, the case study on baking will be
placed in its proper perspective. If the importance
of baking as a whole is not known, then the relative
importance and weight which ought to be given to the
case study will likewise not be known.

Selection for representation is therefore
accomplished by stratifying the population into
major components based on the best global data
available. If the cases must be drawn in a truly
haphazard fashion, there is no way to know how to
interpret the results. In saying that careful stra-
tification will increase the representative nature
of a series of case studies, it should be remembered
that there is little basis for choosing the enterprises or households to be studied within the
stratum, and it is impossible that one single case
could be statistically representative of the group
as a whole. To achieve statistical reliability from
case studies, there would have to be at least 30
cases from each stratum; and by the definitions used
in this manual, the study would then be a "sample
survey" and not a case study.
2. Selecting for comparisons. A continuing
emphasis in the data requirements for project
analysis has been the need for comparative data of

168

many types. Data with and without project activities and data to compare and search for differences which may help identify project activities with significant potential. The selection of cases will have a direct impact on the ability of the analyst to make these comparisons and should be kept in mind during the process of identifying cases.

If, for example, the case-study method is adopted in an evaluative context to provide data for estimating project impact, then cases would need to be selected which match cases for participants with those for nonparticipants, or which treat "before" and "after" cases on the same enterprises or households. If the case-study method is adopted to estimate project potential, selected cases would need to include enterprises with and without the interventions proposed .

The use of data for comparison can contribute added detail for analysts and should be seriously considered whenever a micro-level analysis is chosen.

Training. One of the principal advantages of the case-study method is that subject-matter specialists are the ones who normally conduct the actual fieldwork. This implies that there is no real need for training. The difficulty is not in training the personnel involved in the case study, but in selecting them. The general style of most case studies tends to be highly personal; that is, it tends to depend very much on the choice of interviewer. Two different interviewers may unfortunately come away from the same case with different viewpoints and different data. In case studies, the potential for bias is much greater than in sample surveys because of the weight carried by personal interpretation. Much of this bias, however, may be reduced by the use of comparably specific instruments as discussed below.

Design and testing of instruments. The use of instruments (questionnaires) is closely related to the degree of standardisation imposed on a case study. Case studies vary greatly in the degree to which the interviewer attempts to ask standard questions to complete a preset format or conducts an open-ended discussion and interviews with the intent of reaching his own judgments.

There are many problems with standardisation, but on balance the attempt should be made in case studies to force standardisation as far as the professionals involved in the actual interviewing will permit. There is an obvious difficulty in making

each situation fit into a standard format; each
enterprise or household is a different experience,
and there is strong resistance on the part of the
subject-matter specialists to having their role
reduced to simply filling out preset questionnaires.
If no reasonably consistent format is adopted,
however, the potential for personal bias, for seeing
what the specialist wanted to see, is strong. Over
and over, the results of case studies can be seen to
correlate with the field and even personality of the
interviewer. If he or she is an industrial engineer, then the problems always turn out to be engineering problems. Problem identification for a
marketing specialist usually turns out to focus on
marketing problems, and so on. To use so-called
generalists (sociologists, economists) is not a
satisfactory solution since one can identify the
specific area of interest even of generalists and
see that same interest crop up as a defined
"problem" in the conclusions.

Without a standard or nearly standard instrument, the case-study approach blends almost indis-
tinguishably into the field trip method for generating data in which subject-matter specialists travel
to the field to observe and identify problems and
solutions through "development tourism".

Analysis and interpretation. For the case
study the issues arising from analysis and interpretation are again related to the degree to which an
instrument is used. If no instrument is used, it is
likely that the fieldwork is the analysis, or that
all that is left is to write up the conclusions
already arrived at in the field. In the event that
there are instruments and those instruments contain
the kind of micro-level data and comparisons
described in Chapters 3 to 6 and 9, the analytical
phase should attempt to produce the results
described in these chapters.


## The Use of Informal Methods

The central burden of gathering data for a
project analysis is normally borne by field trips
and interviews with officials. While these methods
are generally inadequate because of their inability
to provide even token reliability and overcome
personal bias, there are situations in which they
are the only acceptable mode of data gathering. The
attempt to focus aid efforts into projects in which
the poor participate in their own development has

increased the difficulty of relying on field trips and informal discussions as the basic sources of data. [1] Before going on to a discussion of the disadvantages of these methods, recognition should be made of the situations in which they are the best methods of gathering information.

Advantages of informal methods. Where data to be gathered relate to the commitment of an institution to a proposed project activity, the best way to gather that information is by direct discussions with the institutions concerned. There may be objective indications in the form of documentary commitments of funds, or other indicators, yet direct discussion is probably the best method for ascertaining intent. Institutional capability may be assessed most adequately in these informal ways with experts whose long experience in similar situations qualifies them to draw conclusions regarding capacity from face-to-face interchanges. Outreach capacity is an exception to this general rule; statistical evidence of historical accomplishments is superior to discussion as a source of data.

Informal methods have the advantage that they can fit the time frame of almost any project, deal with almost any problem, in any season, and require only limited administrative support. Their flexibility is at once their principal advantage and disadvantage.

Disadvantages of informal methods:

1. Personal and professional biases. There is an old axiom about consultants: you can predict the outcome of a consulting visit if you know well the consultant, his field and his interests and opinions. This axiom embodies one of the principal disadvantages of the less-structured methods of data-gathering, and field trips and informal discussions are the least structured of all. In these methods the biases of the analyst may surface virtually untouched by the realities of the situation. To be sure, if the analyst is a particularly unbiased person this may not be damaging, yet even professional training gives economists, engineers, extension specialists, agronomists and all other competent professionals a particular outlook or focus or approach to problems. It is not difficult to understand why the sociologist fails to identify the engineering obstacles as the central issues, or why the engineer does not usually identify religious attitudes as constraints.

2. High cost per observation. While informal methods may seem inexpensive because the total cost

is easily manageable, if the amount of data gathered
per unit of expenditure is calculated the method
turns out to be one of the most expensive ways to
obtain information.  To most professionals a field
trip is not justifiable as a "data-gathering"
exercise; most who think that field trips are beneficial would argue for them on the basis of the
"field sense" that is obtained by simply spending
time probing haphazardly.  While it may be easy to
argue for this, it is difficult to counter the
overwhelming conclusion that few cases exist where
minds were changed by a field visit.

## Using Existing Sources of Primary Data

Without undertaking fieldwork, a wide variety
of data may be available in original form which can
be used for project analysis.  These are most often
in the census offices, in institutional files and
records, or are the result of some earlier project
evaluation or record-keeping system.

Data from industrial censuses or interim
surveys.  In contrast to population censuses, industrial, commercial and service census questionnaires
contain considerable accounting information which
can be useful at all stages of project identification and design.  Standard topics include:

- personnel, employment and wages;
- data on seasonal operations;
- equipment inventories;
- inputs of primary materials;
- consumption of fuels, lubricants and
  energy;
- other costs;
- output by product type; and
- other sources of income.

It is not uncommon to find 500-600 items reported
for medium- and large-scale enterprises and 200 or
more for small-scale ones.

Institutional files and records.  Credit institutions often gather balance-sheet information and
sometimes more complete accounting information on
applicants for loans.  Such information is normally
considered confidential insofar as individual cases
are concerned, but it may be possible to aggregate
and then average data for different types of firms
or scales of operation.  The records of cooperatives, industrial associations and other institu-

tions may likewise be examined to ascertain the
utility of the data contained in them.

Both bilateral and multilateral donor agencies
have mounted data-gathering exercises over the
years. Accessing these sources of data may be
easier than gaining access to the files of local
institutions, and there is usually less concern with
confidentiality if data were gathered with funding
from an international donor. Because much of these
data will have been collected in the context of
identifying and designing a wide range of types of
projects, they will often be particularly useful for
testing hypotheses and estimating the potential of
agribusiness and rural enterprise projects.

## Sample Surveys

The most comprehensive method for obtaining
data which are representative of the target population as a whole, and of its principal components, is
a sample survey. By a sample survey, what is meant
is a carefully selected subgroup of enterprises
and/or households whose resemblance to the total
population can be predicted with standard statistical techniques. Information from the sample will
represent, at some measurable level of reliability,
the characteristics of the enterprises not surveyed.

There are many decisions to be made regarding a
sample survey. The discussion here is decision-
oriented, with its objective being to provide a
project-design team with the level of understanding
necessary to write a scope of work for a survey, and
then monitor the process. It is not possible to
condense into a treatment of this size all of the
necessary information to allow managers to become
research statisticians, but it is possible to make
certain that managers get what they want.

At each decision point in a survey there are
options. This section attempts to outline these
options, but without detailed description, and to
suggest the pros and cons of each. There are six
principal areas of choice:

- A method for selecting the sample must be
  chosen and the size of sample determined.
- The number of visits for each case must be
  specified (one visit, weekly, etc.).
- The instrument must be chosen and/or designed
  (questionnaire, records, direct measurement,
  etc.).

- The methods of selection, training and supervision of field workers must be chosen.
- The approach to coding and data processing must be selected.

Each of these topics is discussed separately below.

1. Sample selection

   Definition of the unit of observation.

The first step in sample selection is to define the unit of observation. This can best be done by describing concisely who we want to respond and on whom and what the respondents are to provide information. It is important to be comprehensive in the definitions so that there will be few exceptions to the definition. For example, an agribusiness and rural enterprise survey might have one of the following definitions of the unit of observation:

The survey should include households outside urban areas (urban areas or their environs with more than 100,000 population in the last census) where any household member owns or operates a nonfarm enterprise. The respondent should be that member of the household most familiar with the management of the enterprise. The target area includes provinces A, B and C. An enterprise for the purposes of the survey shall be any nonfarm business engaged in selling goods or services excepting services paid for by wages or salaries.

In the above definition, the enterprise-owning or -operating household is the unit of observation. The respondent will be answering questions about the household or its enterprise(s). The definition should be such that there is sufficient detail and clarity so that one can easily tell whether or not a particular household qualifies. There is an issue missing from the above definition which deals with the size of the enterprise and/or the wealth of the household. Under the definition, even the wealthiest of rural households (perhaps one owning a large sugar mill, for example) would be included. A simple addition to the definition, such as "Households owning or operating enterprises which employ more than 10 workers should be excluded" would solve that problem. It may be however that such households, even though they are outside the target group on income grounds, should be left in the sample. First, they are likely to be relatively rare and will not therefore consume a large amount of time and, second, if left in the sample, can give some idea of the relative importance of different scales of operation in the target area. The simple importance in terms of employment may be reason enough to include them.

Determining sample size. Having defined the unit of observation (for example, households owning rural enterprises), the next step is to determine the size of the sample, that is, the desired number of households to be included in the survey. This step is one of the most technical in the whole survey process, and what is said here is oversimplified. Even though the choice of sample size may be technical, the basis on which it is decided is essentially nontechnical and must be determined by the users of the survey rather than by statisticians. The basic choice relates to the level of detail and reliability desired in the final results.

The project analyst must decide how detailed comparisons or measurements need to be; that is, how many subgroupings of the surveyed enterprises or households will be wanted. Will the analyst want to see provinces A, B and C separately, or is it good enough to have them all together? Do large enterprises need to be separated from small ones, or will it be necessary to have three or four different groups to represent the various scales? Will the analyst want to compare findings between different types of enterprises; if so, how many different types will be necessary? Will it be important to compare truly rural enterprises to those located in towns and villages; if so, will there need to be comparisons between small villages and towns? These choices, which relate to the final use of the data, need to be answered in detail before the sample size can be determined.

The reason for following this sequence grows out of a fundamental principle of statistical sampling which is important for the project analyst to understand. A short quotation introduces this principle [2]:

> The greatest hurdle to the acceptance of sampling concerns the reliability of estimates. The potential user of survey research will often ask how one can possibly take a sample of 2,000 people in a country of over 200 million people and arrive at a reliable estimate of the number of ... potential voters who favor one or another candidate and so forth.

> Usually the most important factor in reducing the standard error is the <u>absolute size</u> of the sample. ...Newcomers to the field sometimes advance the common-sense hypothesis that sampling error depends primarily on the <u>proportion</u> of the sample to the total population. They might argue, for example, that a 5 per cent sample of a national census will be five times more reliable than a 1 percent sample, a 10 per cent sample twice as reliable as a 5 per cent sample and so on. While this argument may seem plausible, it is erroneous.

The size of the target group does not centrally influence how many enterprises or households need to be surveyed. The number surveyed depends on how detailed the subgroupings in the analysis need to be, since each subgroup roughly doubles the number which will need to be surveyed. For example, let us assume that the number needed to provide a reliable estimate is 30. If we wish to have results comparing enterprises using credit with those not using credit, we need 30 for each of the two groups. If we want further to compare these two groups for each of three subregions in the target area, then we will need 30 for each of the two groups (credit and noncredit) in three subregions, for a total of six subgroups with 30 in each, or a total sample of 180 enterprises or households. If the type of enterprise is important and there are six types of enterprises, then the sample size would have to be 1,080 (6 types x 3 regions x 2 credit categories = 36 subgroupings x 30 per subgroup = 1,080 total sampled enterprises).

If certain of these subgroupings can be made without having at the same time to maintain another subgrouping, the total number can be reduced. For example, if we wish to make the geographical comparison, the type-of-enterprise comparison, and the credit comparison all at the same time, we would need the 1,080 sample size. If, however, we allow the comparisons to be made in separate tables, one at a time, we would only need 180 sampled enterprises. We could still compare enterprises by subregion, and then in another table compare them by type, and then by credit use (though with some loss in statistical reliability). What we could not do with the smaller sample size of 180 would be to compare enterprise type and subregion. The difference in cost and time for a survey of 180 enterprises is substantially different from a survey of

1,080 enterprises, and the only difference is in the type of comparisons which the analyst must have to complete an adequate project design or evaluation. It is therefore worth considerable thought to determine the level of detail which is needed in the data to be obtained from the survey.

This decision is not one which can be delegated to the sample designer; it is an issue for the user of the survey results. Once these basic issues have been decided, it is simply an arithmetic exercise to determine the total sample size. For rough estimation purposes, the survey designer may use the number 40 (to allow for possible mishaps during the survey) as the appropriate number of households or enterprises needed per subgrouping in order to give reasonable levels of reliability. The final number of usable responses usually lies somewhere between 30-35, which is about the minimum required to give acceptable levels of reliability. To get a general idea of sample size, the nonstatistician may first estimate the number of subgroupings he will need for purposes of analysis and multiply that by 40.

Choosing a method for selecting the sample. There are two basic methods of sampling: one based on lists and the other on maps. These two alternatives are usually called "list" or "area-frame" methods. The best method is always the list method if it is possible and practical. Area frame methods are a compromise on statistical reliability but have the significant advantage of being generally cheaper and faster.

- Using lists. If the group to be studied consists of enterprises with loans from an institution, then the easiest and best method is a list frame sample. It is likely that all borrowers from the institution are contained on some existing list, or on records from which a list could easily be compiled. If the number to be sampled (determined by the process outlined above) is 200 of these borrowers, then the 4,000 names of the borrowers on the list could be put into a hat and 200 of them drawn at random. This would yield a statistically pure sample and would be cheap and simple to construct. This is known as a simple random sample (SRS), and it is the ideal which all other sampling techniques strive to equal. Where there is an existing complete list of all households or enterprises fitting the definition of the units we wish to study, the choice of sampling technique is simple--use that list and take a SRS from it. If you cannot draw from a hat, then number the names and draw numbers, or take every twentieth name (4,000 divided by 200 = 20) from the list. All of these, and many other randomising techniques, will work satisfactorily. If there is no existing list, then it will be necessary to compile one; the only requirement is that the list be complete; that is, it should include all the enterprises or households which will qualify under our definition of the group to be studied. If it is impossible or impractical to compile a complete list, then the very attractive properties of an SRS must be foregone and the more complex area-frame techniques must be used. In many cases it is possible to create a list by conducting a field census, but the costs of generating the list are even higher than those of using an area frame. Where list-based samples are not used, it is usually because of the costs of generating a complete list where one does not exist.

- Area frames and cluster sampling techniques. Where the population of interest has not been listed or would be too expensive to list, area-frame samples are a viable alternative. While they compromise the statistical reliability of an SRS, they can yield acceptable confidence levels if properly administered. Suppose that the project analyst wishes to learn more about rural small-scale enterprises in an area. Using available maps, the target area could be divided into three subareas outside the major city. First might be towns, villages and rural groups of more than 10 houses. Second would be areas of farming. Third would be lakes, swamps, mountains and other virtually uninhabited areas. Expecting that enterprises will be rare in the third area, this might be disregarded completely (unless, of course, forestry and fishery enterprises were known to exist in the area). By looking at the list of subgroupings desired, the designer finds that he wants to compare town and village enterprises with farm-based ones. The town and village areas which constitute the first set of areas on the map could be an essentially separate sample from the farming areas. Reviewing the list of subgroupings may suggest other subdivisions on the map which will dictate how the areas are to be structured.

The next step is to divide each of the villages into equal-sized segments on a map in such a way that the dividing lines between segments can be identified in the field as well as on the map. This means following streets, fences, rivers or other natural and observable boundaries. Let us suppose that there are 546 of the villages and that there are 1,352 equal-sized segments in all of the villages, some villages having as many as 14 of these segments and many villages containing only one segment. By visiting a haphazard group of just 10 of these segments, we find that there are about (as a very rough estimate) 3-5 nonfarm-enterprise-owning households in each segment. From the list of sub-groupings, it can be seen that for the village enterprises we need a large enough sample to divide them into 10 subgroups (five enterprise types and two scales of enterprise). This means that approximately 400 enterprises will need to be drawn from the village areas (10 subgroups x 40 per subgroup). If we are right that there are 3-5 enterprises in each village segment, the about 100 segments would yield the necessary 400 enterprises. If our estimate of 3-5 per segment is too high, we may have less than 400 and be able to have less detail (for example, perhaps only four enterprise types) in the results.

Knowing that we wish to sample about 100 village segments, we can now simply number all of the segments from 1 to 1,352 and put these numbers in a hat and draw 100 of them. These 100 selected segments could be found on the map by the field survey personnel and the interviews conducted. The same procedure could be followed for the nonvillage farming areas.

There are many variations which can be made on the general idea presented as the model for the area-frame sample method. If the survey wishes to focus on a certain type of enterprise--fruit and vegetable processing, for example--it may be necessary first to enumerate all enterprises in a larger number or larger sized set of village segments with a questionnaire which is very short, asking each household only if it owns or operates an enterprise and if it is a fruit and vegetable one. Then a random sample could be drawn from the list of fruit and vegetable enterprises for the final detailed interviews. This design would then be a combination of list and area-frame methods.

Without undue delay it is possible in most settings to design a sampling method which will yield acceptable results once the definition of the target group and the level of detail desired in the analysis have been specified.

    2.   Determining the method and frequency of field observations

The three basic methods of observation are recall, record-keeping and direct measurement. All three of these may be used in the same survey or each may be used separately as the sole technique of observation. A discussion of the situations in which each is most appropriate is contained at the end of Chapter 7.

Interacting with methods of observation is the frequency of visit. For some types of data a single annual visit will suffice; for other types of data, daily visits over a 30-day period or weekly visits over a year will be required. The number of visits will probably depend not only on the type of data but also on the methods of observation selected. If recall is the method, then the number of visits will be used to adjust the recall period and the number of events to be recalled.

If comparisons are intended in the analysis between two well-defined groups, then the structure of the sample and the number of visits will be affected. For example, if it is decided that to estimate the potential of a technical assistance project, it would be useful to estimate the income of enterprises with and without technical assistance in the target area, the structure of the sample would obviously have to adjust to this design.

Longitudinal comparisons ("before and after") are common in evaluative designs, and it is obvious that multiple visits (at least one before and one after) are required by such a design.

3. Instrument design and testing

The design and testing of the instrument (questionnaire, record-keeping formats or forms for direct measurement) are important parts of the survey process. This is perhaps the stage at which experience is most required on the part of the personnel involved in design. Familiarity with the alternative types of questions which might be effectively used to elicit usable data is one critical element. A second is linguistic familiarity with the local terms for the items to be included in the survey. Local personnel with a close working familiarity with the area must be involved at this stage.

Once the questions have been selected and the general structure of the instrument is known, professional help in designing the questionnaire so that it will be easy to administer, code and process is an investment well worth the cost.

With a draft questionnaire it is important to administer a field test to see if the design will function in practice. This test should be coordinated in such a way that it can be undertaken by the

supervisors and interviewers who will take it to the
field for the actual survey. The field test also
serves as a method for training the personnel to be
involved in the survey.

4. Supervision and training

After randomising the selection of the
sample, supervision is perhaps the second most
important element in conducting a successful survey.
Many surveys attempt to correct in the office, after
fieldwork is done, errors and inconsistencies which
appear in the data. This is unfortunately too late
for such corrections. Once data have been taken out
of the field, there is little chance that useful
corrections can be made. The time to make these
corrections is while the team is still in the field;
in fact, while the team is still in the area a re-
interview is possible. To catch these kinds of
errors, there must be a field supervisor with the
time to review all of the instruments within a day
after they are administered to detect errors and
omissions so that the household or enterprise can be
revisited. This generally means that there must be
one supervisor for every three or four (at maximum)
interviewers.

The training of interviewers and supervisors
should be conducted at the same time that the draft
instrument is field tested. Before actually beginning the survey, each supervisor and interviewer
should have completed at least three actual interviews. This initial experience should be followed
by time in a classroom setting to discuss problems
encountered with a highly experienced trainer.

5. Data coding and processing

With approaches involving case studies and
informal methods, the coding and processing of data
seldom arise as issues of choice. Where sample
surveys are used however or data from secondary
sources are reprocessed, these choices become important.

There is now a very wide range of options open
for the processing of data--ranging from manual
extraction and tabulation through desktop microcomputers to institutionally operated mainframe
computers--and the choice will influence the coding
scheme used. Perhaps surprisingly, it can often be
faster to obtain selected results by manual processing from a simply coded set of data than to enter
the data into a computer and process it electroni-
cally, particularly where staff require training in
computer-based procedures.

The guiding principle is whether the main

emphasis is on obtaining limited results quickly or on obtaining a full depth and breadth of analyses from the data collected. Normally the project analyst requires the former while the latter is of more interest to academic and other researchers. It is well worth repeating Robert Chambers' cautionary note about the practical worth of much data [3]:

> There has been an overkill in data collection. ...Much of the material remains unprocessed, or if processed, unanalysed, or if analysed, not written up, or if written up, not read, or if read, not remembered, or if remembered, not used or acted upon. Only a minuscule proportion, if any, of the findings affect policy and they are usually a few simple totals. These totals have often been identified early on through physical counting of questionnaires or coding sheets and communicated verbally, independently of the main data processing.

Precoding possible responses into as few categories as possible (but leaving the option for "open-ended" responses) and using clerical staff to tabulate the results are an approach likely to satisfy the immediate requirements of most project designers and analysts. The same data sets used in the design stage can, of course, be entered onto appropriate computers as the first entries in what may become a growing database on a project if it is approved and funded. Normally, however, this will not be a major priority unless data used in design have also been deliberately collected as part of a systematic baseline survey of the project's target group.

NOTES

1. Robert Chambers stresses that many of the "professionally respectable" methods of rural research are all-too-often inefficient and calls for "approaches which are open to the unexpected, and able to see into, and out from, the predicament of the rural poor themselves" (Robert Chambers, Rural Development: Putting the Last First (London, Longman, 1983), p.74). See particularly his chapter 3.
2. Donald Warwick and Charles Lininger, The Sample Survey: Theory and Practice (New York, McGraw-Hill, 1975), pp.82,92.
3. Chambers, 1983, p.53.

CHAPTER 9

IMPLEMENTATION, MONITORING AND EVALUATION

The first half of this chapter outlines some of the principal themes related to the process and methodology of implementation as they specifically apply to agribusiness and rural enterprise projects. The treatment given the subject here will of necessity be less complete than would be possible in a manual dealing only with implementation. The second half of the chapter goes on to discuss the evaluation of agribusiness and rural enterprise projects.

BASIC CONCEPTS

Implementation is defined here as the period in a project's life, after design is completed, when planned activities are carried out. It is the direct action phase. While volumes have been written on methods of project design and evaluation, comparatively little has been written on methods for improving implementation. The analysis of implementation has been called the "missing chapter in conventional analysis" [1] and, despite the existence of copious documentation, there can be little doubt that implementation remains the stage most ignored by analysts.

This chapter distinguishes between two types of activities which take place during the implementation phase of a project. The first of these is termed implementation and the second monitoring. Implementation is taken to be the project activity itself, the undertaking of project tasks; while monitoring is defined as information-gathering and reporting which provide those who monitor and manage projects with the knowledge about progress necessary to allow them to improve the process of implementation.

Most agribusiness and rural enterprise projects involve the provision of some financial, technical or physical input to participating enterprises. Critical to this process is the entrepreneur's taking business risks, integrating project-supplied inputs into his business and seeking increased income and welfare as a result. Even research and infrastructural projects fit this pattern, although in a less direct way than credit or technical assistance projects. Viewed in this light, implementation might be redefined as the process of getting project resources (advice, capital, goods) to risk-taking entrepreneurs.

Since risk-taking entrepreneurs are at the heart of most projects, it may be fairly said that most of these projects involve a "private sector approach". This is not to suggest that public entities are not central to the projects. Public development banks and research and technical assistance agencies may play vital roles, but the most important link is to the private entrepreneur. The private sector, represented by businesses of many different scales, is the final part of the implementation system in most projects; and it is important to approach implementation with a view to making certain that it complements rather than undermines existing financial structures and systems of resource distribution.

Beyond the immediate concerns of those involved with implementing a project is a second set of issues relating to whether the project, as designed, achieved its intended objectives and whether it is worthwhile replicating the design elsewhere. The most immediate purpose of evaluation therefore is to determine the effectiveness of a particular project.

The evaluation should be planned around a logical framework (called a logframe by some aid agencies), which states the project's overall objective and relates this to indicators of the achievement of sub-goals and performance of activities. These indicators should be used to evaluate project performance and to provide a structure for the evaluation effort, since in a sense the logical framework may be viewed as a plan for evaluation at a general level. Evaluation exercises may be undertaken during the course of a project to provide project managers with mid-course information on project performance, but they are more commonly conducted as ex post exercises, particularly for projects of short duration.

DESIGN CHOICES AFFECTING PROJECT IMPLEMENTATION

Problems during implementation can be anticipated through adequate project design work. Various
design choices will have fundamental impacts on the
nature of the implementation process, and the major
design options and issues with critical implications
for implementation are discussed in this section.

## Implementation Problems: Prevention or Cure

If the analytical process outlined in Chapter 6
is followed before projects are approved, many of
the problems which later surface during implementation will be prevented. An analysis of institutional feasibility conducted during the design phase
should suggest areas where implementation bottlenecks are likely to arise and where increased staff,
staff training or added resources and assistance
will be required to prevent subsequent crises.
There is great benefit in early identification of
problems; in many cases the sheer momentum of a
large project prevents the solving of problems which
were not identified early enough. Changes made in
the design phase are relatively painless, while
modifications made later are costly, if indeed they
are possible. One way to get a project design which
can be implemented is to include the people who will
have to implement the project in the team respon-
sible for elaborating its design. Those who are
faced with the responsibility of actually undertaking activities are often more serious about
making certain the design is institutionally
feasible.
Institutional feasibility relates not only to
the entities involved in providing resources or
technical assistance to enterprises but also to the
institutional and organisational feasibility of
project activities within enterprises. Enterprises
vary widely in the early stages of their development
and in the ability of their management to absorb and
benefit from project interventions, and care must be
taken to assure that proposed project activities fit
the development stage of the enterprises to be
assisted.
In addition to institutional feasibility and
its implications for implementation, there is the
important issue of the demand for project services
and resources. If there is no viable market for the
output of enterprises, there are likely to be major

problems of implementation. There are also likely to be problems if there is inadequate demand for project services by agribusiness and rural enterprises of the right numbers and types.

A few extra weeks of careful analysis of institutional feasibility, and of the demand for project-supplied services and resources, at the design stage can prevent months of struggle with bottlenecks later during implementation.

## An Experimental Approach to Implementation

More than three decades of experience with inadequately evaluated development assistance projects has left a legacy of uncertainty about which technical assistance and direct investment approaches work. In this setting, it is not easy to design projects around tested principles, yet the project review process demands a decisive and definite tone in proposal documents. Project designers feel compelled to claim to know the right way even if they are uncertain. While there is in reality much that is experimental in almost all agribusiness and rural enterprise projects, design teams rarely express the experimental nature of proposed activities, and more importantly, almost never design the implementation process as a conscious experiment.

At a variety of decision points in the design process, analysts will face several different options, none of which is clearly superior. Instead of establishing the project as a format for finding out which of the options works best, most design teams select one with very little rational reason to explain the choice. Experimental implementation need not be elaborate. Experiments can be as simple as varying the ratio of rural credit officers to vehicles from one to three in different areas to see if the added investment really results in sufficient added lending activity to justify it. Experiments are not without their problems however, and design and budgets need to be flexible to adjust to the results of even simple experiments. But even with the added difficulties which may be associated with experimental approaches, they have significant potential to assist learning from the experience of implementation.

Agribusiness and rural enterprise projects operate in risky environments and must somehow build in adjustment mechanisms to accommodate to their

realities. Risk is an explicit part of private
sector lending, and allowance for risk is an integral part of every private sector financial and
business institution and organisation. Public
sector programmes are unable to deal with risk in a
flexible and agile fashion. Business risks make
every investment or technical intervention in
support of small-scale enterprises an experiment,
and explicit provisions should be made for mechanisms which deal with isolated business failure
without casting a cloud over the entire project.
Being able to cut losses and redirect investments
easily is a central part of the flexibility inherent
in private sector activities and one which
government- and donor-agency-funded projects would
do well to imitate.

## Flexibility in Project Design

An important choice which will affect the
implementation process is that of the level of
detail in the design. A very highly detailed design
leaves little flexibility to make mid-course adjustments based on changed circumstances and mistaken
perceptions on the part of project designers. An
overly flexible design, on the other hand, leaves
too much to be decided during implementation and may
be the same as issuing a blank cheque to the
implementing entity or recipient of the project's
resources. It is important that a middle ground be
found which leaves the necessary flexibility in the
hands of the implementing bodies yet assures the
funding body that the project will not drift from
its original intent.

A useful mechanism for finding the appropriate
middle ground is to be absolutely clear about the
objectives of the project and the principal means
which are to be used to achieve them. Beyond that
core, which would not be amendable or subject to
review, there could be specific mechanisms for
review and revision built into the design to allow
all parties to participate in deciding mid-course
adjustments to important elements of the project.
All those other areas of decision-making which can
legitimately be left to the unilateral judgment of
the implementing agency without affecting the intent
or principal means of the project should be relieved
of the necessity for complicated and cumbersome
approval procedures.

## The Project Implementation Calendar

Project design involves establishing a chronology of project activities and estimating completion targets. These targets often impose a structure for implementation which is unrealistic, and it is very common to encounter delays in implementation.

Setting an ambitious calendar for project achievements may be used as an explicit mechanism to encourage hard work and to place a certain amount of constructive pressure on personnel concerned with implementation. The difficulty with this approach is its potential for creating just the opposite effect--if fund disbursements and reviews and documentation are keyed to the same calendar, problems may be caused for implementation by unrealistic targets. Time pressure may be useful, but it can also cause inefficient allocation of resources; that is, both time and money may be unwisely spent to meet artificial deadlines. A reasonable solution is to set targets but at the same time create a mechanism for revising the calendar. This will allow monitors to "manage" the time-pressure factor and prevent it from becoming counterproductive. It is important that concern about disbursement rates on the part of funding agencies not dominate the design and implementation process. Multi-year funding can be a useful mechanism for reducing pressure on the implementation calendar and allowing for adequate staging and flexibility during implementation.

## Planning of Disbursements

Choices about the procedures required for release of funds and project resources can have a significant impact on implementation. As in the areas already discussed, there is a tension between emphasising flexibility and ensuring that project objectives for appropriate shares of financial participation by both government and the funding body are met. Elaborate arrangements for the disbursement of counterpart funds may ensure the participation of local agencies but also place burdens on implementation. A balance must be arrived at which includes enough complexity to distribute risk, assure participation and commitment, and protect the integrity of project funds. At the same time, however, procedures must allow sufficient speed in operation so that funds are available when badly needed. Project designers should always ask them-

selves how long it will take to process the counterpart and disbursement arrangements required. If the
period is unreasonable, ways must be found to
simplify procedures.


## INSTITUTIONAL MECHANISMS

### Delivery Channels for Access to Agribusiness and Rural Enterprises

If the number of enterprises is small, relatively little work will be needed to build and
refine access channels. If the project involves
large numbers of small-scale rural enterprises,
delivery systems for services and resources will be
a major concern during implementation. In most
cases there are optional public and private channels
for the delivery of services and resources. For
example, in the case of credit, there are public
development banks, and in the private sector there
are commercial banks, moneylenders, suppliers'
credits, and so on. Care should be taken to explore
all options. Where viable private channels are
available, there are significant advantages in utilising and improving them. In many cases, however,
public channels are the only viable option.
Each case is individual and the channels for
outreach to enterprises must be determined on a
case-by-case basis. It is important that the
channels be well outlined and, if possible, an
analysis should show evidence of their capacity for
the type of outreach implied by the project's objectives.


### Private and Public Intermediaries

Many systems and mechanisms can be found
for extracting maximum benefit from joint public and
private sector participation. It is up to each
project manager together with government and the
funding agencies to decide which mechanisms, or
combinations thereof, are most appropriate. The
ultimate choice will depend on the sophistication of
the infrastructural system in the country and the
capacity of the private and public sectors. Before
private sector mechanisms can function so as to
achieve the desired benefits, government must take
steps to ensure that the implementation process can
proceed. This is done, as noted in previous

chapters, by having government policies give priority to reorienting and synchronising private and public activities in support of agricultural and small-scale enterprise development.

Where public or private programmes exist, advantage should be taken of them. Programmes such as those conducted by the University of the Philippines Institute of Small Scale Industries (which assists entrepreneurs in preparing, formulating and analysing the feasibility of proposals and presenting them for government and commercial funding) have led to the funding of a significant number of projects. Government subsidy or incentive programmes might encourage urban enterprises with an agribusiness focus to consider rural market towns and villages as alternative locations to larger cities. [2]

Improvements in project design and the planning of production and marketing to benefit entrepreneurs can be made through government training and extension assistance. In most developing countries, agribusiness firms tend to have a centralised management structure, and there is a scarcity of trained managerial personnel. Implementation procedures should assure that a move away from centralisation to the rural areas is accompanied by initial management training programmes and subsequent follow-up. For example, industrial extension services in India, Japan and Korea provide prospective entrepreneurs and owners of small-scale rural enterprises with advice on production options, plant layout and machinery installation and operation. Demonstrations of efficient technical processes are conducted by extension service centres in India, reaching rural areas with small mobile workshops. [3]

Limited knowledge of accounting and financial analysis and of banking and credit procedures, as well as the complexity of requirements imposed by lending institutions, make it difficult for small-scale rural enterprises to obtain credit. New mechanisms must be found to counteract these factors if implementation is to proceed by bringing more enterprises into production. Both entrepreneurs and credit personnel need to be trained in accounting, financial analysis, borrowing procedures and loan negotiation. Mechanisms must be decentralised so that institutions and personnel are located in the same rural areas as the enterprises themselves.

It is not enough to assume that the proper mechanisms will fall naturally into place. Special efforts may be needed to create "integrated lending packages" for agribusinesses and rural enterprises to combine credit, technical assistance, design and marketing advice and managerial training. Appraisal and lending procedures may have to be liberalised and should be based on the merits of proposals rather than on credit ratings of borrowers.

Active cooperation between large and small enterprises is another method of linking agribusinesses, agroindustries and agroservices in the process of expanding participation in agricultural and rural development. Larger firms can usefully contribute inputs and assistance to small-scale rural enterprises through technical assistance in organising and supervising production processes, controlling the quality of products and providing managerial training to satellite industries.

Expansion of export potential for the products of agribusinesses and rural enterprises will be important in some countries and could alleviate problems related to inadequate domestic demand and low levels of production. One way to tap the necessary expertise and training is through organisations that specialise in this area. One such is the World Trade Institute, which promotes export expansion in developing countries through training, workshops, market studies, design of production processes and identification of export opportunities. Another organisation which performs essentially the same services is the UNCTAD-Gatt International Trade Centre.

Another approach is linking private intermediary bodies to food and fibre delivery systems in the project country. Examples include both non-profit and profit organisations, multinationals and other firms. A number of intermediate organisations have created some promising new initiatives to utilise the skills and resources of large corporations in the development of food systems. In essence these organisations serve to link corporations to the local political and social environment and to the needs and aspirations of the country in which they operate. The new processes they have developed use local labour, capital and natural resources, plus modest outside capital, to create viable enterprises which would not otherwise emerge. Their projects all emphasise the transfer of technological and management skills to nationals in the project country. Most, although not all, manage to operate on relatively modest budgets.

Sources of expertise frequently overlooked

during implementation of externally funded projects
are local institutions. On all projects, a determination should be made regarding local capacity to
overcome most, if not all, barriers to rural development. Possible arrangements include hiring or
contracting local business schools, development and
commercial banks, credit unions, marketing and production cooperatives, subsidiaries of multinational
firms, indigenous private sector firms and local
universities and technical colleges. All of these
are potential sources of managerial and technical
personnel and could be utilised in both the design
and implementation phases.

## PROJECT MANAGEMENT

In sharp contrast to the analytical skills
needed in the design stage of a project, the implementation stage requires capable managerial skills.
Project management presents many challenges, some of
which international development agencies are not
inherently equipped to confront. [4] Management
can be a problem due in part to the fact that, for
many projects, indigenous management is not sufficiently trained or experienced to handle all aspects
of complex implementation processes.

## Participation in Project Management

A common thread running through much of the
recent literature on development policy relates to
the extent of local "participation". As it relates
to agribusiness and rural enterprise projects, participation implies the active involvement of beneficiaries (entrepreneurs and benefiting families) in
the managerial process of the project. Since many
studies support the importance of participation in
determining overall project performance, decisions
should involve participating entrepreneurs and producing families to the greatest extent possible.
As a practical matter, it is easier to involve
participants in design than in implementation and
administration. Obtaining the ideas of local,
small-scale entrepreneurs about existing critical
constraints and potential solutions to their
problems is an integral part of the analysis process
outlined in Chapter 5. Gleaning local ideas and
perspectives is a much easier process than involving
a widely dispersed and heterogeneous group of small-

scale entrepreneurs in the day-to-day work of
project implementation. If only a handful of enterprises is involved, as in the case of projects
dealing only with large-scale agroindustrial firms,
the difficulty is lessened and intimate involvement
of local entrepreneurs in the decision-making
process is more feasible. Where large numbers of
households are involved, participatory management
presents a range of practical difficulties; yet the
evidence of its importance is such that project
planners should be encouraged to move in this
direction as rapidly as possible.

"Participation", of course, whether organised
or not, results from the activities of implementing
agribusiness and rural enterprise projects; because
projects operate directly with the private sector,
local individuals must participate.

## Personnel Management and Training

The most obvious gap in all implementation
processes is the availability of capable and motivated people to act as managers. Even a poorly
designed project in the hands of effectively trained
and motivated managers has a very good chance of
success. Implementation is more likely to be
affected by success or failure in attracting competent management than any other single factor.
Analysis of institutional competence will not substitute for the "analysis" of personnel. The competence of the handful of individuals who end up
managing the project, and not the general competence
of the organisations involved, will probably be the
predominant factor influencing the success of implementation. It is important that the dominating
influence of individual managers not be overlooked.

While the capacity of local managers may be an
important constraint [5], it is also true that
there are likely to be many capable people who may
be drawn to project management if the project offers
sufficient incentives and opportunities for initiative. While there is no simple solution to this
problem, an important contribution is a personnel
management plan integrated into the project's
design. It is unfortunate that while almost all
analysts of development recognise the importance of
personnel management, it is rare indeed that a
project design devotes much time or energy to a plan
for personnel management and incentives. "Personnel" as a subject is dealt with as one of the four

or five standard blocks of knowledge taught in management schools, yet it is almost always ignored as a subject in project design. There is seldom any systematic plan for ensuring that the best knowledge in each field is employed to contribute to project success.

Where the capabilities of managerial and other personnel, however selected, are weak, a training component will be a vital part of project design. Funding and planning will be required to make this component an efficient and effective tool for improving implementation. [6]

## Formal Project Management Systems

Many of the informal elements of knowledge about project management have been incorporated into formal management systems. These tools are aimed at providing effective management control and information. [7] Where logistics represent a relatively large share of the burden of project implementation, these techniques are of comparatively greater utility. Projects may benefit from the explicit inclusion of one or more of these formalised systems into their implementation plan. [8]

## PROJECT MONITORING

Monitoring involves the provision of information, and the use of that information, to permit project management to assess the progress of implementation and to take appropriate decisions at the right time to ensure that progress continues according to plan.

## Monitoring Institutional Development

An important element in most agribusiness and rural enterprise projects is an institution-building focus which seeks to strengthen an existing institution, or in some cases to build a new one. Monitoring the progress of these institution-building objectives differs so widely, depending on the particular institutional aspects to be assisted, that general guidelines on method are virtually useless. Specific objectives and targets should be set, and the performance toward these targets should be tracked.

Implementation, Monitoring and Evaluation

Much more can be said about monitoring non-institution-building objectives of projects. In many ways adequate monitoring implies a flow of information which allows for serious assessments of progress. The possibility that such assessments can be based on statistical evidence of project impact is very slight. The simple realities of field administration preclude this from happening. What is possible is to structure those elements of the evaluation design that are practical into a monitoring system. Two major segments of this monitoring system are explored below: first, a system to track intermediate flows of goods and services and, second, some modest tracking of final household- and enterprise-level impacts.

## Monitoring Intermediate Flows of Goods and Services

The project's logical framework contains the basic structure for fleshing out a monitoring design. Projects are based on the assumption that outreach will take place and that it will be appropriate in nature and quality. These two simple assumptions which appear in different forms in most project logical frameworks provide the basis for a sufficiently complex monitoring system to track adequately the intermediate part of project objectives.

Monitoring service outreach. The first element which may require monitoring is the outreach of services. While this task may be simple in concept, it requires an information system to be established in the implementing entity to record numbers of visits to enterprises, numbers of training courses given with numbers of participants, and numbers of demonstrations and attendance. Monthly or at least quarterly progress reports with this standard set of data would be an improvement over what passes for monitoring in most projects.

Monitoring the quality of service. The ultimate test of the appropriateness and quality of services is their impact on enterprises and the incomes of participants. There are, however, other tests and data which can be used to monitor quality. Spot-checks on quality may be made through regular supervisory visits by representatives of the funding body, or by contract personnel in charge of the training of extension or outreach agents. If such staff are unable to formulate a system for judging the quality of the final services, it is unlikely that they know enough about the process to implement a useful programme. If these spot-checks on technical-assistance visits, courses and demonstrations can be made at random, the results should provide a reasonable idea of gradual changes in quality of the services.

## Monitoring the Intended Final Impacts of Agribusiness and Rural Enterprise Projects

Tracking the intended final impacts of projects on beneficiaries during the implementation stage raises a number of problems. First, it is probably true that the intended impacts at the level of households will not mature in the early stages of implementation. Second, even after they do begin to mature, it is largely inappropriate to evaluate such impacts as a part of the monitoring system, since a mid-course evaluation is probably already built into the project's evaluation plan. The role of monitoring final impacts during implementation may be seen, however, as providing a different perspective on final results than a mid-course evaluation. It may, in fact, be very useful to begin gathering data on final impacts even before they would be anticipated to materialise.

*Monitoring final impact as a method of improving quality of services.* A useful objective of early monitoring of intended final impacts is that the very process of gathering data and training project personnel to interpret and utilise such data will have an impact on the quality of the technical services. For agribusiness and rural enterprise projects, the nature of technical assistance provided will depend on the type of enterprise, the stage of entrepreneurial development and many other factors. A frequent danger in technical assistance is that the package of interventions fits poorly with the needs of the target group. An adequately designed monitoring system which seeks to identify how technical assistance services are actually changing and improving businesses can be one of the best ways of fine-tuning the technical package. One would not expect to see changes in operations or in household incomes during the first few months of implementation. The operation of a household-level, impact-monitoring system, however, will probably have a significant impact on the quality and perhaps even the structure of the services themselves.

Methods for monitoring intended final impact.
It was noted earlier that impact monitoring is much
like a mini-project evaluation. This concept may be
broadened to the statement that the basic methods
outlined for the project evaluation should be used
in the monitoring stage. The instruments designed
to measure final impact and project "success" should
be applied in miniature to serve as impact-
monitoring tools. If, for example, a survey of a
control group is contemplated as part of the evaluation methodology, the same questionnaires, indicators, etc, could be used as monitoring tools but be
administered to only a small sample of enterprises.

As the project operates over time, the monitoring results will become part of the evaluative
design. Not only will the assessment of progress
toward intended final impacts enhance implementation
by signaling changes needed in direction and
emphasis, but also this assessment should provide a
sound basis for ex post evaluation.

## EVALUATING AGRIBUSINESS AND RURAL ENTERPRISE PROJECTS

The most immediate purpose of evaluation is to
determine the effectiveness of a particular project,
but evaluation also has important implications for
improving the design of future projects.

## Guiding Project Design from Project Evaluation

Beyond the obvious need to record information
on performance, there are other potentials in the
process of evaluation. Designing effective projects
requires a wide variety of information about implementation mechanisms which work in practice. All
international agencies have expended considerable
effort to improve their project design work and have
encouraged the governments with which they deal to
do the same. Additional analysis is now conducted
before making funding decisions to assure that
projects have a good chance of making a cost-
effective contribution. There are, however, many
factors which hinder pre-project analysis and render
it relatively impotent in practice. This section
argues that, for both practical and conceptual
reasons, evaluation of previous projects of a
similar type usually benefits design work more than
analysis undertaken at the stage of project design.

Analysis to assist design is not likely to be as useful as evaluation of prior projects because the programming activities of most aid agencies allocate little time and few resources to project design. There is often little chance of undertaking the necessary data collection and analytical activities necessary to allow project choices to be made wisely. Annual budget allocations, the project identification and review cycle, and the ever-present necessity to commit funds all make the likelihood of depressurising the design and approval process unlikely, and perhaps even inadvisable for many organisational and managerial reasons.

Even though it may be virtually impossible to improve the design process significantly, evaluation is not limited by the same constraints. Evaluation is different from design both in terms of time pressure and limitations on resources. Most development projects probably have time horizons of only two to five years, although it is often accepted that their impacts may take at least a year beyond disbursement to materialise.

Another, and perhaps the most convincing, reason for emphasising evaluative analysis, even at the expense of analysis of design, is that evaluation is carried out in the situation which would be ideal for analysing design. In designing a project, the analyst wishes to determine what will work, to estimate the potential impacts of doing one project rather than another, or doing the project one way in contrast to another. In the design stage, the project's potential can be estimated either by the educated guesses of experts or by the analysed experience of past interventions. Certainly time will not permit the planner to analyse past interventions carefully if that work has not already been done; the designer must rely upon a personal best-guess, which can hardly be regarded as "analysis". If information to permit effective evaluation is not available, the analysis of design must be superficial because there is no analytical background upon which the designer can build. Moreover, there has been a tendency for evaluations to concentrate more on detecting faint traces of "success" rather than to conduct sober and objective appraisals of why success is so hard to find: what went wrong and why. Effective evaluation would gradually build a reservoir of information on project design and impact which would reduce the burden of pre-project analysis and would help alleviate the bureaucratic and practical problems which beset aid programming.

## Evaluation of Intended Final Impacts on Households in the Target Group

The chain of causation. For the purposes of evaluation, it is useful to outline a chain of events which causes a project intervention to have a favourable impact on households in the target group. While any causal chain involving human behaviour is endlessly complex in reality, simplified versions may help to structure a useful analysis. An extremely simple, generalised chain of causation for agribusiness and rural enterprise projects can be constructed by distinguishing changes or impacts which occur at three different and sequentially related levels:

1. Institutions--institutions make available credit or provide technical assistance;
2. Enterprises--enterprises increase output with the increased credit, or efficiency with the technical assistance; and
3. Households--household members obtain more net income or enjoy a higher level of welfare as a result of the increased output or efficiency.

These are only examples and, it must be emphasised, very simple ones, but the three levels defined can be used to fit most, if not all, rural enterprise projects.

This particular conception of a chain of causation is useful because it provides a structure for evaluation and fits neatly into the logical framework, which should be an already functioning part of the project programming cycle and documentation. Each of the three levels should include an evaluative component so that results can be used to draw judgments about the performance of the project evaluated and to provide guidance for design in the future.

The importance of focusing evaluation on households. After a long period of preoccupation with examining institutional changes, most aid agencies now insist upon at least equal attention being devoted to securing evidence that their programmes have beneficial effects at the level of the household. If an evaluation does an acceptable job of measuring and evaluating impacts at this level, it implies that the other levels--institutions and enterprises--have also received adequate attention. It would be conceptually and operationally impossible to determine adequately what the final impacts of a project are without making the

necessary connections to intermediate enterprises
and institutional factors. The converse, however,
is not true. It is possible, indeed easy, to review
institutional changes without ever recording any
impacts whatsoever at the level of households. In
practice, almost all evaluations resemble this
latter type of review. They examine (adequately or
inadequately) institutional performance without any
measurement of what impact was actually achieved at
the enterprise or family level.

Another reason to focus evaluation on the
household level is that knowledge as to what institutional interventions really cause improvements in
family welfare is the missing piece of the project-
design puzzle. Much is known and discussed in the
development literature about what institutional
instruments are available and how to use and adjust
them, but there is only a handful of studies that
actually measure the benefits of these interventions
at the household level. As mentioned above, project
design is an activity with an insatiable appetite
for this kind of information, but for bureaucratic,
budgetary, organisational and conceptual reasons it
seldom has access to such information.

Evaluation in a systems framework. Family
income and other welfare for the rural poor engaged
in agribusiness and other small-scale enterprises do
not derive exclusively from these enterprises.
Employment in other activities, such as a family
farm or other family-owned businesses, may represent
an important source of income. Changes in the
family enterprise must be viewed as part of a larger
system or the results of evaluation may be misleading. For example, family income may actually be
reduced by an increase in income from the family
enterprise if this increase comes from displacing
family resources (whether labour or money) from
other pursuits.

All agribusiness and rural enterprise projects
attempt to make some type of change in an enterprise
to increase the welfare of its owners and/or
workers. While the enterprises may operate on a
small scale, they are nevertheless complicated businesses. An intervention or change in one part of
the business may cause changes in another. It is
important, therefore, that change be viewed as a
systemic phenomenon. Resources, new inputs and
credit are all fungible at the level of the enterprise. It is not enough simply to identify whether
the project intervention has been completed and
completed on time. It is also necessary to identify

if the expected, or other, unexpected, changes have occurred in the enterprise system.

## Institutional and Project Inputs

In addition to evaluating the impact of the project on the enterprise, evaluation is needed of the institutional process by which project inputs or interventions are provided to the target enterprises. Much less quantitative precision is needed at the institutional level, but compensating increases are required in the organisational sophistication of the evaluative design and much higher levels of local awareness are necessary in the personnel conducting the institutional evaluation.

## DATA FOR EVALUATION

The importance of project-specific data cannot be overemphasised. Almost all evaluations proceed without data bearing directly on enterprises or households in the project area. Collecting data from households and enterprises is a long, difficult and painstaking process; as long as evaluations are accepted which avoid this effort, there are few incentives to undertake it; indeed, many documents reveal that evaluators saw their role as one of interviewing various officials to glean their opinions as to what happened. Such collections of "official" impressions and opinions, linked to at times insightful observations about the institutional process, have in some quarters come to be widely accepted as adequate project evaluations. There are exceptions, of course, and it is important to note that they are more distinguished by the data gathered than by the methods used to analyse them. The gathering of basic data, not its interpretation, is the hardest part of carrying out an adequate evaluation. More effort needs to be made to develop reliable data-gathering methods than to refine statistical techniques for analysis. If the data-gathering effort is poorly structured and inadequately controlled, no amount of sophisticated analysis will be able to salvage meaningful results. [9]

A necessary but not sufficient condition for a good evaluation is an appropriately designed and carefully managed system of gathering primary data at the level of the enterprise. While many other elements are also needed, the absence or incorrect application of this one will ruin the attempt to conduct a sound evaluation.

## Using Comparison to Assess Impact and Causation

The most basic method to determine whether objectives have been achieved is by using comparisons as both an analytical and a data-gathering method. The data themselves must be gathered in such a way as to permit valid comparisons. The task can be defined as gathering comparable data and comparing the right things at the right times. The analytical method outlined in the section following this will add very little to the comparisons which could be made using raw data if gathered correctly.

Comparisons function better at the level of enterprises and households than at that of institutions simply because large numbers of the smaller units will probably be excluded from participation. There are two reasons why observing larger numbers of units (households or enterprises) makes results of any analysis more believable. The first reason is simple logic. The more cases that fit the rule or the finding, the more secure one feels in the finding itself. The statistical corollary to this intuitive judgment states that results obtained from samples with less than certain numbers of observations lack reliability when generalised or extended to cover the whole population from which the sample is drawn.

There are basically two types of comparisons which can be used to provide conclusions on impacts for evaluative purposes. The first is comparisons of participating households, enterprises or institutions in "before-and-after" fashion. The second is comparisons between participants and nonparticipants with similar characteristics. In the first type (comparisons over time) we are attempting to see if the project has changed the particular entity from what is was before, with the implication (later to be examined) that the difference is "caused" by the project. This type of comparison of the same households, enterprises or institutions over time is called a longitudinal comparison.

In the other case, where participating enterprises are compared with similar nonparticipating enterprises, we wish to observe differences, which by implication are "caused" by the project, since they are the only differences between the two groups of enterprises. A comparison made at the same time between two different groups of households, or enterprises, is termed a cross-sectional comparison.

In both longitudinal and cross-sectional comparisons, analysts are trying to isolate influences due to the project from the endless other influences which can change households or enterprises in order to identify changes which can reasonably be associated with the project's activities in a causal way. Since no one believes in causation by a single factor, the project evaluator is not looking for the true "cause" in the strict sense of the word. Instead evaluation analyses impacts associated with the project, changes related to the project and changes strongly influenced by the project.

The process of isolating project-specific influences from others is an imperfect one, but it is inescapable if choices in project design are to be enlightened by experience. The discussion which follows outlines the logic and explains the procedure by which various types of comparisons may be used to draw conclusions or inferences about impact.

## 1. Longitudinal Comparisons of Enterprises

The design of a longitudinal comparison for evaluating the impact of a project on rural enterprises or households often begins with what is called baseline information on the participating enterprises or households. Let us simplify the impact which is to be measured in order to explore the data-gathering technique. Assume that we wish to measure the impact of the intervention on the volume of production in participating rural enterprises. To assess what the project has done to production levels, we would take the requisite numbers of randomly selected enterprises. (See Chapter 8 for discussion of sampling and surveying.) We would then go to each enterprise before its entry into the project and obtain from the proprietor the amount of production over the past year. Then, each year after the project begins, we would return to the same group of firms and obtain the same information for the ensuing years.

If we find that production has increased by 40 per cent each year, we might say the project has been successful. There are, however, other factors in the environment of the enterprise which influence levels of production and which have nothing to do with project interventions. Credit may have become scarce and more costly for firms outside the project, or prices may have made production more profitable and hence more attractive. The weakness of longitudinal comparisons is that exogenous changes may invalidate or distort the association between the observed change and the activity intended to promote change. Longitudinal comparisons control the enterprises by insisting that the same ones be observed over time. We still deal with the same enterprises but fail to control the changes in the environment in which they operate.

## 2. Cross-sectional Comparisons of Enterprises

Cross-sectional comparisons between participating and similar, but nonparticipating, enterprises present almost a mirror image of the strengths and weaknesses of longitudinal comparisons. In a cross-sectional comparison, we select a group of enterprises about to participate in the project and match these enterprises with similar enterprises which are not going to participate. This group of nonparticipating enterprises is commonly, although somewhat erroneously, called a control group. [10] No comparisons are made between the two groups until after the project has been implemented because they are by definition and by selection similar before the project begins. The comparison after implementation is between participating and nonparticipating enterprises. The idea of the cross-sectional comparison is that the only difference between the two groups is participation in the project, and therefore any significant differences that emerge during the course of implementation can reasonably be attributed to participation in the project.

Since cross-sectional comparisons are made simultaneously, there is no distortion from changes in the environment over time, fluctuations in demand, changes in prices and all the other external factors influencing enterprise. These factors remain constant for both participating and nonparticipating groups because the comparison is made at the same time.

The absence of external distorting influences is the main strength of cross-sectional comparisons, in contrast to longitudinal comparisons, where it is the main weakness. The principal weakness of cross-sectional comparisons, however, is that they admit distortion based on uncontrollable differences within enterprises between participating and nonparticipating groups. It is impossible to match participating and nonparticipating groups so well that the only difference between them is participation in the project. It is always possible therefore that an observed difference in some indicator, such as level of production, between the project group and the "control group" is due not to participation but to some internal difference in the firms which is not related to the project.

3. Combining Longitudinal and Cross-sectional Comparisons

The strengths and weaknesses of the two comparative methods are mirror images of each other. Longitudinal comparisons hold internal characteristics of enterprises constant by using the same firms as units of observation before and after, but influences outside the project may change over time and distort the findings. Cross-sectional comparisons try to hold outside influences constant by taking measurements simultaneously in project and nonproject groups, but internal differences between the two groups, however much we may attempt to adjust for them, may distort the results.

An obvious solution to the relative strengths and weaknesses of the two methods is to combine them. This can be accomplished by taking before-and-after data from participating firms and a group of nonparticipating firms. In this combined approach, the basic comparison is longitudinal--examining the before-and-after state of participating enterprises--but changes in the environment over time are "controlled" by following a second group--previously matched, nonparticipating enterprises. Changes observed in the participating group can then be scaled, or "deflated", by changes which are occurring naturally in the nonparticipating group. For example, if it were observed that output increased by 80 per cent compared with the level before the project began, this increase would be reduced by the increase in production which occurred for the nonproject group of enterprises. Thus, if production for nonparticipating firms had increased by 35 per cent, the increase which might reasonably be associated with the project would be 80 - 35 = 45 per cent.

This type of combined cross-sectional and longitudinal comparison is considerably more involved than either of the others, since it involves the more costly and time-consuming elements of both.

4. Comparisons Based on Random Samples

Impact can also be assessed using simple cross-sectional random samples of firms and analytical groupings and statistical techniques. Because of their complexity, these methods would require a separate manual to treat them satisfactorily; yet it may be useful at least to make planners aware of the possibility.

There are two approaches. The first involves constructing groups based on observed character-istics of randomly sampled participants or of all enterprises in the region. For example, a random group of participants might be surveyed. If the intervention is technical assistance, these enter-prises might be placed in three groups after the survey: those receiving minimal technical assis-tance (perhaps less than 3 visits), those receiving moderate amounts of assistance (3 to 8 visits), and those receiving intensive attention (more than 8 visits). If those with a substantial amount of input perform the same as those with almost none, it creates a presumption that the intervention has had little impact. To strengthen the conclusion, there will probably be some enterprises sampled which intended to participate but for some reason did not get assistance, and these might be used after the fact for comparative purposes. If their performance were significantly poorer than that of those who received project inputs, the inference would be that the project had a significant beneficial impact. With some reflection, it can be seen that this method is attempting to do, with less precision and care, what the longitudinal and cross-sectional comparisons are designed to do.

The other approach is to use regression and correlation techniques, and preferably a combination of the two, to identify those factors which cor-relate highly. The argument is that a high degree of correlation implies a causal relationship; however, if the direction of causality is to be determined using these techniques, the requirements are very careful construction of analytical models and insight into both the techniques being used and the nature of the assumed causal relationships in the project. If, for example, technical assistance and increased output happen together (that is, are highly correlated), then the tendency is to assume that they are somehow causing each other. Which causes which, however, is far from clear. For example, it may be that higher production causes increased technical assistance rather than vice versa; it may be that technical assistance personnel tend to visit aggressive and progressive firms.

The major problems with this type of analysis are that it may take an extended period of time, requires access to computer facilities and demands a relatively high level of statistical and analytical training on the part of the personnel using it. More fundamentally, those conducting this type of analysis tend to allow it to drift off into the realms of academic research with very limited application to either project design or implementation. It should be noted that in both longitudinal and cross-sectional comparisons the basic ideas are simple and, except for the techniques used in data collection and skills in data-processing, no specialised analytical training is required to administer the process or extract commonsense conclusions from the results.

## ANALYTICAL METHODS FOR EVALUATIVE COMPARISONS

This subject requires a manual of its own if it is to be treated thoroughly, and the discussion here only attempts to outline a few simple approaches and to raise some of the issues encountered in analysis.

### Direct Comparison of Averages

The simplest method for making comparisons is to measure the average of some important indicator, such as the level of output, both before and after the project (for a longitudinal comparison) or for participating and nonparticipating groups (for a cross-sectional comparison). For example, in Table 9.1, production per hectare is compared between participating and nonparticipating groups of small-scale farmers.

### Estimating the Reliability of Comparisons

Control group reliability. The problems inherent in both cross-sectional and longitudinal comparisons have been discussed above. To minimise these problems, the two methods can be combined and groups matched with utmost care. There is no acceptable way to estimate quantitatively the possible distortions from a lack of care in matching or of

207

Table 9.1.--Average Value of Production of a Sample
of Participating and Nonparticipating
Small-scale Farms

| Farm size | Value of output per hectare of arable land | | Level of significance |
|---|---|---|---|
| | Partici- pants | Nonparti- cipants | |
| (Ha.) | (US$) | | (Value of t) |
| 0 to <1 | 1,221 | 446 | 3.80 |
| 1 to <5 | 401 | 384 | 0.70 |
| 5 to 10 | 303 | 296 | 0.08 |

uncontrolled distortions over time.

Survey quality control and reliability. The
largest sources of error in most analytical work
relate to difficulties of a practical nature in the
survey work, or nonsampling errors. These difficulties (discussed at length in Chapter 8) relate to
quality control of interviewers, coding, training,
supervision and designing satisfactory survey
instruments, or questionnaires, for obtaining information at the level of the enterprise.

Statistical reliability and sampling error.
The third type of reliability is called statistical
reliability and refers to the reliability of working
with results from a sample rather than the whole
population of enterprises. Assume, for example,
that the results in Table 9.1 come from a sample of
1,600 small farms (with equal numbers of participating and nonparticipating farms). If some 6,000
farms participated in the project, the 800 represent
a sample from the "universe" of 6,000. It is possible to estimate statistically what the probability
is that the comparisons based on the sample are the
same as a similar comparison based on a survey of
all 6,000. This test is known as the t test; if the
value of t (an algebraic computation the method for
which can be found in any elementary statistics
book) is high, it means that there is a very high
probability that the sample results are "reliable",
meaning that they would not be significantly different if we had surveyed all of the participating
firms and not just a sample.

The t-test depends not on the absolute size of
the observed difference but rather on its stability.

For example, in Table 9.1 it would be possible to get a high value of t from a small difference such as that found between participants and nonparticipants in the 5-10ha category. The t-test in Table 9.1 indicates that the reliability of the finding that participants had higher output is only good for the smallest farms (0 to <1ha) where the t-value is 3.8. This means that we can feel confident that if all participants in this size class had been interviewed, they would have shown a similar margin of superiority over nonparticipants as that shown by the sample. For the other two size groups (1 to <5 and 5-10ha), the results are very unreliable. There is no assurance that the same margin of difference would have occurred in the rest of the farms which were not sampled. The t-test helps us to decide how much confidence to put in observed differences from a comparison based on a sample survey.

## Using Indices to Evaluate Impact

Considerable attention was given in an earlier section of this chapter to the importance of tracking project impacts on both households and enterprises. The idea was to be able to see how different parts of the enterprise or family "income system" contribute to the results achieved by the project. Simple comparisons of averages such as those described above do not help this process, since all that is known when the comparison is finished is that output (or income or any other indicator of achievement) has been influenced and by how much. The intermediate mechanisms by which the project interventions stimulated this impact are obscured in these simple comparisons. Slightly more complex methods are required to conduct evaluations which get at such interrelationships. The more sophisticated of these methods (multiple regression analysis, production function analysis, etc.) are not discussed here simply because these techniques would require time, resources and skills out of reach in the analysis of most rural enterprise projects and because their practical usefulness is dubious. A technique which has been successfully used within these limits is the elaboration of simplified indices to capture the contribution apparently made by a number of factors.

For this technique to work, there must exist a simple arithmetic and accounting framework in which any result is the sum of a series of component

factors. This technique works well for business
enterprises where the objectives are increased
output or profit since the internal sources of
increased output may be divided among the sources,
as shown in Table 9.2.

The following example will show how indices
might work in evaluating the impact of a rural
enterprise project. Assume that a project focused
on providing three major inputs to a group of brick-
making enterprises and had the single objective that
these three interventions would increase the level
of output of the participating firms. Assume
further that the evaluative design involves a longitudinal comparison of a sample of participating
firms before and after project implementation. The
comparison indicates that production increased in
participating enterprises by 48 per cent, and there
is no reason to suspect that anything but the
project inputs caused this increase. The three main
project inputs are: technical assistance to get
entrepreneurs to use better technologies, credit to
expand production, and provision of energy-efficient
heat sources for reducing the cost of firing kilns.
The intent of the indices is to attempt to understand how the enterprises achieved higher (by 48 per
cent) levels of output in order to illuminate how
much of that increase came from changes the project
hoped to make and to help design other projects by
understanding the process of beneficial change.

The application of indices is best understood
by identifying the sources of the increased output
in terms of certain accounting concepts of the
enterprises before and after project intervention.
What things might be different about the firm before
and after which could have given rise to the
increased output? First, entrepreneurs may have
increased the size of their productive capital base.
Second, they may have increased the level of output
from the previously existing capital base either by
using the same capital better (through increased
managerial efficiency) or they may have changed the
type of capital through changes in the productive
technologies that produce more output per unit of
input. Third, entrepreneurs may be producing the
same physical volume of output but are obtaining
higher prices for each unit sold, with the result
that the value of output obtained from a fixed
capital base has increased. This increase in prices
may have been obtained by different marketing
arrangements or improvements in the quality of the
products. Finally, the value of output may also

have been increased by changes in the mix of
products produced without any corresponding change
in capital invested or efficiency of operations.
While these causes could be broken down still
further, the discussion above serves to illustrate
the use of indices for attributing proportional
contributions among several different factors. The
value of each of these factors would be compared
before and after the project, and indices would be
used to associate a proportion of the total increase
in output with each factor, as shown in Table 9.2.

Table 9.2.--Decomposition of Output Gains Across
Contributing Factors*

| Contributing factor | Proportion of increased output in participating enterprises associated with each factor |
|---|---|
| | (Per cent) |
| Increased value of capital | 38 |
| Increased yield from capital | 2 |
| Increased prices for outputs | -6 |
| Changed mix of products | 14 |
| Total increase in value of output | 48 |

Note: Data are hypothetical.

The example shown in Table 9.2 implies that
credit may have played the most important role since
most of the increased value of output was due to
increases in scale (the capital base), which is what
one would expect from an infusion of credit. The
change in the mix of products suggests that technical assistance may also have made a substantial
contribution, but additional information should be
sought from those involved or from project documents
to see if changing the mix of products was one of
the major focuses of technical assistance. It
should be noted that prices obtained for products
actually declined, and this drop could indicate one
or more of several things. The lower prices may
reflect a drop in quality or some sort of marketing
problem. On the other hand, prices may have dropped
simply as a consequence of increased production and

Table 9.3.--Sources of Increased Production among
Participating Small Farms, Guatemala

| | Farm size in hectares | | | | | |
|---|---|---|---|---|---|---|
| | 0-<1 | 1-<3 | 3-<5 | 5-<10 | 10+ | All farms |
| | | | (Per cent) | | | |
| Mean increase in total output per farm | 147 | 37 | 20 | 12 | 17 | 32 |
| Sources of difference in output: | | | | | | |
| Differences in land use: | | | | | | |
| Increases in farm area | 6 | 9 | 1 | 3 | 7 | 17 |
| Intensification of land use | -8 | 10 | 15 | 14 | 18 | 18 |
| Shift to higher-valued crops | 154 | 15 | -8 | -1 | -1 | 0 |
| Increased yields | -4 | 1 | 15 | 2 | 0 | -3 |
| Increased prices | -1 | 2 | -3 | -6 | -7 | 0 |

Source:   S. R. Daines et al., The Impact of Small-
          Farm Credit on Income, Employment and
          Production (Washington, United States
          Agency for International Development,
          1975), p3.

competitive marketing of larger supplies.  If this
is the case, it suggests that consumers of the
products have benefited from lower prices, while
participating enterprises have benefited in a
variety of ways.  Such an outcome, however, is
likely to have had adverse effects on nonpartici-
ting enterprises because it is likely that they now
face lower prices for unchanged levels of output.
     Technical assistance aimed at making enter-
prises more efficient by increasing the yield from
existing capital or changing the types of technology
embodied in capital seems not to have worked well,
since only 2 per cent out of the 48 per cent
increase appears to have come from this source.  The
technique of using indices helps to sort out causation and to associate impact with specific compo-

nents of a project with multiple interventions. It should be noted that the technique does not attribute causality with any high degree of precision, but it does help to raise or support hypotheses about the causes of project impacts.

An actual example of such an evaluation is shown in Table 9.3, which uses indices to divide the increased output associated with a project among a series of contributing factors. The enterprises in this example are small farms, not agroindustries or other small-scale rural enterprises, and hence the categories are not the same as those outlined for applying the technique to rural enterprises.

NOTES

1. Allison favours increased emphasis on methods of implementation and argues that policy analysis pays little attention to the problems encountered in implementation. See Graham T. Allison, "Implementation Analysis: 'The Missing Chapter'," in R. E. Zeckhauser et al. (eds.), Benefit Cost and Policy Analysis (Aldine, Chicago, 1975).
2. D. A. Rondinelli, "Small Industries in Rural Development: Assessment and Perspective," National Productivity Council Journal, 1978.
3. Ibid.
4. Rondinelli and Radovich show that management and administrative difficulties appear in almost all projects. Two further conclusions from their review are relevant here. First, they observe that knowledge of implementation problems does exist within development agencies, although this knowledge is not effectively utilised due to inadequacies in institutional learning. Second, they suggest that a relatively simple diagnostic study can be used to identify major problems or deficiencies that can affect project performance through succeeding stages. See D. A. Rondinelli and H. R. Radovich, A Study of Development Project Administration: Diagnostics for Improved Implementation (Vanderbilt University, Memphis, Tennessee, 1975).
5. For a more complete treatment, see Robert Chambers, "Executive Capacity as a Scarce Resource," International Development Review, vol.11, 1969.
6. There is a large and growing literature on design and planning considerations for training programmes in public management. A useful overview is Morris Solomon, Flemming Heegaard and Kenneth Kornher, "An Action Training Strategy for Project

Management," International Development Review, vol.20 (1978),pp.13-20.

7.  A range of models of formal project management systems exists upon which planners and designers can draw. The following sources provide a guide to some of the documentation based upon practical experience: D. K. Leonard, An Evaluation of the Programming and Implementation Management (PIM) System, Institute for Development Studies, Working Paper No. 89 (University of Nairobi, Kenya); Peter Delp et al., System Tools for Project Planning, International Development Institute (Indiana University, Bloomington, Indiana, 1977); and H. R. Radovich, "Development Project Management: An Integrated Approach to Project Planning and Implementation," Planning Processes for Project Management, vol.1, Graduate School of Management (Vanderbilt University, Memphis, Tennessee, 1974).

8.  Increasingly attempts are being made, with greater and lesser success, to incorporate microcomputers into formal management systems, but the inconsistent experience has yet to be systematically documented. Forthcoming joint work by the World Bank, the Food and Agriculture Organization and the International Fund for Agricultural Development should provide useful guidelines if preliminary work is indicative. See Jean-Marc Boussard, "The Use of Computers in Monitoring and Evaluation of Rural Development Projects" (Institut National de la Recherche Agronomique, Paris, 1986).

9.  Two excellent and practical references are D. J. Casley and D. A. Lury, Data Collection in Developing Countries (Clarendon Press, Oxford, 1981) and, by the same authors, Monitoring and Evaluation of Agriculture and Rural Development Projects (Johns Hopkins University Press, Baltimore, Maryland, 1982).

10.  The terminology has been borrowed rather uncritically from scientific research. See the two works by Casley and Lury for the reasons why the identification of such groups may be difficult any why resources are often not allocated for the study of them.

# CHAPTER 10

## SUMMARY

While agribusiness and rural enterprise projects have very attractive potential for generating growth with equity, such a result is not automatic; considerable care in design and implementation is required to achieve significant and positive results, and project failures are far from rare events.

Careful analysis is required initially to contribute to an understanding of the setting in which it is proposed that agribusiness and rural enterprise projects will operate. The nonpoor are comparatively agile in most rural and urban situations. It is they, the nonpoor, who can usually take advantage of new resources, new government programmes and incentives, new market opportunities and the like. The nonpoor are the ones who by and large have the skills and mobility to shift, to adjust and to capture the benefits of most realignments in the rural economy. Perhaps the best way at least to reduce the natural advantage of the nonpoor is to design projects so as to incorporate the poor and their resources directly and actively into the interventions proposed.

Three principal recommendations are made in this volume to increase the probability that projects will generate positive employment and income impacts for the rural poor without the benefits being syphoned off by those who need them least. The three recommendations all have a common focus of building on existing structures and of maximising the involvement of the poor through the utilisation of their skills, resources and products. The basic recommendations apply to all types of interventions and constitute an analytical checklist against which to test each intervention and its components.

Summary

First, all interventions should be designed so
as to focus primarily on the use of the most
important resource possessed by the rural farm and
nonfarm poor--their labour.  There are two basic
ways to ensure that agribusiness and rural enterprise projects maximise their impact on employment
creation:  by favouring the production of goods
which use large proportions of labour relative to
capital and land and by using methods of production
which utilise higher proportions of labour.

Second, all interventions should be designed so
as to focus on the second most important resource of
the nonfarm rural poor--their small-scale enterprises and the entrepreneurial skills they have
developed to operate them--in order to harness the
entrepreneurial capabilities of the poor in the
solution of their own problems and to reduce the
leakage of benefits to the nonpoor.

Third, all agroindustrial interventions (those
using farm products as inputs) should be so designed
as to draw their raw materials from the small-farm
subsector in such a way as to develop further
existing entrepreneurial skills and maximise the
benefits of backward links.

This checklist provides a framework for
selecting activities and interventions which will
maximise the benefits of agribusiness and rural
enterprise projects for the rural poor.  The actual
instruments chosen through which to implement an
intervention may encompass a considerable range,
including training, research and advisory services,
credit programmes, facilitating procurement of raw
materials and/or equipment, aids to marketing, and
the like.

Two concepts--appropriate technology and local
participation--need to be borne in mind in applying
the approaches set out in this volume because both
incorporate implicitly the notion of significant
local involvement in the definition of problems and
the possibility that purely indigenous solutions may
be found.  Both concepts can serve as important
focusing devices in project design.

While it is difficult to summarise adequately
the full range of techniques used in project identification and analysis, the point of departure is the
creation of a backdrop for rational identification
of project opportunities.  [1]  This is done through
preparation of a profile of an agribusiness and
rural enterprise structure.  Next comes an orderly
process of project identification based on a ranking
of constraints and the delineation of qualifying

groups in the population. This step is followed by
the estimation of project potential in terms of the
magnitude and probability of improvement in target
group welfare and a rough assessment of whether a
project is feasible and whether likely benefits
justify the anticipated costs. Finally, a full
comparative analysis is made of the potential
benefits with the costs of undertaking an agribusiness and rural enterprise project.

The range of data required to conduct a full-
scale, pre-implementation analysis of a potential
project is wide, and the demand for data once implementation is underway is--while quite different--
potentially as far-reaching. A typology is elabo-
rated covering data utilised in the various stages
of analysis and design, and an inventory is provided
of optional sources of data and methods of acquiring
the data required. The emphasis is placed strongly
upon exhausting all possible sources of secondary
data before even contemplating an exercise to
collect primary data.

If all the stages outlined in the first eight
chapters of this volume are followed, the likelihood
is that a sound project concept will have been
developed into a viable and focused set of activities. On the premise that there is more money
available for development efforts than there are
good projects, a project designed in this way and
addressing the issues raised in this volume should
find little difficulty in attracting the resources
necessary to launch the project. With the beginning
of implementation, one is in the direct action phase
of an agribusiness and rural enterprise project. In
this phase, two major types of activity take place:
the carrying out of the tasks designed into the
project and the systematic gathering and reporting
of information to permit decision-makers to improve
project performance. The improvement of performance
is an immediate objective for all current projects,
but there is also a longer-term goal of learning
from current experience so as to improve the design
of the next generation of projects.

Finally, both before any activity begins and as
project implementation proceeds, information will
need to be generated relating to the effectiveness
of agribusiness and rural enterprise projects in
terms of wider developmental goals. This continuing
analysis needs to be just as painstaking as was the
initial analysis if staff in carefully designed
projects are not to lose sight of broader objectives
and drift into a preoccupation with the mechanics of

217

keeping day-to-day activities going according to plan.

NOTE

1.    Excellent references for the desks of staff concerned at a high level of detail with the activities of identification and analysis are James Austen's two volumes, Agroindustrial Project Analysis and Rural Industrial Development. The former is also particularly well suited as a text for training in these areas.

BIBLIOGRAPHY

Allison, Graham T. "Implementation Analysis: 'The Missing Chapter'", in R. E. Zeckhauser et al. (eds.), Benefit Cost and Policy Analysis (Aldine, Chicago, 1975)

Anderson, D. and Leiserson, M. W. Rural Enterprise and Nonfarm Employment (The World Bank, Washington, DC, 1978)

Austen, James E. Agroindustrial Project Analysis, Economic Development Institute, The World Bank (Johns Hopkins University Press, Baltimore, Maryland, 1981)

_____. Rural Industrial Development: A Practical Handbook for Planners, Project Managers and Field Staff (Cassell, London, 1981)

Banco de Guatemala. Prestamos Concedidos por el Sistema Bancario a la Industria (Guatemala, 1976)

Bhalla, A. S. "Choosing Techniques: Handpounding v. Machine Milling of Rice: An Indian Case", Oxford Economic Papers, vol.17, no.1 (1965), pp.147-57

Boussard, Jean-Marc, "The Use of Computers in Monitoring and Evaluation of Rural Development Projects" (Institut National de la Recherche Agronomique, Paris, 1986)

Casley, D. J. and Lury, D. A. Data Collection in Developing Countries (Clarendon Press, Oxford, 1981)

_____. Monitoring and Evaluation of Agriculture and Rural Development Projects (Johns Hopkins University Press, Baltimore, Maryland, 1982)

Chambers, Robert, "Executive Capacity as a Scarce Resource", International Development Review, vol.11 (1969)

# Bibliography

_____. Rural Development: Putting the Last First
(Longman, London, 1983)

Daines, S. R. Analysis of Industrial Structure,
Technology and Productivity in the Food
Processing Sector of Brazil (Massachusetts
Institute of Technology, Cambridge, Mass.,
1975)

_____. Columbia Agriculture Sector Analysis (United
States Agency for International Development,
Washington, DC, 1972)

_____. Brazil, El Salvador, Costa Rica. Agro-
industrial Profile (United States Agency for
International Development, San Jose, Costa
Rica, 1976)

_____ and Smith, G. Guatemala Rural Enterprise
Sample Survey (United States Agency for International Development, Guatemala, 1978)

_____ et al. The Impact of Small-Farm Credit on
Income, Employment and Production (United
States Agency for International Development,
Washington, DC, 1975)

_____ and D. Steen, El Salvador Agroindustrial
Profile (United States Agency for
International Development, San Salvador, 1977)

Delp, Peter et al., System Tools for Project
Planning, International Development Institute
(Indiana University, Bloomington, Indiana,
1977)

Esman, Milton et al. The Landless and Near Landless
in Developing Countries (Cornell University,
Ithaca, New York, 1977)

Bhatt, V. V. "Financial Innovations, Transaction
Costs and Development," Development Digest,
vol.16, no.3 (1978)

Bouman, F. J. A. "Indigenous Savings and Credit
Societies in the Third World," Development
Digest, vol.16, no.3 (1978)

Chang, Yen-Tien. "Land Reform and Its Impact on
Economic and Social Progress in Taiwan"

Fundacao Instituto Brasileiro de Geografia
Estatistica. Censo Industrial, (1970)

Government of El Salvador. Industrial Census (San
Salvador, 1971)

Government of India. Annual Survey of Industries
(New Delhi, 1965)

Government of Jamaica. Department of Statistics,
Production Statistics (Kingston, 1977)

Harper, Malcom. "The Employment of Finance in Small
Business," Journal of Development Studies,
vol.11, no.4 (1975)

# Bibliography

Hirschman, A. O. The Strategy of Economic Development (Yale University Press, New Haven, Connecticut, 1958)

Ho, Y. and Huddle, D. L. "The Contribution of Traditional and Small Scale Culture Goods in International Trade and in Employment," Program of Development Studies, Paper No.35 (Rice University, Houston, Texas, 1972)

King, R. P. and Byerlee, D. "Income Distribution, Consumption Patterns and Consumption Linkages in Rural Sierra Leone", African Rural Economy Paper No. 16 (Michigan State University, East Lansing, Michigan, 1977)

Kochav, D. et al. Financing the Development of Small Scale Industries (The World Bank, Washington, 1974)

Leonard, D. K. An Evaluation of the Programming and Implementation Management (PIM) System, Institute for Development Studies, Working Paper No. 89 (University of Nairobi, Nairobi, Kenya)

Liedholm, Carl and Chuta, Enyinna. "The Economics of Rural and Urban Small Scale Industries in Sierra Leone," Africa Rural Economy Paper No.14 (Michigan State University, East Lansing, Michigan, 1976)

Meyer, Richard L. "Financing Rural Nonfarm Enterprises in Low Income Countries," Economics and Sociology Occasional Paper No.522 (Ohio State University, Columbus, Ohio, 1978)

Molenaar, N., El-Namaki, M. S. S. and van Dijk, M. P. Small Scale Industry Promotion in Developing Countries (Research Institute for Management Science, Delft, the Netherlands, 1983)

Morawetz, D. "Employment Implications of Industrialisation in Developing Countries: A Survey", The Economic Journal, vol.84, no.325 (1974)

National Council of Applied Economic Research. Study of Selected Small Industrial Units (NCAER, New Delhi, 1972)

Oshima, H. T. "Labor-Force 'Explosion' and the Labor-intensive Sector in Asian Growth", Economic Development and Cultural Change, vol.19, no.2 (January 1971), pp161-83

Von Pischke, J. D. "A Critical Survey of Approaches to the Role of Credit in Smallholder Development" (Paper presented to the Eastern Africa Agricultural Economics Society Conference in Lusaka, Zambia, May 1974)

Bibliography

Radovich, H. R. "Development Project Management: An
     Integrated Approach to Project Planning and
     Implementation", Planning Processes for Project
     Management, vol.1, Graduate School of Manage-
     ment (Vanderbilt University, Memphis, Tennes-
     see, 1974)
Rhee, Y. W. and Westphal, L. E. "A Micro-econometric
     Investigation of the Choice of Technology,"
     Journal of Development Economics, vol.4, no.3
     (1977)
Rondinelli, D. A. "Small Industries in Rural
     Development: Assessment and Perspective",
     National Productivity Council Journal (1978)
_____ and H. R. Radovich, A Study of Development
     Project Administration: Diagnostics for
     Improved Implementation (Vanderbilt University,
     Memphis, Tennessee, 1975)
Rusch, W., Mann, F. and Braun, E. "Rural Coopera-
     tives in Guatemala: A Study of their Develop-
     ment, and Evaluation of A.I.D. Projects in
     their Support" (1975)
Solomon, Morris, Heegaard, Flemming and Kornher,
     Kenneth, "An Action Training Strategy for
     Project Management", International Development
     Review, vol.20 (1978), pp.13-20
Staley, E. and Morse, R. Modern Small Industry for
     Developing Countries (McGraw-Hill, New York,
     1965)
Steel, W. F. Small-scale Employment and Production
     in Developing Countries: Evidence from Ghana
     (Praeger, New York, 1977)
_____ and Takagi, Y. The Intermediate Sector,
     Unemployment and the Employment-Output
     Conflict: A Multi-Sector Model (The World
     Bank, Washington, DC, 1978)
Tayengco, Edward S. (ed.), Agro-Industry Management:
     Case Materials (Asian Productivity
     Organization, Tokyo, 1984)
United Nations Industrial Development Organization.
     Technical Services for Small Scale Industry
     (United Nations, New York, 1970)
United States Agency for International Development.
     Agribusiness and Rural Enterprise Project
     Analysis Manual (Washington, 1980)
Warwick, Donald and Lininger, Charles. The Sample
     Survey: Theory and Practice (McGraw-Hill
     Book Company, New York, 1975)
World Bank. Development Issues in Rural Non-Farm
     Employment (Development Economics Department,
     Washington, DC, 1977)

Bibliography

_____. Employment and Development of Small Enterprises (Washington, DC, 1978)

_____. Employment Creation and Small Scale Enterprise Development (Washington, DC, 1977)

INDEX

Printed in the United States
by Baker & Taylor Publisher Services